NAME ZARA
DATE OF BIRTH 70/11/3
HOME ADDRESS Fitzrandolph Ave

Month DNR 9/87

WITHDREW
RETURN
WITHDREW
☐ Graduation

PREVIOUS SCHOOL ATTENDED (last only) WEST

DATE ENTERED YEAR 84 MONTH 9 DAY 5

SUBJECTS	GRADE & YR	CODE	MARK	CR.
		E214	D	5
		A214	C	
		C254		
English 9b	9th 84-85	M914	D	2½
Art I		S113	D	2½
U.S. History 1b		S123	D	2½
Intro Algebra		P123	D	5
Phy Sci I b ½ yr		P113		
Phy Sci II b ½ yr				
Health I ½ yr		E414	F	0
Phy Ed I ½yr		S434	B	5
English 10b	10th 85-86	Z224	D	5
Biology b		M414	D	0
Piano Lab I		A214	P	2½
Intro Geometry		B214		
Art II		P323		
Typing I		P313	F	
Health II		E113	F	
Phy Ed II		F373	F	
Legends repeat	11th 86-87	B113	F	
Idol Lit		B733	F	
Legends		J256	F	
Creative Writing		Z424	F	
German I		B513	F	
Piano Lab II		J256	F	
Computer Data Process		P523	F	
Computer I		P513		
German I				
Health III				
Phy Ed III				

3 PHASE DRIVER EDUCATION

KEYS TO MARKS:
A - EXCELLENT
B - ABOVE AVERAGE
C - AVERAGE
D - BELOW AVERAGE
P - PASSING THROUGH EFFORT,
    ACHIEVEMENT FAR BELOW
    AVERAGE
F - FAILING
X - NO CREDIT, INSUF-
    FICIENT ATTENDANCE

M - MEDICAL
CP - CLASSIFIED
     PROGRAM
W - WITHDREW
  - SUMMER
  - GRADE

5 CREDITS - 5 CLASS PE

HAMILTON TOWNSHIP SCHOOL RECORD

Trenton, New Jersey 08610

Accredited
By The New Jersey State System
And the Middle States Association

ENROLLMENT IN GRADES

NUMERICAL EQUIVALENT
A=4 | B=3 | C=2 | D=1

☒ PUBLIC SCHOOL
HONORS A&B
PASSING D&P

SUBJECTS	GRADE & YR	CODE	MARK	CR.

Year 9/87

3 PHASE DRIVER EDUCATION PROJ.

M - MEDICAL
CP - CLASSIFIED PUPIL/SPECIAL
     PROGRAM
W - WITHDREW
  - SUMMER SCHOOL
  - GRADE TO DATE

KEYS TO MARKS:
A - EXCELLENT
B - ABOVE AVERAGE
C - AVERAGE
D - BELOW AVERAGE
P - PASSING THROUGH EFFORT,
    ACHIEVEMENT FAR BELOW
    AVERAGE

EXPLANATION OF COURSE SYMBOLS
(a) ABOVE AVERAGE, ENRICHED
(b) AVERAGE
(c) BELOW AVERAGE, ADJUSTED
(c) ADVANCED-SELECTION BASED
    ON HIGH ACHIEVEMENT
    TEACHER RECOMMENDATION

MARK	CR.
D	5
C	5
	2½
D	2½
S113 D	2½
S123 D	
P123 D	5
P113	
E414 F	0
S434 B	5
Z224 D	5
M414 C	0
A214 D	2½
B214	

LAST NAME ZARA
DATE OF BIRTH 70/11/3
HOME ADDRESS Fitzrandolph Av

PREVIOUS SCHOOL ATTE

DATE ENTERED
YEAR 84
GRADE & YR
9th
84-85

FIRST NAME

UNEDUCATED

UNEDUCATED

A Memoir of Flunking Out, Falling Apart, and Finding My Worth

CHRISTOPHER ZARA

Little, Brown and Company

New York Boston London

Little, Brown and Company
Hachette Book Group
1290 Avenue of the Americas, New York, NY 10104
littlebrown.com

First Edition: May 2023

Little, Brown and Company is a division of Hachette Book Group, Inc. The Little,
Brown name and logo are trademarks of Hachette Book Group, Inc.

The publisher is not responsible for websites (or their content)
that are not owned by the publisher.

The Hachette Speakers Bureau provides a wide range of authors for speaking events.
To find out more, go to hachettespeakersbureau.com or call (866) 376-6591.

ISBN 9780316268974
LCCN 2022939872

Printing 1, 2023

LSC-C

Printed in the United States of America

For my mom, who would have looked great in a cap and gown

Contents

Contents

Part III

Author's Note

What is the true value of higher education? Praiseworthy books of every imaginable genre have tackled this question over the years, from breezy novellas to the densest academic tomes. While their diverse size and scope might suggest a robust debate from all perspectives, blink and you could easily miss one homogeneous detail: almost every book about college is written by an author who graduated from one.

What does it say about our society when the national conversation about higher education is driven almost exclusively by people who have benefited from it? To the millions of American adults who have no college degree, it sends a stinging message that their voices have no place in this important debate, that non-college-educated people are to be talked *about*, not engaged with.

I started writing this book because I wanted to describe what the education gap looks like from the wrong side of the diploma divide, what it's like to be shut out of careers that expect impressive credentials, jobs that reward top-tier pedigrees, and entire industries that subsist on talent pipelines supplied by a handful of elite schools. I didn't initially set out to write such a deeply personal story, but the more I dug into the vocational and economic realities of non–college graduates and high-school dropouts, the more I was forced to confront uncomfortable questions about what it meant to be a dropout myself—a topic that I had been too ashamed to talk about for most of my seventeen years in journalism. Key to that exploration was understanding why I had failed so miserably in school to begin with. I hope what I've put down on paper adds something valuable to the discussion.

Author's Note

Everything in this book actually happened, but much of it was written from memory, which is a strangely subjective thing. Where possible, I've tried to confirm details and verify that my account of events was accurate. In some cases, I've approximated dates, numbers, and the order of certain occurrences to the best of my recollection. I've also changed some names and identifying details, whether or not I note it in the text. As you read this story, you'll see that I have good reasons to start it with a disclaimer about the fallibility of memory, especially my own, which has admittedly suffered a few blows over the decades. Had I gone to college and taken a more traditional route to my chosen profession, I'm pretty sure I would have a few million more intact brain cells. If nothing else, maybe that's a nice metaphor for what we lose when we miss out on school.

Which brings me back to the original question: What is the true value of higher education? I don't pretend to believe that a single book can answer it. But maybe the more critical question is who gets to ask it.

Monopoly on the Twenty-Ninth Floor

I SHOULDN'T BE HERE.

Not a day goes by at *Fast Company* magazine when that doesn't pop into my head, often several times an hour. I walk through the revolving glass doors at 7 World Trade Center on a Tuesday morning, passing a herd of crisply dressed finance bros from Moody's before swiping my Silverstein Properties ID and heading to the elevator. Everyone's shirt is tucked in except mine. *I shouldn't be here.*

I have the anxiety-inducing experience of running into our editor in chief near the marble-lined elevator bank that goes to the twenty-ninth floor. We ride up together. We're about the same age and she went to Northwestern. One of our younger staff writers who works under me also went to Northwestern. The two of them have a lot to chat about. *I shouldn't be here.*

We arrive for the first editorial meeting of the week. It's in a spacious corner conference room we call Jail, a name that makes more sense after you learn that our entire floor is modeled on a Monopoly board because our old CEO thought that was clever and the billionaire entrepreneur who owns our magazine went along with it. Each of the lockers in the center hallway has a yellow magnet on it that says COMMUNITY CHEST, and we have conference rooms called Boardwalk and New York in opposing corners. Now you can picture it, right? The office is spiffy overall, but Jail is the most impressive part. It has a giant monitor, a high-tech sound system, floor-to-ceiling windows, and beautiful views of the 9/11 memorial and New York Harbor. The picturesque scene outside the southern window is dominated by a large swath of One World Trade Center, which sparkles on a sunny day like a giant blue fortress from the future. Being in Jail for a big editorial meeting makes you feel like you're in one of those movies that still depict the magazine industry as glamorous because it's clear the screenwriters know nothing about the magazine industry. This is the Nora Ephron version of a magazine job. *I shouldn't be here.*

At the meeting we discuss all our big editorial packages, and in case I haven't mentioned it yet, *Fast Company* is one of the country's leading business magazines, with a focus on innovative leadership, technology, design, and start-up culture. As the senior editor on the news desk, I get to touch every one of those topics on a daily basis. It's all very cool stuff in the purest sense of the word *cool,* and you can tell we're writing for a first-rate audience by the caliber of the feedback we receive. For our readers, college isn't just an expectation — it's a birthright. The only time our magazine speaks directly to people without college degrees is when it runs one of those clicky listicles about — oh, I don't know — ten great jobs that don't require a college degree, which don't really matter to anyone who works at *Fast Company* because they all have college degrees, including the people who write those listicles.

We're not talking about four-year degrees from mediocre state schools here. Journalism is one of those shiny white-collar industries that both attract and favor people from the same handful of shiny institutions. Columbia. NYU. Maybe Boston University, if you want to shake things up. Established journalists adore people from these schools, and established business journalists adore them even more. For all the talk of making media more accessible and inclusive, we're basically an insular profession built on relationships, and those relationships rely on tight-knit networks furnished by very selective, very expensive institutions of higher learning.

Suffice it to say, if you want to work in media and you go to a great school, you have a shot at getting your foot in the door. And if you go to an Ivy League school, you might even get to work at *The New Yorker.*

Then there's me. I mean, how do I even begin to describe my education? Technically, the highest level of schooling I completed was tenth grade. That's the last time I made it through an entire school year. I remember it vividly because I was fifteen, which is the same age I was when I had my first kiss, my first date, and my first breakup, all of which coincidentally happened near the entrance of the same Lord and Taylor. Our family lived in a lower-middle-class neighborhood in Trenton, New Jersey, a once-great manufacturing center that was already well into its postindustrial decline by the time my brothers and I were born. Our playgrounds were abandoned factories where they used to make things out of rubber and steel and iron. Perhaps we were white trash, but I can't recall anyone using that term as an actual pejorative. So, yeah, at fifteen, I thought things were basically good and pretty normal.

But somehow it all seriously spiraled out of control about seven months later, in my junior year of high school, when I was ejected for behavioral problems and locked up for a short stint in a mental institution. The school system gave me the label *emotionally disturbed,* so determined by a team of teen-crisis experts whose teen-crisis reports were riddled with typos. I know this because I stumbled on a copy of it years later in my parents' filing cabinet and became annoyed by the idea of having had my mental competence evaluated by people who didn't hyphenate their compound modifiers. Around the time I was institutionalized, I also sank into a deep depression and attempted suicide. And then, a few short months later, I found myself somewhere I never thought I would be in a million years: on the campus of Princeton University, awestruck by its stately neo-Gothic buildings, leafy open spaces, and ivy-covered walls. No, I wasn't a student — that would have been impressive — but I spent the summer of 1987 there working as a dishwasher and food runner at the Cloister Inn eating club. During special events, I'd serve finger foods to upperclassmen in Izod shirts and penny loafers who wouldn't say two words to me, and my bitter disdain for privilege and snobbery grew more ossified with each shrimp cocktail I doled out. To get through the experience, I'd sometimes make inappropriate jokes to coworkers about Brooke Shields, who was an actual student there at the time. And I pondered — a lot. The future is hard to imagine when you're sixteen and even harder when you have no institutional guidance. But I did find myself wondering if formal education, perhaps even at an esteemed university like Princeton, could be a part of my future.

I got an answer that fall when I was required to attend a high school for troubled youth located in a decaying building with walls covered in moss and mold, not ivy. We called it "the special school." I could write volumes about the word *special*, but I'm pretty sure no one wants to read that kind of book. I lasted at the special school for only about a month, partly because I was threatened with physical violence on a daily basis but mostly because I was too embarrassed to ride the short bus that showed up at our house to pick me up. The taunts of other kids yelling "Tart cart" as we drove away were simply too much.

Early one morning, I plunged my feet into my steel-toe boots, threw on my tattered trench coat, and stepped out into the chilly fall air. Instead of waiting for the short bus like I was supposed to, I just kept walking until I hit the end of our street. From that distance I stood and watched the short bus arrive at my house, its mustard hull vibrating rebelliously as if to keep from freezing over. The driver idled there for several minutes. I imagined him calling me a stupid son of a bitch or a dickhead—he didn't like me anyway, and now I was making him wait. I hid behind a neighbor's bush until he finally drove off, and then I began a day of roaming the streets of Trenton. The control felt good. It was as if, for the first time in my life, I was shaping my own destiny. I didn't have to go to school. I didn't have to do anything. It's funny how that feels like a revelation to a moody teenager. This was before I learned that doing things is actually not so bad and that not doing things was probably the main source of my mood swings.

Special schools, it turns out, have little tolerance for truancy, so it didn't take long before I got kicked out of a second high school that year. At least, that's how I remember it. Maybe we just mutually agreed that I was not a good fit. Not that it mattered, because I had a real plan to show them all: I would complete my high-school education on my own. And I did, that very same school year. At seventeen, I joined the small percentage of dropouts who earned their GEDs, a rare moment of academic pride. What I didn't know at the time was that the GED would be the zenith of my formal education.

Fast-forward a few decades, and I don't mention the GED very often to my colleagues in journalism, for much the same reason I didn't want to ride the short bus in the 1980s. It feels, instinctively, embarrassing. Well-meaning people sometimes tell me that I should be proud of having built a career without a traditional education to springboard me into all the right opportunities. But that's the paradox of marginalization, isn't it? How you can be both proud of the thing that pushes you into the margins and simultaneously terrified to discuss it in certain company. The result of those feelings is a strange form of denial that compels me to disengage and deflect when the conversation veers into uncomfortable territory. I've learned to throw up roadblocks to certain topics. "My twenties? Oh, they were a blur," I'll say with a low-key indifference that I hope discourages further inquiry. "How about this weather?" The self-preservation becomes so pronounced that a perfectly normal question—Where did you go to school?—feels like a violent interrogation. To answer would be to surrender to the crude Darwinism of demographics, to watch as my interrogator tries to reconcile his preconceived ideas about what a high-school dropout looks like with the reality of who I actually am. A person. A professional. An equal?

And why should people understand? I look around our newsroom each day and I'm reminded of my outlier status by endless discrepancies, subtle and not-so-subtle differences between my educated colleagues and myself. It could be situational, that gap year someone spent backpacking across Europe when he was twenty-two, an age I spent jobless, strung out on heroin, and living at home. Or maybe it's financial: All the younger reporters complain about student-loan debt. I just have debt. No matter how disparate and diverse my coworkers seem, they all share a collective experience—the college years and the college friends—that's completely foreign to me. I'm an anomaly here at *Fast Company* and in the broader world of media for sure. Current statistics are hard to come by, but the last estimate I saw of journalists without a college degree was somewhere around

8 percent, and that was in 2013. In New York City, it's probably even lower, and at 7 World Trade Center, on this floor, well, I may very well be the only one.

Of course, that doesn't matter if I can successfully argue that people without college degrees have something meaningful to contribute beyond scooping ice cream, sweeping floors, and assembling picture frames—all jobs I did before I became a journalist. And that dovetails into the more philosophical question of whether people without college degrees are actually different from their college-educated counterparts, separated by the sheer force of demography.

Without a doubt, I can say that we are, if only because society never lets us forget it. From our perspective, the world is a rigid system of credentials and tiers that stifles those of us on the wrong side by design, from the unpaid internship that demands a four-year degree to those annoying LinkedIn notifications that remind you to "complete" your profile with the name of a university because fifteen years of experience apparently counts for nothing. Hell, even the robots are against us. As a fun game, try submitting an online job application through one of those automated systems without checking off at least a bachelor's degree. You will typically not get past that first rudimentary algorithm, the one that is programmed to filter out spammers, drive-by applicants, purported Nigerian princes, and you, the person without a degree. If your degree-free résumé does make it to a human being through some fluke of omission, you can bet it will raise red flags. I once landed a job interview with an executive at a fast-growing digital-media company who just assumed he was missing a page. "You seem like a great fit, but I think your résumé got cut off," he told me, flipping through four pages of my work history that I had dressed up with kitschy adjectives like *lightning-fast* and humblebrags about how I'd reported from four continents.

"I can't find the part that says where you went to college."

"I didn't."

"At all? Oh."

"Um."

That admission tends to elicit many different types of responses. In this case, much to my relief, my interviewer just made light of the situation. "Eh, our CEO never finished either," he said with a chuckle.

We had a good interview after that.

I never heard from him again.

The editorial meeting in Jail is nearly finished, and not a moment too soon. The sun has moved to an inconvenient position in the western sky, flooding the giant corner conference room with blinding light like that scene in *Close Encounters of the Third Kind* where the kid opens the door and sees the UFO. Plus, it's almost two o'clock and everyone is thinking about lunch. But before we adjourn, we come to my favorite part of the meeting: a creative brainstorm where the editors and writers are asked to suggest ideas for future stories. It's a great window into people's headspaces. What matters in the world right now and why? No one is forced to participate in this exercise, but it's always fun to see who doesn't and who does, who looks up from their phone or laptop long enough to proffer a suggestion. Even more telling are the ideas themselves, because they exemplify many of the biggest fault lines along the educational divide.

Not to suggest that the ideas are bad. We should absolutely care about the student-debt crisis and eco-friendly shopping and green energy and workplace microaggressions and meditation apps. (Okay, maybe not meditation apps.) But as I watch my educated colleagues identify, debate, and prescribe solutions to society's ills, I realize it's impossible to talk about those fault lines without being honest about who draws them. It's the educated who decide where social classes begin and end, people within the halls of academia, the offices of media, and the boardrooms of corporate America. And there's a fence, a wall, or armed security separating each of those spaces from the outside world. It's the educated who write for professional journals, who commission studies, who green-light TV shows, who join think tanks, who fund the arts, decide court cases, and run the government. The educated, as a category, have a stranglehold on power and influence that is impossible to escape. If you're one of them, if you've gone to college, you might not notice. You might not even think of "educated" as a single category. But if you're like me, you see it every day. It forms around you like a giant Monopoly board, like the very floor in this building, a floor I shouldn't be on, a game I shouldn't be allowed to play.

Education is a net good for society. It lifts people out of poverty and provides opportunity. It's valued because it's necessary. I realize that, and it is probably the thing I find most painful about not having a degree. Would it have killed me to suck it up on that chilly fall morning in 1987 and ride the stupid short bus? I have no idea where I'd be now if I'd made a different choice, graduated high school, gone to college, earned a degree. Maybe not here on the twenty-ninth floor, working a dream job, looking at Greenwich Street below and thinking about how it seems like such a long way down. Depth is an illusion. The truth is, I could hit that pavement in five seconds.

PART I

CHAPTER 1

Look Good on Paper

THE LITTLE CLASSIFIED AD SEEMED to be winking and nodding at me from the back of the *Village Voice,* four compressed lines, sandwiched between an ad for a cashier and another one for a lab technologist. *INTERNS: For editorial dept. of busy entertain newspaper,* it read. *College Stu/Grad....No Pay. Great Oppty! Tim.*

It was day four of my new life as a New Yorker, and my SRO on West Ninety-Fourth Street was feeling claustrophobic. The smell of mold. The sound of day-drunk neighbors. There was a reason they rented this room by the week. My daily job hunt went from six in the morning until eleven at night. Craigslist was the platform of the moment in 2005, but I couldn't spend all day scouring its depths without going crazy. The *Voice,* though not the gold mine of opportunity I recalled it being in the nineties, still had the occasional gem. Thumbing through it in a coffee shop felt like a trip to the day spa, even if this mysterious ad gave me pause. No job description? No listed qualifications? And what kind of lazy fake name was Tim?

I wasn't a college stu or grad, but I figured there was no harm in calling and inquiring about the internship. To be honest, I didn't really know what an internship was. Why would I? My working life up until that point had been little more than a loosely rhythmic procession of three phases: not having a job, applying for jobs, and working at whichever retail establishment hired me. Ice cream stands. Cookie stores. Frame shops. Quit, step, repeat.

The idea that there was this limbic stage of career development in which inexperienced job candidates worked unpaid for companies that would probably never hire them seemed sketchy on its face, but I assumed it was the price one paid to gain experience in a glamorous industry like newspapers. Plus, I remembered I'd once seen an episode of *Friends* in which Chandler Bing became an intern at an older age in hopes of breaking into advertising. At some point, he's actually offered a job because his maturity and life experience turn out to be assets or whatever. I mean, I knew it was only a dumb show, but I also secretly thought my own experience as an aging intern seeking a fresh start could mirror the type of neatly wrapped story arc one might see on an NBC sitcom. It was the best reference point I had.

Within seconds of dialing up the mystery entertainment paper, I was put at ease by the pleasant-sounding young man who answered the phone. His name was Kevin. Tim wasn't available, Kevin explained, but he'd be happy to discuss the internship with me. He had the disarming disposition of a trained receptionist but spoke in short sentences that suggested a hectic newsroom behind the scenes. Unseen excitement, in my mind. I pictured Kevin in a sprawling lobby of tinted glass walls sitting behind a large L-shaped desk, pushing buttons with the dexterity of a concert pianist while the blinking lights of an office phone yielded to his commands. I liked Kevin instantly. He seemed cool under pressure. If he was the type of person who worked at this paper, then I wanted to work there too. At one point during the conversation, Kevin said the name *Show Business Weekly* and I nearly flipped. That was huge. Or at least it sounded like something I should have heard of. To my great relief, he did not ask me if I was affiliated with a college or why I wanted the internship or much about my background at all. He invited me to come in for an interview later that week.

"Bring a cover letter and résumé," he said.

So began a crisis of conscience. *What do I put on my résumé? How do I pave over the cracks in my background?* Structure was not an issue; I'd read more than enough how-to articles on résumé building to understand the formatting basics. Work experience went first. Then education. The Objective section was optional, and there were lots of conflicting opinions about whether you should include one at all, but I personally found it impossible to write an objective without sounding like a creepy stalker. In the end, I just added some vague facts about myself, which were all true but probably no less creepy. Work experience was the easy part. Even though I had written only a handful of freelance magazine articles up until that point, I was confident that I could flesh out those accomplishments and fill at least three-quarters of a page. Bullet points helped. I recommend the triangle-shaped ones.

But what to do about education? How do you dress up a tenth-grade education, a GED, and a few random community-college classes? Every résumé draft I sketched out felt like an instant checkmate. I wasn't about to put down anything about high school—for God's sake, I was thirty-five. Similarly, I didn't think the name Mercer County Community College would score many points, and in fact, I was sure it would raise more questions, since I didn't even have an associate's degree. Part of me thought it was better to simply leave education off my résumé altogether. I'd let the power of purposeful omission work its magic and hope—pray—no one noticed.

There was another option: I could lie. People lied on their résumés all the time, I reasoned, and who really looks up someone's school? It seemed like a ridiculously simple solution to a problem that had been gnawing at my sense of self-worth ever since my life first fell apart, back when abandoning the idea of school seemed like my only choice. Nine years earlier, desperate and addicted to heroin, I used the money from a Federal Pell Grant to move far away from the Northeast and escape the open-air drug markets that were so prevalent in New York City in the nineties.

Now, in 2005, I was back and looking for a job. Couldn't I just fill in the blanks? Pick a school, choose a major, and call myself a college graduate? Surely moral relativism gave me some leeway here. I knew I was good enough to be a professional journalist, that I would do a great job if given the chance. *A system that locks people out solely on the basis of educational attainment is inherently unfair,* I thought. *Are we bound by ethics to play by the rules of an unfair system? Fuck the rules.* Here I was in New York City, the place I'd dreamed of living my entire life, the place everyone tells you they're proud of you for moving to even though they're secretly waiting for you to fall on your face. "Good luck," they say. What they really mean is *You'll be back.*

But I'd been in town less than a week and already the perfect career stepping-stone was presenting itself: a real internship, whatever that was, in Midtown Manhattan at *Show Business Weekly*, which I was definitely almost positive I'd heard of. I only got one shot at this.

The story of how journalism became the near-exclusive domain of college graduates is a complicated one. By some accounts, it starts with the yellow journalism of the late nineteenth century, when the bitter newspaper war between Joseph Pulitzer and William Randolph Hearst produced a brand of reporting so sensationalistic and fact-averse that no sound person of the era would have considered journalism a respectable profession. It was an intensely competitive time, with Hearst's *New York Journal* going head-to-head with Pulitzer's *New York World* in a battle for the precious attention of Gilded Age Gothamites. They defamed enemies, mocked rivals, even openly campaigned for war. Pulitzer wanted to at least try to elevate the practice. In 1892, he offered to fund a journalism school at Columbia College—a wild idea at the time—but the school said no, thanks. After all, Columbia, not yet the sprawling university it is today, was in the process of trying to elevate its own status. To make that leap, it needed to align itself with the right people—meaning not journalists.

But Pulitzer wasn't the only journalist who thought the profession needed to pull itself out of the gutter. In 1908, Walter Williams, a high-school dropout from Missouri who rose through the ranks in the newspaper business and went on to become an influential voice in journalism ethics, founded America's first journalism school, at the University of Missouri. "I believe it is possible for this school to give dignity to the profession of journalism," the university's president said at the time. *Dignity* is the key word there. It's what separates work and career. People with dignity have careers. People without it work.

As for Pulitzer, he too was ultimately successful—or at least his money was. He left the school two million dollars in his will, and the Columbia School of Journalism opened in 1912, shortly after his death. Today it is considered among the most prestigious journalism schools in the world.

Journalism schools did not immediately drive non-college-educated reporters and editors into extinction. As late as the early 1970s, journalists without college degrees still represented more than 40 percent of employees in the media. The divide is notably depicted in the 1976 movie *All the President's Men,* about the two investigative reporters who broke the Watergate scandal. Carl Bernstein, a college dropout who started in newspapers as a copy boy at the age of sixteen, is portrayed by Dustin Hoffman as the polar opposite of Bob Woodward, a handsome Yale grad who was polished enough in real life to be believably played by Robert Redford. The movie sets up the contrast between the two characters as a subtle plot device, but the conflict in journalism between scrappy, of-the-people reporters and the glossy professionals churned out by college journalism programs was real.

In the decades that followed, it became clear that the Bob Woodwards of the world were winning. By 2003, almost 90 percent of working journalists had college degrees.

I didn't know any of those statistics when I started writing as a freelancer that same year, and if I had, I probably would've stopped there. Editors typically do not ask freelancers where they went to school. All you have to do is bring them an idea they love and convince them you can write it. I know that because the first magazine editor I ever pitched gave me an assignment. I was living in Seattle, depressed, desperate for money, and I happened to come across one of those how-to books about selling magazine articles. Getting a yes on my first pitch was beginner's luck, I quickly learned, but it was enough motivation for me to keep pitching other editors. Before I arrived in New York, I'd worked up a small portfolio of clips that way.

But now that it was time to interview in a real office — to be judged on a résumé — I wasn't ignorant enough to believe that my lack of an education would be overlooked. Which brought me back to my original quandary: To lie or not to lie? Would the advantage of adding a false alma mater be worth the risk of getting caught? I admit it was rather enjoyable to think about which fake school I would pick. NYU or Columbia seemed too obvious, given the likelihood that a hiring manager would have gone to one of those. The University of Washington is a good school, and I actually did live in Seattle for three years. Princeton—ah, yes, my old dream, but would anyone believe it?

These were questions I tortured myself with as I sat alone after my phone call with Kevin, who I assumed was the first line of defense in an army of gatekeepers at *Show Business Weekly*. I imagined he'd have a stack of résumés waiting for him at the end of the day, having put off going through them for as long as he could, because who likes going through résumés? Five minutes before it was time to go home, he'd rocket through the pile and look for reasons to toss them in the trash. Who knew what Kevin's individual red flags were? Those are often dictated by personal pet peeves, which is one of the main reasons I hate gatekeepers. I know, I know, everyone hates gatekeepers, but I actually reserved a spot for them in the map of hell I've drawn in my head.

Also, personal pet peeves were less relevant in this case, because I was certain that having no education would be a red flag for pretty much every gatekeeper.

As the hours wore on, the street noise on the Upper West Side got quieter and quieter until the only sound that remained was the high-pitched hiss of my tinnitus. The emptiness uncorked a torrent of self-judgment. How had I managed to accomplish so little by thirty-five? My thoughts drifted back twenty years, to a fifteen-year-old with red-and-black hair and spiked bracelets who has this whole résumé scam figured out. Lying on a bare mattress, feet propped up on the wall, spongy headphones over his ears, he sneers along to the song "Terminal Preppie" by the Dead Kennedys, a satirical attack on for-profit higher education and how the system concentrates power in the hands of the privileged. Jello Biafra, the group's front man, performed the song in first person, as he often did, thereby assuming the identity of the very thing he was attacking. In this case, his target was the power-seeking alpha sheep who pursue college. One lyric has always stuck with me:

My ambition in life
Is to look good on paper
All I want is a slot
In some big corporation

Here I was all these years later doing exactly what those terminal prep-pies were derided for doing, except that without college as a foundational résumé builder, I didn't look good on paper. I couldn't. And now that I needed to, it was too late. That's something the song leaves out. Somehow, I'd managed to betray my fifteen-year-old self and let down Jello Biafra all in one night.

A crushing flood of holiday shoppers filled Herald Square as I walked hur-riedly toward Midtown East, where the *Show Business Weekly* office was located. I wore dress shoes for the interview, but I did not own a tie or know how to tie one. It was a chilly afternoon in late November, the week of Thanksgiving, and it seemed as though everyone in the world was already on vacation. Where there was no room on the sidewalk, I moved onto the street. Pushing and shoving my way through crowds of people gawking at window displays felt like a small victory.

My actual destination was not especially impressive. The office, about a block from Grand Central, was in a beat-up old building set back so far that it could not even be seen from the street. But the thrill of being there, in the shadow of the Chrysler Building, the mustard blur of taxicabs zip-ping by as I braced for an actual interview to work in media, erased all traces of objective reality. I arrived about forty-five minutes early and waited in a nearby Starbucks. My plan was to show up exactly on time. Not five minutes early or three minutes late. Right on time. For some rea-son, I had it in my head that hyper-punctuality was a subtle but effective power move that lulled the interviewer into a less defensive posture. Plus, being on time was something I could control. There was always a Star-bucks to wait in right outside.

Exactly two minutes before the interview was scheduled, I entered the building and was sent to the third floor. The creaky elevator went up, and my stomach stayed behind, dropping out from under me as a cold wave of anx-iousness took control of my body. This was it. *Am I even prepared?* I caught a glimpse of my newsboy cap in the metal trim along the elevator wall and sud-denly felt ridiculous. I wore it so often to hide my hideous bald head that I felt naked without it. I knew a hat was an inappropriate look for a job interview, but if I took it off and went full Yul Brynner, I'd feel less comfortable, which would make me visibly more nervous, which would ruin the interview. It was a lot to ponder during a twenty-second elevator ride. As the doors swung open, the hat came off my head and went into my messenger bag.

At the office, Kevin answered the door personally and looked exactly as I'd imagined he would: thin, dark hair, glasses, twenty-three. He wore a dress shirt and skinny tie but also jeans and sneakers, precisely the kind of hybrid style you want to have in a creative but professional media environment. The giant lobby and bustling newsroom I'd pictured during our phone call were nonexistent. In fact, the office contained no more than eight or ten desks, and there was not another human being in sight. It was Thanksgiving week, after all. There was no actual Tim working there, Kevin said. Tim was short for "Tim House," a fake account executive whose name was placed in job ads so Kevin would know who was calling about the internship. *Okay, that's a little odd, but I'm glad we cleared it up.*

With pleasantries out of the way, Kevin led me to a small round table and asked for my résumé. At some point—I was too nervous to fully process what we were talking about—I realized that he was not sitting me down in a waiting area and sending in the interviewer. He *was* the interviewer. Kevin told me his title was editorial assistant and that he himself had been an unpaid intern only a few months earlier. After a recent staff upheaval of some sort, the publisher and owner of the newspaper apparently put a team of interns through a secret test of their abilities and plucked Kevin out of the lot.

"I guess I passed," he said with a smile.

Now Kevin was running the show and looking for his own team of unpaid interns. This was 2005, and that concept had yet to receive the full legal scrutiny it would get a few years later when unpaid interns started suing their employers for back wages. Unpaid interns were basically still the lifeblood of many media outlets. With no oversight, employers in competitive industries like media and entertainment figured that if they could get away with using free labor in lieu of paid employees, they would. And they did.

I didn't know any of this when Kevin told me his story. He seemed to treat the intern-mill concept as a completely normal thing, and I certainly didn't question it. He explained that the duties of an intern at *Show Business Weekly* included editing news copy, formatting audition notices, and assisting with other random odds and ends around the office. If the boss liked your work, there could be some news writing involved, and you might even get to review plays and musicals around town. It all sounded great. That the job was unpaid made complete sense to me, since none of it sounded like work in the way that I understood the word. To me, work was building picture frames, helping asshole customers pick out mats while their kids ripped all the Velcroed samples off the walls. Work was handing out ice cream samples to packs of teenagers at a shopping mall. This sounded like fun. And Kevin—smart, easygoing, agreeable—seemed like a great person to work with.

Or for. I admit, having a boss so young would take some getting used to, but I was game if he was.

Kevin stared at my résumé for what felt like hours. He did not see a college or university falsely listed anywhere, because in the end I decided against that. Instead, I made no mention of education at all. It was the truest thing I could do. It's not that I felt an overwhelming moral compulsion to play by the rules of a system I deemed inherently unfair. But the fear of getting caught, the idea of living with that fear for an entire career, knowing that I could get a tap on the shoulder at any time by a superior who was diligent enough to check, was too much to bear. I had enough trouble sleeping as it was. Plus, I wasn't that good a liar. What would I say when Kevin asked me where I went to school? I honestly hadn't rehearsed it.

"When would you be able to start?" Kevin asked. "Because I want to hire you."

"Next week? Today? When do you need me?"

I still don't know if there's anything to all this purposeful omission stuff. Maybe Kevin was just so green that he didn't catch the obvious red flag of my not having a college education. Or maybe he took pity on a guy twelve years his senior who was seeking work as an unpaid intern. Who can really say? I don't know and I never asked. It's entirely possible that he saw the same episode of *Friends*.

CHAPTER 2

All Work, No Pay

THE FIRST TIME I MET Gus Gary, he did not seem like the kind of person who would kick me out of his apartment when I had nowhere to live, but then I probably did not strike him as the type who would pee in his Che Guevara mug.

I was on my best behavior on the evening of our first encounter, a visitor to his spacious two-bedroom in Washington Heights who hoped to become a roommate. Gus Gary wanted something more: a companion, a TV buddy—not a best friend, necessarily, but someone with whom to share occasional meals and art-house movies. He made all this abundantly clear when I showed up, a packet filled with landlord references and previous employers in hand. I nodded attentively, as one does, when he described his vision for the living arrangement, how we would do things together and be chummy.

"That sounds great," I said.

It did not sound great.

One Hundred and Seventy-Sixth Street felt like another world, a subdivision within an enclave where all the buildings stopped at six floors and nothing new had been built in the past fifty years. Who knew Manhattan street numbers went up this high? My living situation, in a place eighty-two blocks down, was unsustainable. I was shelling out way too much money each week for an SRO that smelled of mold in an expensive neighborhood. If I had any hope of staying in New York, of starting my internship at *Show Business Weekly* in six days, I needed a steady income and a more affordable place to live. The income part was remedied with a part-time job in a picture-frame shop on the Upper West Side not far from the moldy SRO. It was owned by a Turkish entrepreneur who preferred to hire Uzbeks over Americans but for some reason offered me a job on sight. The pay was eleven dollars an hour, enough for me to squeak by. Now it was time to find a permanent place to live, and the clock was ticking. Each week in the moldy SRO drained hundreds of dollars from my bank account, almost all the money I had.

I didn't really want to become someone's roommate at thirty-five. For starters, it flew in the face of my loner proclivities. But circumstances dictated it, and Gus Gary seemed a perfectly suitable means to an end. Neatly dressed with close-cropped salt-and-pepper hair and well-placed smile lines, he described himself as divorced and "in my fifties," which I took to mean fifty-nine, even though he looked younger. He was an editor for a labor union newsletter and liked to talk about left-wing politics. I must have admitted that I didn't know much about that topic, because he seemed especially invested in getting me up to speed on Karl Marx before the end of the evening.

"If Communism was such a good idea, why did it fail?" I said to provoke him.

"It didn't," Gus Gary said. "It's complicated."

I guessed I'd take his word for that. I was too busy scoping out the apartment, with its high ceilings, pretty molding, and large windows. A slow pan of the interior also revealed two cats, a ten-speed bicycle mounted on the wall, and a picture of Huey P. Newton in the living room. I honestly thought all that stuff about us spending time together was just stuff people say.

On the first day of my internship at *Show Business Weekly*, I was greeted at the door by another intern, Lori, who was the only person in the office. I introduced myself, and she smiled at me through braces.

"Nice to meet you," Lori said. "What school are you from?"

I explained that I was not in school but merely new in town, which in hindsight doesn't really make sense. Nevertheless, Lori seemed happy to meet a fellow unpaid laborer, and I did not mind being mistaken for a student, ridiculous as the notion was. We redheads do tend to age over-night. We walk around looking like teenagers until one day we wake up to find our bright, smooth, freckled skin is all dried up, flaky, and dead-looking. This can happen when we're twenty-two or thirty-two or forty-two, but it happens eventually. Overnight. Suffice it to say, on the first morning of my internship, I had not hit the redhead wall yet. Although the day was young.

The office was even smaller than I recalled from the interview, cavern-ous and dark, with smudged-up walls and rows of aging iMacs that ranged in color from bluish green to greenish blue. Tabloid-size newspapers, piles of them, bundles of them, unread, took up every square inch of spare space. A red banner across the front pages said *Show Business.* The sole window was tiny and looked out onto a charmless sliver of East Forty-Third Street. Lori told me to take a seat at any of the iMac stations, and I followed her direction, picking one of the greenish-blue ones. At some point, a third intern entered the picture, this one a tall, skinny student named Steven. The three of us chatted for several minutes like unsuper-vised children. Clearly there was no work to do until Kevin returned. Our twenty-three-year-old boss was out running an errand, I was told. Okay, but did anyone else work here? Perhaps that question could wait until my second day.

When Kevin entered, we three interns straightened our backs, perking up in unison. He began doling out tasks like a pro: Lori would download and type in new casting notices. Steve would comb the dailies looking for news leads. Kevin's easy manner made the assignments sound more like suggestions. At first, he didn't seem to know what to do with me, as several long minutes passed between his welcoming me to my first day and finding something for me to do. The waiting was painful: Was I just supposed to know? Finally, he printed out a feature story and dropped five or six pages on my desk.

"Can you edit this?"

I nodded. Of course I could. Just find the mistakes and correct them with a red pen, Kevin instructed. Great.

But when I looked down at the pages, the words made no sense. The letters were familiar, but I couldn't grasp the syntax. What was happening? Had I forgotten grammar? As I pulled the words closer to my eyes, the pages wobbled between my index finger and thumb, following the rhythm of my bounding pulse. Still nothing. What the hell? I knew these rules. I edited my own writing all the time, and I was always the first person my friends turned to when they needed something proofread. Except I'd never been asked to proofread something on command before. Performance anxiety had seized control of my frontal lobe, and I was suddenly useless. *What if I actually can't edit things in front of other people?* Beads of sweat began to form on my temples as I fought the instinct to walk out right then and there. I'd done it before. There was that time I tried to do telemarketing and another when I thought I could haul bags of rice on a loading dock. Neither lasted more than a few hours; I hated bothering people at home and I wasn't strong enough to carry the rice. But this was different. I actually wanted to be here, to work in media, to learn the ropes.

It suddenly occurred to me that maybe this was what people learned in college, how to overcome impostor syndrome, how to function in a real office. Maybe unpaid internships were really just a way to weed out the weak. *Breathe.*

The anxiety that snatched my capacity to think, to edit words on a page, was the product of a deeply ingrained sense of inferiority whose grip on me I had not completely come to terms with. It was a small prelude to an unpredictable range of symptoms that would reappear and worsen in the years ahead: Shaking hands. A tightening voice. Abrupt chills. Worst of all, a blank mind. These manifestations were somehow easier to tame when I was working a retail job, perhaps because the biggest price of failing in a job you don't care about is losing a job you don't care about. But walking into that office, meeting the other interns, amplified a sinking belief that I had skipped a step. Lori was finishing her degree at Stony Brook — in comparative literature, I think, or some other subject I'd never heard of. Steven, studying film theory, was an aspiring public intellectual in the mold of Roger Ebert. Who the hell was I? Some rube who saw an ad in the back of the *Village Voice*.

Thankfully, Kevin was a calming force that stopped my downward spiral of self-doubt from spinning out of control. He had a chatty way of starting conversations at just the right moment, when the awkward silence of the office became too much to bear. He talked about his large Chinese American family, how they liked to eat too much at Thanksgiving. I remarked that my dad's large Italian American family were the exact same way. Kevin seemed to have a deep passion for online culture and said he and his college buddies were launching a website that would blend the sophisticated humor of *The New Yorker* with the web-savvy snark of *Gawker*, whatever that was. I appreciated his casual asides. They made my being in the office feel natural, instead of the abomination that I feared it was.

By early afternoon on that first day, it was all starting to fall into place. I had successfully edited the feature story with the red pen and was now writing a news item about a new theater space in Chelsea. Lori and Steven were cutting up, making fun of the movie *Hitch*, because it was formulaic and unfunny and what had happened to Will Smith? Inoffensive indie music was playing on Sirius satellite radio, some band called Franz Ferdinand. *My God, is this really how the other half works? I sure could get used to it.* Then the office door swung open, and the airiness of the room gave way to a cyclone of dark psychic sludge. A voice screamed Kevin's name, then barked something about an insertion order for a quarter-page ad from the Stella Adler acting studio. "Where the fuck is it? Kevin, is it on my chair?" I kept my eyes down on my news story, but in my peripheral vision saw a blur of slick black hair and aviator sunglasses. This was my first glimpse of Mr. Chieftain, the publisher and owner of the newspaper. As he disappeared into his private office, Kevin responded, cool as ever, "On your chair."

The room got eerily quiet. Even Franz Ferdinand was gone. Did Kevin shut it off? Within seconds, Mr. Chieftain was back in the main office and circling the periphery, rifling through papers, his small brown eyes burning with intensity, piercing, a deep scowl that made him look borderline Cro-Magnon. He was barely five foot seven, but the room felt too small for his presence. Our eyes met for a split second and he seemed to have no idea what I was doing there. That made two of us.

"What are you working on?" Mr. Chieftain asked in a way that implied I'd better have a good answer. Except he didn't give me time to come up with one. "You're working on that. Okay. You're working on that."

Mr. Chieftain moved on to Lori and said something about needing her to run across town to the Farley post office to pick up a package. He repeated the directions twice and told her not to write them down because it was easy and she should be able to find it.

"I'll just write it down," Lori said.

"Don't write it down."

Off she went.

Mr. Chieftain stomped back to his private office and summoned Kevin to follow. Through the thinly constructed wall that divided us, I could hear that they were going over editorial copy—reviews, feature stories, and the like—as Mr. Chieftain complained about a litany of perceived grammatical offenses. He was clearly no fan of the word *thespian*. "Just say *actor*," he said. "Kevin, do you tell these writers? Can they just say *actor*?"

"I tell them," Kevin said.

"Everybody's a genius," Mr. Chieftain continued, emphasizing the word *genius* to such an extent that I could feel his scorn for mediocrity through the wall. "Everybody's a *geeeeniusss*."

As I sat there and eavesdropped, I thought about how the office had changed when Mr. Chieftain entered the room, how the energy immediately shifted and how it suddenly felt like I had a real job, whether I was getting paid or not. I felt stupid for allowing myself to believe, even for a second, that a job at a New York City media company could be easy and fun. If it were easy and fun, wouldn't everyone do it?

CHAPTER 3

Long Game

NIGHTS AT THE FRAME SHOP on the Upper West Side often went late. Bobir, one of my Uzbek coworkers, was a frenetic frame-building machine who liked to keep going well into the evening, long after the shop was closed and it was just the two of us tinkering around, cutting mats and mounting posters. The pace was exhausting, but Bobir was so fascinating to talk to that it made the nights fly by. Having grown up poor in Tashkent in the 1980s, he relished his life as a modern twenty-something New Yorker, and no amount of Western culture was too much for him. He nicknamed me "Christopher Lambert." He bought all his clothes at Daffy's. And God help you if you got him started on Scarlett Johansson.

Hanging around the shop with Bobir reminded me of being in school during those rare times when I had a male friend with whom I actually connected. Looking back, I could count them on one hand. What I loved most about Bobir was that even though he worked like a madman, he never took the work seriously. If a picture had a piece of dust behind the glass, he'd insist the customer wouldn't notice. He was always right.

The ride uptown on the 1 train to Washington Heights tacked another twenty-five minutes onto my already long nights, but Gus Gary always seemed to be waiting up for me, often in boxers and a T-shirt, watching the Science Channel or PBS. We'd share a beer and chat about current events—the guy hated Bush with a passion—and then I'd quickly make an excuse for why I needed to go into my bedroom and close the door. A freelance assignment. A phone call. Whatever; I'd make something up. As my first few weeks in the apartment wore on, beer time with Gus Gary got shorter and shorter. I could tell he was disappointed when I abruptly disappeared into my room, but even though I felt wholly indebted to him for letting me move in, I couldn't let the living arrangement rob me of the alone time I desperately needed. Between the internship and the frame shop, I was working seven days a week, and I needed to decompress alone — without Gus Gary and his thoughts about labor rights or Marx or Bush.

Alone time is like water to an introvert, and I was becoming dehydrated, which is to say cranky, irritable, and just generally unpleasant. I tried to control these baser personality traits when I got home, but they possessed minds of their own. Occasionally, Gus Gary would make small overtures in an attempt to bring more substance to our home life. "I have something for you," he said one day when I arrived after work. Then he handed me a copy of *The Communist Manifesto*, fresh off the shelf, nicely packaged in paperback form with a glossy red cover. He'd picked it up at the Barnes and Noble in Lincoln Center. It was too early for Christmas. *What gives?*

"It'll help you understand what we've been talking about," Gus Gary said. "It's all here — the history of class struggle, of labor dynamics."

I found it intriguing that Gus Gary so fervently wanted me to understand class struggle, Gus Gary with his salt-and-pepper hair and his editor job and the fancy degree that I assumed he had. I might have been more receptive to the gift had I not been so worn out from my shifts at the frame shop and my unpaid internship. Whenever the subject of my work situation came up, Gus Gary's face would fold into a sour grimace. He said I was being fleeced. He'd point to my news stories in *Show Business Weekly* and explain that I should be paid for those contributions, no two ways about it.

"You should march in there tomorrow and say, 'Let's talk turkey,'" he said, genuinely furious that I had not negotiated at least a modest hourly wage for the internship. On the one hand, I appreciated that he was looking out for my welfare, but on the other hand, what world did he live in? Did he not realize how lucky I was to catch this break, that I'd already agreed to work for free? Who talks turkey after the fact? Turkey is for the bargaining stage. It's strictly pre-closure. But that didn't matter, Gus Gary insisted, because the newspaper had taken advantage of my vulnerable position when I applied for the job. I had no power, he said.

"I had the power to say no," I countered.

On any given day at *Show Business Weekly,* Mr. Chieftain could take the concept of the asshole boss to radical new places. You weren't allowed to cough, for one thing. And he only allowed pens in the office that had black or red ink. Blue pens went right in the garbage. He hired lots of ad sales-people, but they never lasted very long because he would lose patience with them the minute they ran out of new leads, which usually took about a week. The newspaper was aimed at the New York City acting commu-nity—people looking for audition notices and trying to break into the-ater—and there were only so many acting schools and voice coaches and sleazy photographers willing to pay to reach that audience. "Make phone calls!" Mr. Chieftain would bark at his salespeople whenever he heard stretches of silence, but after Shetler Studios and that weird guy who did headshots from his Hell's Kitchen apartment said no for the third time, what could you really do? This was all compounded by the fact that we already had a much larger competitor, *Back Stage* magazine, which had cornered the market on audition notices long ago, to say nothing of all the upstart casting websites that were popping up at that time.

Poor Kevin bore the brunt of Mr. Chieftain's excitable nature, because he did practically everything *except* sell ads. He wrote features, assigned and edited every theater review, scoured the internet for news, kept track of invoicing, and God knew what else. On my first Friday in the office, I saw him laying out the newspaper—something he did at the end of each week on a design program called Quark—and searching Google for images that could be used for the front cover. "Don't newspapers usually have art directors?" I asked.

"Thank you," Kevin said in a rare acknowledgment that too much was expected of him.

But it was always what Kevin didn't do, or forgot to do, or didn't do fast enough that set Mr. Chieftain off—a misplaced folder, an unpaid invoice—and the boss would make no secret of his disappointment, openly chastising his twenty-three-year-old editorial assistant in front of the entire office. I honestly couldn't fathom how Kevin let Mr. Chieftain's rantings roll off his back so easily, how he managed to stay so calm in the face of belittling rhetorical questions like *Why would you do it like that?* and *What, do you have amnesia?* Maybe Kevin was so agreeable because he had to be. Once in a while, when Mr. Chieftain would shout his name from the next room, Kevin would wince in disgust, his nerves clearly frayed, but he never let Mr. Chieftain see that side of him.

Fortunately, Mr. Chieftain rarely talked to us interns. Kevin was the strategic buffer who kept us from having to deal with him directly. Mr. Chieftain would bark and bellow and rant, and Kevin would calmly communicate what needed to be done. He always asked and never ordered. "Could you do me a favor and download the new casting notices?" he'd say. How can you say no to doing someone a favor?

Despite the buffer zone, interns were still frequently rattled by Mr. Chieftain's gruffness. Some went out for lunch on their first or second day and never came back, which I found very perplexing, even though I'd basically done the same thing that time when I couldn't carry the bags of rice. My own capacity for dealing with Mr. Chieftain got its first test on the day he barreled in complaining that he hated all the house ads in the newspaper. "We need a new campaign," he told Kevin. "These ads suck. Kevin, can we fix these ads?" I had the misfortune to be two feet away when this happened. Mr. Chieftain stared me up and down.

"You. How are you with ideas?" he asked.

"I'm...I'm an idea guy," I squeaked.

He opened a copy of the paper, showed me one of the ads he hated, and asked what I would do to make it better. He was right in that it was objectively bad. It said something about "getting in on the act," which was like, come on. I blurted out a fix that seemed entirely 100 percent not terrible: "Perhaps we could say how a subscription to the newspaper is an investment in their acting career, like—"

"Conventional," Mr. Chieftain responded without hesitation. "Do you even know where you work? Do your homework."

* * *

Alone in my bedroom that night, I stewed. *How could I have let him speak to me like that? What happened to punk-rock me? Why didn't I tell him off or walk out?* I was angry at Mr. Chieftain for putting me on the spot and even angrier at myself for caring. The clock ticked along in slow motion. At some point Gus Gary went to bed, giving me a chance to take a trip to the bathroom and the fridge without the fear of an awkward conversation about the history of collective bargaining. Glancing in the bathroom mirror — always a mistake on a sleepless night — I noticed one of those red marks emerging on my left cheek, the slow-growing kind that usually sticks around for several days. By morning I knew it would be swallowing my whole face. One more thing to worry about.

One a.m. turned into three a.m., and any hope I had of a good night's sleep slipped further and further away. But silence and insomnia can be a stimulating cocktail, because they triggered a memory: I had an old version of Quark, the program Kevin used to lay out the newspaper, installed on my Dell laptop. I didn't recall how it got there, and I surely didn't know how to use it, but theoretically, I could teach myself some tricks over a few weekends, make some ad mock-ups, and bring them in to impress Mr. Chieftain. It was a great tentative plan, the kind of benign revenge fantasy one entertains when the chemicals responsible for inducing sleep refuse to cooperate. Except that just fantasizing about it didn't help me sleep, and now three a.m. was becoming four a.m.

The hell with it. No time like the present.

The following afternoon, Mr. Chieftain charged in as he always did, passing the large corkboard that was mounted outside his private office. He stopped in his tracks when he saw two ads that I had designed thumbtacked to the board. "What is this?" he said, pulling them down for closer inspection. Kevin, a great pitchman, explained that I was simply doing the "homework" that I'd been assigned. Mr. Chieftain looked at me, then back at the ads, then back at me. "You made these?"

I nodded. In retrospect, the ads were not good. As a Quark neophyte, I committed several unforgivable design crimes: Warped text. Faux bolds.

Clashing typefaces. But Mr. Chieftain liked the idea for the campaign — a series of ads debunking common entertainment-industry myths. ("Entertainment Myth No. 31: Anyone Can Act!") More important, Mr. Chieftain seemed taken by the idea that I had worked these ads up on my personal time.

"Kevin, why can't you come up with more ideas like this?" Mr. Chieftain said. "You're the one getting paid."

It's hard to say which one of us should have been more offended by that statement. Of course Kevin had no time for extracurricular activities like designing house ads. I felt instantly guilty that my act of initiative had been perceived by Mr. Chieftain as a shortcoming on Kevin's part, and yet my perspective on my own self-worth shifted dramatically that day. For the first time, I could see the difference between my status as an unpaid intern and Kevin's as a paid editor: an imaginary thing separated only by opportunity. It took Mr. Chieftain acknowledging that my work had value for me to realize how much I was being devalued.

After fawning over the ads for a few more minutes, Mr. Chieftain set me up at a better computer station, one with Quark installed, and asked me if I wouldn't mind staying late and coming up with a few more ad concepts. That is, unless I had somewhere else to be.

CHAPTER 4

Traitor

A COLD WIND STUNG MY face as I darted across 175th Street, defying the first of many Don't Walk signs. I stopped for a moment to yank my knit hat down over my cheeks, and a second wind whipped me even harder from the other direction. Ouch. This bullshit weather was definitely not something I'd missed about the Northeast. An endless stretch of upper Broadway rolled out ahead, and that was just the first leg of this trip. How was I expected to make it all the way to Midtown on foot?

I was one of millions of people walking to work on that frigid morning in December 2005, day three of New York City's first transit strike in twenty-five years. Subways and buses were shut down and there was not a cab in sight—not that I could have afforded one. Gus Gary thought I was ridiculous for walking halfway down the island to get to an internship I wasn't being paid for, and he wasn't wrong. But I didn't feel that I had much of a choice. When I'd spoken to Kevin about it earlier that morning, he'd made it clear that my presence was needed in the office. "Just do what you have to do to get here," he said. It was the only time I can recall him *telling* me to do anything. Tension between Kevin and me had risen in the weeks since I brought in those ad designs. I was emerging as Mr. Chieftain's star pupil, the intern he'd call on for special tasks, and I could see Kevin was conflicted about it. The easy banter Kevin and I once shared gave way to personal digs, like the time I made a crack about his frequent smoke breaks, because it was 2005 and who still smoked? "Maybe I'll quit by the time I'm your age," he responded.

Little by little, Mr. Chieftain was giving me more to do. When he heard my ideas for news stories, he invited me to the editorial meetings, which were often just Mr. Chieftain, Kevin, and a few freelance writers who randomly joined. When he found out I could write well without using the word *thespian,* he gave me first dibs on any new Broadway show I wanted to review. I'd never even seen a Broadway show before. Kevin might not have been especially thrilled with all this, but he liked having the extra help. Each task I took on was one he didn't have to worry about. On that December day, when I finally arrived at the office — my face frozen stiff and my feet blistered from the ten-mile walk — Kevin rattled off something about a story deadline and the casting notices that still needed to be inputted and a bunch of other chores that I now knew how to do. Oh, and could I take out the garbage?

By the time I made it back to Washington Heights that night, city officials had announced that the transit strike was over, and not a moment too soon. I don't think I could've handled another day of it. After trudging inside, I grumbled something to Gus Gary about how the whole thing felt pointless. The union bosses had violated New York State law, I argued, and worse than that, they'd left millions of people with no way to get to work. I mean, I understood solidarity and all that, but I was also tired, frozen, and blistered. "It's hard to know whose side to be on," I said.

"What are you talking about?" Gus Gary snapped. "There's only one side. How can you side with anyone except the workers?"

He wore me down with those kinds of comments, because as offended as I was at the suggestion that I was somehow *not* on the side of the workers — what the hell was *I,* after all? — arguments with Gus Gary forced me to think about why the topic of organized labor made perfectly reasonable people seem so obstinate, and what did it say about me that I was so conflicted about it? Maybe it was because I'd never felt that unions had done anything for me personally. When you bounce around between low-level service jobs your whole life, you don't exactly feel the rising tide of the labor rights movement under your sore feet. But at least Gus Gary never let me forget the bigger picture — that the alternative to empowering workers was handing power over to companies.

* * *

My first spring in New York City was a blur. If I wasn't in the frame shop or at *Show Business Weekly,* I was teaching myself how to use computer programs that I thought would help me in an office setting, like Microsoft Word, HTML, and, especially, Quark. Trying to figure out design software is a bit like learning to play a musical instrument. The first time you open the screen, you are visually assaulted by a jumble of panels and pointers and rulers and *What the hell is that V-shaped thing?* But then, bit by bit, you learn what each tool does, how it functions, why it exists. The layers of unfriendly gibberish slowly peel away, muscle memory guides your fingers to the keyboard shortcuts, and beautiful purpose reveals itself.

By the final week of March, my zeal for self-tutelage had started to pay off because Mr. Chieftain now trusted me to help Kevin lay out the newspaper on the production computer, the "big one," which Mr. Chieftain let only a few people touch. Mr. Chieftain was almost pathologically suspicious of everyone who came into the office. In my mind, he embodied the stereotype of a well-bred paranoid New Yorker, the product of a Manhattan childhood and expensive boarding schools. Too many nannies and not enough love.

In 1941, Mr. Chieftain's grandfather had founded the newspaper *Show Business,* a pioneer of the printed audition notice, and Mr. Chieftain was in charge of keeping the operation afloat in the twenty-first century. His family was not filthy rich, but there was enough money to fight over, often in the courts. Distrust was Mr. Chieftain's default mode. He once fired a young salesperson on her first day because she showed up with a horseshoe septum ring that she had discreetly tucked into her nostrils during the interview process. "False advertising!" Mr. Chieftain said.

Somehow, I was spared the same level of neurotic scrutiny, and I wasn't sure why. Was my quietness working in my favor? I never imagined this instinct would be an office skill. Mr. Chieftain seemed to enjoy teaching me the ropes. On the day he showed me the layout procedures, he displayed all the steadiness and patience of a proud mentor. And yet I couldn't help but think back to an incident just two weeks earlier, when I'd caught him glowering at two interns leaving the office together for their lunch break. "Kevin, can you make sure they go to lunch at different times?" he said. "The interns shouldn't socialize. I don't want them talking."

I recall Kevin chuckling awkwardly at that comment, but Mr. Chieftain did not smile. "I'm not joking you," he added.

I was struck by Mr. Chieftain's willingness to say all this in front of me. Did he not expect me to immediately take this information back across enemy lines? The tricky topic of trust in the workplace weighed heavily on me that week. In the real world, trust is supposed to be earned, built up slowly over months or years. But in the white-collar world, as far as I could tell, it appeared to be based more on forging alliances with the right people. You trusted the people who could help you, and they trusted you, or pretended to.

Internships at *Show Business Weekly* usually lasted five months, and I'd been there for four and a half. The skills I had acquired in my short time there gave me the naive confidence to apply for every halfway decent media job I came across. I scoured online portals like Craigslist and Mediabistro and JournalismJobs, sometimes firing off four or five cover letters and résumés a day. I omitted any information that might give away my age, a ripe old thirty-five and a half. I didn't expect to land a corner office at *Vanity Fair* or run the metro desk at the *Times,* but I was sure the offers for entry-level gigs would pour in. Or at least trickle in. Or something.

They didn't. Not a single interview. Not even a *Thank you for getting in touch.* What was I missing? Was the internship not impressive enough? I suspect I knew the truth: my lack of a college education was a cavity too deep to fill. But I did everything I could to block out that voice of reason. I fooled myself into believing I could substitute a five-month internship for a four-year degree. Some job candidates piled two or three or four internships on top of a master's degree, scholarships, awards, and two years with the goddamn Peace Corps, and they still couldn't find media jobs. But if I let myself accept that, if I focused on what I didn't have going for me, I knew I was doomed. Time was running out. I couldn't work unpaid forever.

* * *

April delivered the first warm weekend of the year, the kind of seductive weather that compels cabin-fevered New Yorkers to spill out onto the streets in droves. Their hurried winter gait slows to a casual stroll, and they gaze at the spiky horizon with fresh eyes, smiling and remembering just how much they love this place. It was my first spring as a New Yorker, and I was discovering the city anew. For me, Manhattan had been a destination for heroin, a den of excess and escape, but those associations were slowly beginning to dissipate. In an unexpected way, that ceaseless New York rhythm made visions of my old life all the more jarring when they'd occasionally come rushing back. A walk through Washington Square Park on that first warm April weekend instantly transported me to a beautiful afternoon in 1994 when I nodded off in the sun on a bench by the fountain as beat boxes blared, street kids and NYU students danced in harmony, and the smell of ganja wafted. Twelve years later, the music and hair styles had changed, but the festive energy was exactly the same. I thought I even recognized that guy with the snake.

When you're a junkie, the bar is low. As long as you have your fix, you can enjoy a nice afternoon in Washington Square Park without strings. Lower Manhattan has everything you need. Years later, when I was a working person, the city was still the only world I wanted, but it all felt too temporary. My internship was coming to an end and there was no career in sight. The only tangible thing waiting for me, the only real thing, was my job at the frame shop. Nothing else seemed attainable. Retail was all I'd ever known, but it was becoming harder to silence the voice in my head that said it was all I deserved. As my internship approached its inevitable conclusion, my bitterness toward having to work a day job began to overpower my career aspirations. I resented having to show up at the shop, having to help well-to-do Upper West Siders pick out stupid mats to go with their stupid Kandinsky prints. "Look, you can't put red with yellow unless you're Ronald McDonald," I'd snap at some poor lady in a turtleneck and oversize glasses who didn't deserve my acrimony. I'd never especially liked working service jobs, but in all the years I'd been doing it, I'd never taken it out on the customers. I could always somehow reach deep down and pull out the part of me that understood and respected the trans-actional nature of my relationship with the people who patronized the business. They were the reason I had a job. And the dynamic of my having to serve them was not their fault.

How many more hours of my life was I willing to sell for eleven dollars a pop? That employers in media did not deem my résumé worthy of even a response pierced my ego and deflated what little was left of it. Retail had long felt like purgatory. Now it felt like prison.

Bobir was the only thing that kept me sane at the frame shop. We spent much of our shift joking around and watching Hollywood movies on his laptop; he fast-forwarded through the dialogue and went right to the special effects. The fight scenes in Peter Jackson's *King Kong* were his favorite. "Whoa!" he'd say, pointing and laughing as Kong ripped open the jaws of a T. rex. "That is so beautiful."

"Bobir, you realize this is a love story, right?"

"No, it isn't."

"King Kong loves the girl. That's what it's about."

"No."

My easy rapport with Bobir stood in contrast to my awkward home life with Gus Gary. Our tense exchanges and bickering over politics seemed to be getting worse by the day, despite my vow to try harder. The more convinced I became that I would spend the rest of my life in retail hell, the more I resented Gus Gary, him with his ideals and his hot takes on workers' rights. It was all so theoretical when you had a cushy editor job. Pledging your solidarity with the subway strikers was easy when you could work from home. While Gus Gary treated Marx like gospel, *Communism* was a dirty word to Bobir. As a Muslim growing up in Soviet-era Uzbekistan, he hadn't even been allowed to pray in school. He was thirteen when Communism collapsed and he remembered it vividly as a moment of sheer joy. Any mention of the Soviet Union set him off on a rant about all the things he believed it had taken away from him. Being Western, which was the thing he wanted most of all, meant the freedom to practice his Muslim faith and watch the fight scenes in *King Kong* in equal measure. No wonder Bobir referred to the frame shop as a "gallery." That's really how he saw it. My prison was his refuge.

* * *

I had to hand it to Kevin. My twenty-three-year-old boss seemed to have more confidence in my ability to find a job in media than I did. At the office one afternoon, I confessed my frustration with my job hunt, how I couldn't even get a response from prospective employers. He seemed almost alarmed at the thought of my leaving. "But my internship is ending," I reminded him. I couldn't just stay there and keep working for free.

Kevin sat me down for a confidential talk. "Keep this between us, but I might be leaving *Show Business Weekly*," he said, pushing his glasses up the bridge of his nose. "I've been thinking about it for a while. Obviously, you'd be more than qualified to take my place. Plus, Mr. Chieftain trusts you, and that's the biggest hurdle here."

After a pause, I responded with what I figured was the most obvious question, really the only question: "Where would you go?"

"Eh, I'm not sure," Kevin said, his eyes now focused on his computer screen as if he had already lost interest in the conversation. "I only graduated from NYU last year and I'm still trying to figure shit out."

Figure shit out? Part of me wanted to shake him, to tell him I'd already figured shit out for him. *There's nothing out there, kid,* I wanted to scream. *The real world is cold and unfeeling, and it will still be here waiting for you when you're done finding yourself.* But the urge to talk sense into him was overridden by something more primal. Inside, I was salivating at the thought of taking his job. "Tell me more," I finally said.

"Working at some trade paper that no one's ever heard of isn't going to help me in the long run," Kevin said. "That much I know."

At that moment the subtext of our conversation became clear. *Some trade paper.* He'd said it with such contempt. *Show Business Weekly* was Kevin's frame shop.

What if Kevin was low-key because he just didn't care? Either Kevin was too young and naive to understand what he had or I was too clueless and ignorant to see the plain truth of what I didn't. His degree from NYU meant that he had options. I didn't. Kevin had options. Lori and Steve had options. The interns who walked out because they were rattled by Mr. Chieftain had options. Me? I was expected to keep working unpaid, to wait patiently in the wings for a younger, more experienced, more creden-tialed professional to figure shit out.

Not long after my conversation with Kevin—a few days or weeks—I checked my e-mail at the frame shop. I hoped to see new responses from prospective employers, but instead I was staring at a spinning circle. We pirated our internet from the grocery store next door, and the connection was lousy. When my in-box finally loaded, it was empty except for an urgent e-mail from Kevin. He wrote that he was quitting the newspaper, giving his two weeks, and that I could expect a call from Mr. Chieftain later that day. "Mr. Chieftain wants to hire you," Kevin wrote.

I must have taken several long seconds to process that information, because Bobir was staring me down hard. He had just seen *Match Point*, the new Woody Allen movie, and was trying to describe the life-affirming experience of watching a wet Scarlett Johansson kiss Jonathan Rhys Mey-ers in the rain. But I was completely unresponsive. What gives? Bobir wanted to know.

"I think…I just got a new job," I said, still staring at the screen.

"A new job?"

"A better job."

"Better than gallery?"

I wasn't sure how to answer. "I mean, it's what I want to do. It's a job in journalism. I'd be an editor at a newspaper."

"Ah," Bobir replied. Then a smile stretched across his face. "Traitor."

He meant it playfully, a one-word eulogy for a workplace friendship we both knew would not survive outside this workplace. I was a traitor, leav-ing a job for the promise of a career, trading shop hours for office hours, sneakers for shoes, a cash register for a desk. Without a degree, I didn't have the options Kevin had, but that didn't mean I had none at all.

I got out of work early that day. Taking advantage of the extra day-light, I walked south through the Upper West Side, the street numbers descending. I counted down one by one as I contemplated the semantics of direction. What is *up* and *down*, anyway? What does it mean to *go north* or *walk south?* For my entire life up until that point, I'd moved from one job to the next with very little thought. Those moves were always lateral, not up or down, not better or worse than what had come before. A job was a job. I've always had a lousy sense of direction—that's why I prefer numbered streets.

By the time I arrived at Columbus Circle, Fifty-Ninth Street, I decided I'd earned a slice of pizza for dinner. After walking thirty-two blocks and spending forty-five minutes in personal reflection, I figured the pizza would be a net gain of ten calories at the most. I popped into one of those unremarkable Midtown pizza places, the kind with smoke-damaged awnings and broken bathrooms. I sat down to eat my slice and fell into a tunnel-vision moment. I don't remember if the pizza was good, although, let's be real, Midtown pizza never is. I also can't recall if the place was busy or where I sat or even what street it was on. I just remember the picture frames on the walls. The mats were faded from the sun, the corners splitting, the glass filthy. Those were not my problems anymore.

CHAPTER 5

Stupid Shy

MR. CHIEFTAIN AND I SPOKE by phone for only a few minutes that night. He offered me the job, as Kevin had predicted he would, and I said I'd be honored to accept. He seemed to like that I used the word *honored* because he repeated it several times. "You're honored. I'm honored. Everybody's honored," he said.

We agreed to work out the details the next day and hung up. Sounds from outside my bedroom rose up through the courtyard, aided by open windows and the dry spring air: Kids playing. A Spanish-language radio station. There was almost always an opera singer with scales to practice. I tried to let my thoughts disappear in the meditative symphony of Washington Heights, tried to prevent myself from obsessing over the professional transition I was about to make. *What if I'm not ready?* I kept thinking. My biggest concern was not knowing the basic rules that everyone else took for granted. I thought back to my first day of the internship, how my mind went blank when Kevin handed me that assignment. What if freak-outs like that kept happening? I wondered again if I had skipped necessary steps in not finishing high school, in not going to college, and whether the things they would have taught me there could be learned outside of a classroom.

Did I fail school or did school fail me?

It's an annoying rhetorical question, and yet I find myself annoyingly asking it whenever I try to retrace the steps that led to my academic collapse. Maybe that's because school started out so promising. In the beginning, the rules made sense. School was a walled garden, a place where I

41

could surrender control to authority, where the constant fear of teachers and nuns and God rendered dissent unthinkable. The people in charge talked about easily digestible concepts like hell and eternal suffering. They shamed us for wanting to dress up like Batman on Halloween because *What about Jesus?* When the bell rang from the copper tower at the top of Holy Angels Church, it meant recess was over. We'd stand there in silence on the blacktop, hands in praying position, and wait obediently for a teacher to direct us back to the classroom. We always walked in single file and never left our places in line. If we acted up, we got detention—or worse. New Jersey was the first state in the union to ban corporal punishment in schools, but teachers could always hand you a wooden ruler and make you hit yourself with it. *Harder, harder—you're not even trying.* Our matching outfits hewed to the dullest of palettes, the boys in blue button-down shirts and clip-on ties, the girls in blue plaid skirts. Conformity was the greatest virtue in this world of rites and rituals, and I was too afraid to be unvirtuous. You might say I was the perfect Catholic-school student.

But it was also a time when the line between fear and phobia was murky. What I remember most about those early years of school is that I managed to get through them by saying as few words as possible. I basically never talked to anyone. When asked questions or prompted to take part in conversations, I froze, just like I froze on my first day at *Show Business Weekly.* Anxiousness and the fear of messing up left my mind in a state of protracted blankness. *Shyness,* they called it then. Not a disorder but the kind of thing you grow out of. My classmates knew better. They were perceptive, as kids tend to be, and instinctively homed in on this weakness, ridiculing me with comments like "Zara, you talk too much."

Adults took a bit more time to understand that something was amiss. Teachers tended to see quietness as a sign that everything was going well. They didn't notice that I was unable to sound out words or that I struggled with fractions. When it was discovered in second grade that I was near-sighted and needed glasses, one teacher asked me why I'd never told anyone I was having trouble seeing the chalkboard. Well, who knew the world wasn't supposed to be blurry?

* * *

I might have eventually outgrown the worst of my introvert tendencies had it not been for the random misfortune of birth order. While I was off being a quiet, God-fearing student, my older brother, Joe — two grades ahead of me — was being the exact opposite. Joe spoke up constantly. He talked in class whenever he had a passing thought. He shifted in his seat, ate his erasers, asked too many questions, and basically drove all the adults crazy. Every nun was at the end of her rope. One nun suggested my mom give him caffeine in the mornings. *Sometimes that'll help settle a hyper lad.* Another suggested Ritalin. *Have you heard of it? Works miracles.*

My mom didn't care for these solutions. She had a mother's protective instinct and tended to find fault in people who were not her children. Joe's attention difficulties, by her reading of the situation, were clearly the result of an inflexible school system, of bad teachers who couldn't grasp the idea that a kid might require a little extra help. He was inquisitive, overactive perhaps, but never malicious, she argued.

At home, my parents were used to Joe's behavior, almost numb to it, perhaps because Joe seemed to lead a charmed life. At two years old, he'd jumped out the second-story window of our row house, narrowly missed a pair of telephone wires on his way down, and landed safely on some scraps of carpet that my dad had thrown in the alley. I was six days old at the time, guzzling baby formula on my mom's lap when she heard an ominous *thump* outside the window. Here was the first home-cooked meal of my life and it was already interrupted by the antics of an overactive older brother. Joe always managed to escape the worst. Charmed life.

The consequence of growing up a couple of years behind a sibling who demands everyone's attention is that you naturally fall into the opposite role. My entire personality was formed like elementary particles after the Big Bang, passively following someone else's orbit. Of course, I wanted to be just like Joe, but there was room for only one. We shared an obvious physical feature, bright red hair, which adults said made us look like fiery twins, but that only sharpened the contrast between our personalities. Joe had a theory that the constant teasing that went along with being a redhead affected us differently as kids. "My red hair forced me to be more outgoing and yours forced you to be more shy," he said.

At Catholic school, Joe was branded a "hyperactive child," which left such a negative taste in my mom's mouth that she ultimately yanked us out of Catholic school and sent us to public school. My parents had moved us a half block over the city border into Hamilton Township, although the post office weirdly still considered us as having a Trenton mailing address. Our front lawn had bald spots, and our porch was sinking into the ground, but Hamilton's public schools were pretty decent, according to adults, better even than Catholic schools. There was just one problem: My mom, the product of Catholic schools herself, had conditioned us to be terrified of *all* public schools. Lairs of depravity, they were. Kids wore whatever they wanted and no one believed in God. "They throw rocks," my mom would say whenever we drove by a public school. Now we were suddenly expected to go to the rock-throwing school, and it felt like a jail sentence.

I went to public school from fourth grade on. No one threw rocks on my first day, but I clearly remember not knowing how to sit as the teacher took attendance. Normally, I would fold my hands quietly at my desk. Now I was afraid someone would think I was praying.

While Joe was commanding everyone's full-time attention two grades ahead of me, my younger brother, Fred, was doing so for different reasons two grades behind me. He was having trouble reading and falling further behind his classmates. What I lacked in speaking ability, he seemed to lack with words on a page, but worse. Letters appeared contorted and unfriendly, sentences unreadable. Tutors and extra time to do homework were not enough, and when Fred was in the second grade, the school decided that he should be held back. Except, for some bizarre reason, this decision was made in the middle of the school year, so Fred suffered the horrifying public indignity of being told this news in front of his entire second-grade class. A school administrator entered the classroom, pointed Fred out, told him to gather his things from his desk, and ordered him back to the first grade.

The scar from Fred's midyear demotion was one that he would carry throughout his time at school, and Fred did not hide his scars easily. He was always a bit hotheaded, quick-tempered, not afraid to pick fights with larger kids if he thought they were trying to make a fool out of him. He wore the permanent chip on his shoulder of a youngest sibling—too young to keep up, determined to do so anyway. But his temper was off-set by a friendly disposition and a steady brown-eyed gaze. That combination helped Fred earn something I lacked in elementary school: the respect and admiration of classmates. Just like Joe, he made friends with little effort.

Even back then, I suspected I was a walking middle-child stereotype—thank you, Jan Brady and Crackle, the goofiest elf—so I guess it was a stroke of luck that my brothers and I got along so well. We were definitely closer than most siblings—we listened to Kiss on eight-track tapes and formed our own secret agency called Expert Spy Kids. On Friday nights, we sat behind foldable TV-dinner tables and watched *The Incredible Hulk*. And one Saturday morning, determined to fly like Superman, we built a hang glider out of a discarded refrigerator box and a broomstick. It was glorious and carried Joe nearly all the way across our front lawn.

By the time I was in fifth grade, my parents had begun to suspect that my difficulties in school went beyond garden-variety shyness. I was starting to lag behind the other students, particularly in spelling and math. My mom decided to have me evaluated by a team of special-education experts at Trenton State College. These experts, in their evaluation summary, noted my tendency to pronounce words and syllables backward—*book* was *koob;* my aunt Peggy was Geppy—and pointed out that I wrote letters in what they described as "mirror image," which sounds like a cool party trick but was really just an early symptom of my lousy sense of direction. "Below-average spatial relations" was their nice way of saying it.

However, I took a series of aptitude tests, and they didn't find much else wrong with me. They noted a history of "perceptual problems" that affected males in my family—my dad and two brothers, especially Fred, all had trouble learning to read—but the team ultimately determined that my own achievement problems in school were not the result of a learning disability as defined by education law. I was not, as they put it, "classifiable."

Granted, my evaluators were not especially impressed with my social skills. "Eye contact with Chris was limited and difficult to obtain and maintain," they wrote. But they didn't spot any red flags that might suggest an academic catastrophe was waiting for me down the line. I guess that's the problem with experts. When they end up being wrong, they usually have the luxury of not being around to find out about it.

CHAPTER 6

The D List

A FEW WEEKS BEFORE MY first day of high school, I had a revelation in church. It had nothing to do with God or salvation, but it was as profound to my thirteen-year-old self as anything I'd ever felt. By 1984 our family had stopped going to church regularly, mostly because my brothers and I were old enough by then to have mastered the art of collective resistance. But this one Sunday, in the thick humidity of late summer, our parents convinced us to attend morning Mass at Holy Angels, probably by bribing us with the promise of a trip to Mr. Ed's afterward for soft ice cream—or "custard," as my dad called it. The church was hot and crowded that morning. As we were shuffling into our wooden pew, my brother Joe, now about to enter his junior year, pointed out a classmate of his who was shuffling in with his own family three or four rows behind us. "That's Lazer," Joe whispered. "He's a punk rocker."

I turned around to see a tall, lanky seventeen-year-old boy in a torn-up tank top, loose-fitting pink pants, and pointy black boots. His hair, bleached almost blindingly white, was sticking straight up in some parts and hair-sprayed flat to his head in others. Earrings dangled from his ears, reflecting bright colors from the stained-glass windows that depicted the stations of the cross. His long forearms were swathed in homemade spiked bracelets, some with three-inch nails piercing through worn leather bands. Old ladies gasped at the sight of him. People several rows away were staring, gawking, whispering. Lazer was unfazed. He stood there in silence and fixed his gaze on the altar, exuding a detached self-confidence. It wasn't that he didn't notice the stares and snickers of the other churchgoers. It was that he didn't care. Even more than that, he seemed to welcome the attention. Somehow he was able to embrace his own weirdness and be indifferent to it at the same time.

I had spent all my years at school up to that point being terrified of not fitting in, praying for invisibility, learning to contort my personality into whatever unnatural shapes allowed me to get by unnoticed. Weird was the worst thing you could be. In Catholic school it would land you in detention, and in public school it would get you ridiculed or punched. By the end of eighth grade, I had developed such a fear of shared spaces that I had not urinated in a school bathroom in three years, a condition I later learned was called paruresis.

But now here, in front of me, was a boy whose existence defied my understanding of what it meant to be different, proof that weirdness could be a strength. Lazer was in color. Everyone else in church that day was in black-and-white.

High school was the horror show I'd expected it to be and then some. The hallways were darker, the classrooms more crowded, the teachers less engaged. The girls who ignored you looked more like women, and the boys who picked on you looked more like men. By the time I started ninth grade, I had shot up to an awkward six feet, but unlike my dad and two brothers, I was not—how to say this—blessed with a trim physique. My dad said I had "the tendency," his not-so-subtle way of telling me that I put on weight easily, as if the heightened self-consciousness of puberty had not already made that obvious to me. "Be careful," he said. "You take after your mother." Unfortunately for me, the tendency began at the worst possible time for my floundering body image, which had devolved into an unhealthy obsession with mirrors. For a while, I thought I could will away my physical flaws if I just stared hard enough at my own reflection, no matter how ghastly and unwelcoming.

I had escaped my share of freshman-year beatings, thanks in part to my last name. Joe already had a reputation for being tough, and when other tough kids learned he was my brother, they would often back off. What they didn't know was that Joe's reputation for toughness was mostly the product of his own creation, stories he made up or embellished, like how he'd cracked some kid's head open. The same talkative nature that used to drive nuns crazy in Catholic school served Joe exceedingly well in high school. He honed his natural gift for gab into the perfect defense mechanism, creating an origin myth that ensured his own survival. And mine.

Joe and Lazer became inseparable that year. They'd roam the halls together between classes, smoke near the bleachers, and drive around after school in Lazer's jacked-up 1972 Chevy Nova, decorated with masking tape to look like the car from *The Dukes of Hazzard*. Only instead of saying GENERAL LEE on the side, it said GENERAL FLEE, like the satirical version of the car that appeared in *Cracked* magazine. Lazer had been held back a few years earlier and was one of the few juniors in the school who were old enough to drive. He seemed to take nothing seriously, even though he put meticulous thought into everything—his clothes, his music, his turns of phrase. On occasion, I would hear him cackling like a wild goose from clear across the lunchroom, apparently laughing out loud at his own wacky ideas. He loved nothing more than pulling off random acts of absurdism. "Joey, let's drive to Pathmark and practice getting into car accidents!" Observing him from a distance, his long jacket with the anarchy symbol flopping along with the jerky movements of his thin frame, I was struck by how much Lazer seemed to enjoy himself. But what I noticed most was that everybody—everybody—knew who Lazer was. *Oh, that crazy punk rocker? What's wrong with that guy?*

I was starstruck the first time Lazer came over to our house. I came down from my room one dark Saturday evening to find him leaning back in a chair at our kitchen table, eating cereal from the box. Joe was off getting ready somewhere. The house reeked of Aqua Net. Lazer peeked out from behind his wide plastic sunglasses, looked at me in my Mötley Crüe T-shirt, and sneered.

"Crüe rots," he said.

Huh?

"They suck."

I was too stunned that he was talking to me to answer. But also, why was he antagonizing me? Didn't he know I was his biggest fan? At some point, Joe came to collect Lazer and the two of them went out for the night, leaving me to ponder my obviously flawed taste in music.

From the Beatles and Pink Floyd albums that Joe had turned me onto when I was eleven, I had progressed to 1980s hair bands, which were the epitome of cool in my mind. "We don't need no education" gave way to "Hot for Teacher." With no friends at school, I spent most of my weekends at home with Fred, putting on long-haired wigs and lip-synching to the likes of Quiet Riot, Ratt, and Van Halen in front of a black-and-white video camera—still a novelty at that time. With VHS tapes, Fred and I created our own television network, called ZTV, for an audience of no one. My gravitating toward heavy metal music was psychologically fraught—these were, after all, the same bands that the burnouts who picked on me at school seemed to embrace. Part of me reasoned that if all of us were scribbling the same Twisted Sister logos on our paper-bag book covers, they'd have less of a reason to pummel me.

But Lazer's offhand comment made me wonder if I had it all backward. Why had I adopted the musical tastes of the people who thought I was a loser? What if music was better enjoyed not as a show of conformity but as an act of rebellion? I wasn't sure I knew the answer to those questions, but I knew I never wanted to wear another Mötley Crüe T-shirt again.

My freshman year ended with another downward slope in my academic success. I got a D in almost every subject that year. Intro to algebra. U.S. history. English. All Ds.

No one seemed to notice that my grades were getting progressively worse. My mom had recently gone back to work for the *Trenton Times*, where she'd begun in data processing but moved on to computers. Unwittingly, she had also been thrown into one of the last great newspaper wars of the twentieth century. Ten years earlier the Washington Post Company had bought the *Trenton Times* with the aim of turning it into an elite journalistic operation that focused on national politics and global affairs, a kind of *Washington Post* North. What the high-minded owners hadn't counted on was the *Trentonian,* a scrappy, saucy tabloid that was the polar opposite of what they were trying to turn the *Trenton Times* into. Even back then, it was rare for a city as small as Trenton to have two daily newspapers, and somehow the Washington Post Company had overlooked the fact that Trenton was a two-newspaper town. Someone must not have done basic due diligence, because the *Trentonian* and the *Trenton Times* had offices very close to each other on opposite ends of Perry Street, each with its own rooftop neon sign that sliced into the night sky with brilliant shades of orange and red. This scene basically screamed, *We're having a newspaper war here, people.*

While the *Trenton Times* sidelined local reporters, imported fancy talent from larger markets, and sought to capture affluent readers from nearby Princeton, the *Trentonian* kept gaining more and more market share by giving local readers what they actually wanted: pictures of kids' birthday parties and lurid headlines like "Mother Knifed, Eaten." The Washington Post Company pumped money into the *Trenton Times* for several years, but in the end, its smaller competitor proved unbeatable. The company finally sold off the *Trenton Times* in the early eighties, and Trenton's great newspaper war became someone else's problem. Katharine Graham, the Washington Post Company's chairman, famously referred to Trenton as "my Vietnam."

Suffice it to say, being a foot soldier in a newspaper war kept my mom very busy. She was determined, in ways that I was oblivious to at the time, to recapture a career that was put on hold when Joe, Fred, and I were born. My mom got her first job in data processing right out of high school. She was driven, intellectually curious, and might have climbed comfortably up the corporate ladder had she not faced the nearly impossible task of raising three boys, one of whom had a propensity to jump out windows. During my first year of high school, my mom was making up for lost time, learning how to use computer software and shoring up her qualifications for a changing industry. Bad grades from a middle son were an easy thing not to notice, or at least not to deal with.

My dad was not very involved in the day-to-day affairs of parenting. He worked third shift for the Department of Labor and Industry, spending his nights in a modernist office building in downtown Trenton surrounded by reels of magnetic tape on giant IBM machines. It was a job he'd had ever since I could remember. He started working for the State of New Jersey at nineteen—stocking shelves right after high school, which he barely finished—and basically stayed there ever since, inching his way up and becoming a supervisor in the computer room. They even held his job for him while he was in the army. My dad seemed to enjoy the quirky rhythm of the night shift, living slightly out of step with the rest of the world, shopping at 7-Eleven at two in the morning, sleeping all day. He thought grades and report cards were things my mom would take care of, if he thought about them at all.

The concept of academic excellence is hard to wrap your head around when passing, or barely passing, is your status quo. Ds on my report card weren't great—I knew that much—but they were enough for me to squeak by, and squeaking by was all anyone seemed to expect from me.

Ninth grade was such a miserable social experience that I was more than happy to leave it behind. I was on the D list in more ways than one. After spending the year as a quiet observer, watching Lazer and Joe and their friends have the run of the school, I became obsessed with reinventing myself. I spent that summer combing through thrift stores for ill-fitting suit jackets and soaking my jeans in bleach. I borrowed a chain collar from our dog, Scamp, and wore it around my neck. I went to the Piercing Pagoda and had holes punched into my earlobe—only the left one, because that's how everyone knew you were straight. My red hair, which had been a magnet of unwanted attention my entire life, was suddenly an asset. Other punks spent small fortunes dyeing their hair bright colors. My hair came that way. I just cut it short and doused it in Stiff Stuff.

The soundtrack to my transformation that summer was exhilarating, a curated mix of underground music discovered on the cardboard-box shelves of independent record stores. Unpolished and intense. Male but not masculine. Bands with names like the Crucifucks and Suicidal Tendencies and Anti-Nowhere League. You couldn't find this stuff on MTV, and they didn't play it at shopping malls. If you were lucky, you could catch the occasional punk segment on WPRB, Princeton's college radio station, but mainstream DJs never touched it. They were too busy with Michael Jackson or Madonna or Huey Lewis, music that suddenly sounded to me like it was going in slow motion. I had barely noticed the overproduced gloss of top-forty radio until I heard music stripped bare, ground to its essence by artists who prized emotional honesty over technical expertise. They pounded their drums, sometimes losing the beat, and let the feedback on their amps run wild. They screamed contradictory lyrics into their microphones, declarations of nihilism mixed with manifestos of uncompromising idealism. The point wasn't to be perfect or even right. The point was to be heard. And I heard them.

This music and the emotional connection I felt with it further validated the revelation I'd experienced at Holy Angels. Individuality was the way forward. That much was clear. All of mainstream society could keep willfully tuning out the truth for all I cared. For the first time in my life, I felt like I knew something that everyone else didn't. This intoxicating blend of arrogance and ignorance did wonders for my ability to mask the social anxiety that had been holding me back. Its effect on my grades was far less impressive.

CHAPTER 7

This Is Not a Democracy

THE CRACKLING NOISE CAME ABRUPTLY from the square-faced intercom speaker that was perched above our classroom door, interrupting an otherwise uneventful eleventh-grade health class. Usually, that sound meant someone was about to be called to the office, and these days, that someone was usually me.

"Tell them I'm in the shower," I joked, which got a rousing laugh from the class.

I was summoned to the office of one of our vice principals. We had four of them at the high school and they seemed to take turns dealing with me. In the months since I began my junior year, I had already gotten in trouble for leaving school grounds, sleeping in class, using the girls' bathroom, mouthing off to a teacher, and setting my locker on fire. I wasn't sure what I'd done this time, although I suspected it had something to do with my T-shirt, across which I had scrawled the words *I'd Rather Be an Asshole* in thick black Sharpie. Teachers had been giving me dirty looks all day.

I took my time traversing the empty hallways on my way to the vice principal's office. I walked in slow, gaping steps, taking in the echoes of my own footfalls, the clanking of chains against my leather boots, the jingle of locks around my wrist. I wondered why other kids didn't try to make noise when they walked. The classrooms were filled with half-conscious students in the thick of third period, that part of the day when lunch is beckoning and the lectures seem like they will never end. Some of the students craned their necks as I passed by the doorways, surely wondering why I was roaming the halls alone.

Everyone at school knew me or knew of me, or at least that's what I told myself. *That weirdo. That freak. What's wrong with that guy?*

Lazer and Joe were distant memories — they'd graduated a whole year earlier — and now I was carrying their torch of strangeness, pushing the envelope with acts of insubordination that would rise like hot air and float along the rumor mill until the facts became indistinguishable from urban legends. *Bro, I heard you brought a dead rat to school.* It wasn't dead and that wasn't me, but I took credit for it anyway.

As I passed by the glass trophy cabinet that honored past heroes from the high school's football team, I caught a faint glimpse of my reflection, my pointy hair and popped-up collar offering the perfect contrast to the boring football jerseys and pom-poms. Mirrors had been a source of dread for me since puberty and the tendency, but now that I was eating mostly cucumbers to stay thin, I could enjoy the way my ripped-up jeans and the flannel shirt tied around my waist hung loosely from my body. On a good day, I could see my own reflection and not feel grotesque.

Back when my dad was in elementary school, he hated reading out loud more than anything in the world. By the time he made it to junior high, he was at serious risk of flunking out, still grappling with the basic rules of spelling and grammar. It was the late 1940s, and Trenton was about as big as it would ever get, its factories clinging to life as workers toiled away in the kinds of manufacturing jobs that would soon be a thing of the past. Clouds of black soot billowed from the skyscraping smokestack at the Roebling manufacturing complex, the company famous for its wire and cable. Here in the postwar era, the capital of New Jersey was still living up to the slogan emblazoned on its landmark bridge — TRENTON MAKES, THE WORLD TAKES — even as the specter of collapse was edging closer.

My dad grew up in a crowded household in Chambersburg where kids learning to read was not a foregone conclusion. His own father, an immigrant laborer from Calabria, never learned to speak English, and most of my dad's twelve siblings did not even graduate from high school. It didn't help that my dad's eighth-grade English teacher seemed to be setting him up for failure. Each day, he would pass a book around the class and insist that every student read a few paragraphs—out loud. My dad would grow nauseated as he watched the book change hands, edging closer and closer to him. And when it was finally his turn, the outcome was always the same: my dad would stumble over the words and the kids would laugh at him.

The teacher didn't try to spare my dad these mortifying moments; in fact, he apparently got a sadistic kick out of them. In my mind's version of this story, he has a hammer-shaped head and glassy eyes and looks like the cartoon schoolmaster from Pink Floyd's *The Wall.* I even imagine him talking with the mock Scottish accent. *Come now, young lad,* he'd say. *Even wee ones know these words.*

One day this teacher's goading went a step too far, and my dad felt his blood come to a boil. He realized, at fourteen, that being forced to read out loud was not about learning. It was about power and control, and he had the power to make it stop. "I won't do it," my dad said, dropping the book and letting it fall to the floor. "Don't ever ask me to read in this class again."

My dad periodically retold this story of his one-person classroom revolt whenever he heard that one of his three sons had encountered a difficult teacher. When Fred's own reading problems caused friction with his second-grade teachers, my dad spun his long-ago experience into a life lesson about knowing when to stand up to authority. "Freddy, don't ever let them make a fool out of you," he'd say in a deep voice, backed by the unassailable weight of moral certitude. "You walk out."

I understood from my dad that he would always take our side in a dispute with a teacher, that deference to teachers should not be automatic. In Catholic school, deference to authority was my default mode of behavior, but in high school I feared I was a weaker person because of it. The real life lesson at the heart of my dad's story was the malignity of public humiliation—being laughed at was the worst thing in the world. *Don't let them make a fool out of you.* Whenever I faced belittling teachers or violent tormentors at school, I heard his voice in my head. "Fuck you" was the best response I could muster, whether I was facing a teacher with an attitude problem or a dirtball in a jean jacket who called me a freak in the hallway. "Fuck you." And because saying it felt good in the short term, I thought it was actually working. I came to see rage as the cure for shyness.

I didn't know how much longer I could sit there and stare at the backs of people's heads. In one sense it was my own fault because I'd picked a desk in the rear of the classroom, but the conditions under which I'd been forced to sit there, in the same spot for the entire school day, were absurd and unjust. The school had instituted this thing called in-school suspension, whereby students who got in trouble were sentenced to what was essentially one full day in classroom prison. You couldn't talk. You couldn't leave the room. And you were supposed to complete some kind of vague assignment, which no one really paid attention to. In the eyes of some New Jersey districts, in-school suspension was less punitive than a conventional suspension because students served out their punishment on school grounds and did not incur any absences. I had already been suspended from school multiple times that year and was very close to the point of no return—automatic failure due to too many absences—so ending up with an in-school suspension was kind of a lucky break. I was sharing the room with about a dozen or so fellow inmates, mostly the usual suspects with cigarette packs wedged in their back pockets but also a big-haired girl in denim who probably would've been more comfortable at the Limited.

The minutes felt like hours, each period longer than the next. At one point, desperate for stimulation, I decided to alleviate the boredom by doodling. I used a ballpoint pen and started drawing one of my trademark cartoon characters—the kind with the bug eyes and mohawk—directly on the desk, pushing with force to ensure that the laminate would absorb the ink. Mrs. Dower, the teacher in charge, saw what I was doing and told me firmly to stop. She was one of those teachers who took discipline seriously; she was tall and fiercely vigilant with roaming eyes that could spot the tiniest wisp of deviant behavior. We'd had a number of fallings-out in the past, and she seemed to have a genuine distaste for me. She'd once berated me for being on the wrong side of the school after the bell rang even though I was legitimately lost at the time. When I tried to explain that my notably terrible sense of direction—documented by experts, as a matter of fact—made navigating the large school difficult, she didn't want to hear it. When I suggested that her unwillingness to hear me out might be part of the problem, she didn't want to hear that either. *School is not a democracy,* she was fond of saying.

Mrs. Dower had little patience for open debate and even less of a sense of humor. She was not amused that time I thought it would be funny to call her by her first name. "I have a title!" she screamed at me that day, yanking me into her office to write me up. "If I met the president of the United States, I would not call him Ron!"

Given that tainted history, it was unfortunate for me that Mrs. Dower had been put in charge of the in-school suspension. But there we were, locking eyes in this dank classroom, me in the back of the room by the storage closets and her at a large desk near the door like a warden. She told me again to stop drawing. I ignored her. She said it again, louder. She meant business. Heads swung around as the other kids looked in my direction to see what the commotion was about. I continued drawing. *Ignore them,* I thought. Lazer wouldn't care about being stared at. The facial features of my cartoon character were starting to take shape. Mrs. Dower had seen enough. She made it clear that I was no longer welcome in the classroom and that I was to go immediately to the vice principal's office. Either that, or she would call the police and have me arrested.

I rose from my chair and slowly made my way toward the door, every eye following me intently as I crossed the room. The clomping of boots and clanking of chains were deafening. The walk felt like an eternity. In my mind, I replayed every event that had led to my academic decline. Every altercation. Every bad teacher. My parents. Some kid who punched me in the head and made my ear bleed. I'd lost track of how many people were at fault for the utter failure that eleventh grade had become. In the haze of assigning blame, I let myself believe that I was blameless.

I stopped at Mrs. Dower's desk, pulled my hand from my trench-coat pocket, and gave her the middle finger, putting it so close to her face that she could have bitten it off. She said nothing as I left the room.

As I walked down the hallway toward the school exit, I suddenly heard Mrs. Dower behind me, enraged, screaming at the top of her lungs. I thought for a moment that she might jump on my back and tackle me, but I didn't dare turn around to see how close she was. "That's right, you little bastard!" she yelled. "You better walk out of here, because if you had touched me, I would have buried you! I would have finished you, you little fucker!"

For a brief moment, her words pierced through my fog of adolescent obstinance and let me see a fuller picture of who she was — not an authority figure on a power trip but a frightened woman who was forced to confront a potentially dangerous delinquent, a woman of color who had worked her way up the administrative ladder only to have her status challenged by a disrespectful white kid with no sense of perspective. Whatever part of me had refused to see teachers as human beings vanished in that instant, but it was a fleeting form of enlightenment.

I didn't go to the vice principal's office like I was told to. What was the point? Another suspension was inevitable. I kept walking, through the large double doors, into the cold, wet air, down the tan concrete steps of the old building. The overcast sky was bright, but I had sunglasses at the ready. The walk home took about twenty minutes, down a crumbling stretch of South Broad Street, with its smelly gas stations and fenced-off buildings and that sad bridal shop that no one ever went into.

I came home to find my mother in the kitchen, sitting silently at the table and twirling the coiled phone cord between her fingers. She had already talked to the school and knew all about what happened. She was surprisingly reserved, almost at peace. My mother had grown used to these phone calls and was clearly tired of making excuses for my behavior. I told her that I was sorry and that all I could do was try to make up for lost time when I went back. "You don't understand," she said. "They don't want you back."

CHAPTER 8

The Quiet Room

It was a Saturday night. Not that it mattered, because every night was the same now. In the six weeks since I'd stopped going to high school, I'd spent nearly all my time in my room, sulking, thinking about death. *Who meets you when you die? Jesus? Dead relatives? I'd love to see my grandfather again,* I thought. When he'd passed away a year earlier, he still had a full head of red hair. Mine was already thinning and I was going back and forth between being in denial about it and believing it was a punishment from God. That's what I got for not appreciating my red hair as a kid.

I couldn't see any kind of future. I hated not having anywhere to go, but the thought of going anywhere repulsed me. I hated my room. It was too familiar, too dirty, too quiet. I thought endlessly about belonging. Even in the uncertainty of this wretched limbo, I knew I didn't belong in a classroom.

The school district sent a tutor to the house for a while, a bespectacled, middle-aged man who sat on his hands when he talked, but he quickly grew frustrated by my lack of interest in his lectures. Child Study Services enlisted more psychologists, more social workers, more learning-disability experts to study me.

"He appears to be in opposition to the demands placed on a high school student," one evaluator wrote. "He has not established career goals...he does not demonstrate the motivation necessary for school success."

My mom, who used to break into my room and physically pull me out of bed when I overslept on a school day, stopped caring how late I slept.

Noon. One p.m. I barely noticed what time it was when I stumbled into the kitchen to heat up an Ellio's Pizza or Steak-Umm. I didn't notice how filthy our house had gotten, the clumps of unchanged cat litter and piles of unwashed laundry, or that my parents had stopped speaking to each other, or that the last family portrait we'd taken, two summers earlier at Kmart, was collecting dust in a corner.

Being up at all hours of the night, I grew used to existing around my dad's third-shift routine. He'd leave for work in the evenings, giving me the option to sneak downstairs, eat whatever was in the house—I went on and off the cucumber diet—and channel-surf, but I'd make myself scarce around two in the morning when he came home for lunch. One reason I knew it was a Saturday night was that he was home, sitting with his feet up in the recliner, watching a Yankee game or an old movie. I was in my room alone, staring into the full-length mirror that hung from my faux-wood-paneled wall and suffocating under the forces of self-judgment. Every imperfection I saw felt like I was being bludgeoned with a club: The oils of my blotchy skin under the sharp light of my desk lamp. The bulbous shape of love handles under my T-shirt. The blue tint of circles under my eyes, matching the blue veins in my hands and neck. My chin fat. My hairline. My curved spine. The more I stared, the more I was overcome by the sensation that something was wrong. I *couldn't* look like this. There had to be a mistake. I don't remember the exact thought that precipitated what happened next, but the feeling of glass against my forehead remains etched in my memory. The mirror smashed when I banged my head against it. Once. Twice. A third time. The relief was instant and freeing, as was the growling sound I produced with the full force of my lungs when I grabbed the nearest object—maybe a desk or a dresser—and hurled it across the room. I must have looked like an apoplectic orangutan. My dad sprang out of his recliner as soon as he heard the commotion; I could hear the thumping of his footsteps up the stairs. Within seconds, he busted through my locked door, grabbed me by the shoulders, wound up, and slapped me across the face.

"What the hell are you doing?"

The slap was meant to snap me out of it. It worked. What the hell *was* I doing? I had no idea. I blurted out something I have no memory of, something about how I was tired of living and I wanted him to hit me again, and the next thing I knew my mom was in the room too. I hadn't even known she was home. My parents just looked at each other with the kind of pregnant expression that two people get when they badly want to say something but are waiting for the other person to go first. They were about to break their unspoken rule of not speaking to each other to figure out what to do with me next.

From a distance, it looked like a ski lodge out of season, a flat stretch of interconnected brick structures with elongated windows and pointy mint-green rooftops surrounded by what seemed like miles of grassy fields. *Behavioral health center*—that was the preferred term. The inviting design made that description almost seem plausible, but I knew what it was. The ER doctors suggested that my parents take me here, because even though I'd insisted that I was not a danger to myself or others, how could you believe that when it came from someone who'd just smashed his head into a mirror? As my parents and I drove up to the complex in our Ford Fairmont station wagon, I took in the pitch-black sky of rural New Jersey. There were so many stars, more than I was used to.

The strip search was unpleasant. Who would even think of hiding a foreign object in such places? My dog collar and boot chains were confiscated and stuffed into a large plastic envelope by attendants in white suits. Same with my spiked bracelets, which were replaced with a rubber wristband that had my last name on it. Next came the tests. Electrodes on my head. Blood. Urine. Reflexes. *Can you follow my finger with your eyes?* After that, I got a tour of the facility, which had the feel of a cheap hotel. Long corridors stretched into brightly lit hallways with pale blue wallpaper and rows of double bedrooms. *Ugly* wasn't the right word for it. *Kitschy*, maybe, but that's being generous. At the back end of the building, they showed me where they put patients who were in distress. The Quiet Room, they called it. "Hopefully, we won't have to put you here," they said. "But you can come and use it anytime if you just want to decompress." It looked exactly like you would picture it: padded walls, no windows. This was not the cliché I'd ever expected to become.

I felt so plain and boring when I walked into the common area of the hospital on that first night, scoping out the other mental patients against the glare of the recessed ceiling lights and large windows. There must have been fifteen or twenty scattered about, some sitting on sofas and chatting, others playing card games or reading newspapers. What was wrong with them? I wondered.

But I was asking the wrong question. That became more obvious to me the following day when I got to know some of them in group therapy and my preconceived notions sank under the gravity of their personal stories. There was Cheryl, fifteen and thin with large glasses, an artist. She would draw ominous-looking pictures of the "stepmonster" who tortured her at home. Mac, thirtyish and stocky, had an addiction problem, but he never seemed to specify the drug. Maybe meth? He was cheerful, with an argumentative edge, a Republican whose attempts to engage me in political debates were completely lost on my apathetic adolescent self. Lorena, a sweet girl about my age, saw her dead grandmother and would sometimes point her out to other people. "She's sitting right there," she'd say, gesturing toward an empty chair. When another patient teased her one day by sitting in the same chair, Lorena screamed and broke down in tears. There was Mikey, short with plump cheeks, not more than twelve years old, but hilarious. At night, he'd run up and down the halls and sing the jingle for Ice Cream Cones, a newly introduced breakfast cereal that was basically a knockoff of Cookie Crisp. "My name's Ice Cream Jones!" Mikey would sing as everyone was settling in to sleep. "I'm bringing the kids my Ice Cream Cones!" Then he'd mimic the part in the commercial where Ice Cream Jones's truck slides down a hill. It cracked me up every time.

My roommate at the hospital, also about my age, seemed to be quite the ladies' man. At bedtime, he would stand in the doorway of our room and chat up some of the girls whose rooms were on the other side of the hallway. They'd giggle and touch his arm. They all seemed like they'd known each other forever.

On the first night, my roommate and I sat up in our matching beds and talked for a long time. He asked me why I was there, but I had no good answer. "My parents put me in here," I said. He told me that the hospital couldn't keep me against my will for more than three days unless I posed a threat to myself or others, and if my goal was to leave, I should be as cooperative with the evaluation team as possible. They'd ask me about drinking and drugs, about suicidal thoughts and homicidal fantasies. They'd ask me about hallucinations and delusions. Just answer "No" to everything, he said. Then he pointed to my right forearm, which was scarred and scabbing from where I had sliced into it with a razor blade some weeks earlier. "They'll ask you about that too," he said. "Hmm— tell them it was a phase."

I grew curious about this boy who seemed to know the ropes, who was clearly self-possessed and happy. If the hospital couldn't keep you against your will, what was he doing here? When I asked him that, he just smiled. I guess it beat school.

Living and bonding with the other patients over the next few days might have been the closest I'd ever come to a dorm experience, but I was too preoccupied by my fear of captivity to give it a chance. I just wanted out. I thought about what people in my life must have thought when they heard I'd been committed—my brothers, friends in our circle. How would I face them? Would they ask me why I broke the mirror, why I had such a distorted view of my body? We didn't talk about such things. We didn't even know that they were things. What I knew was that being in a mental hospital was embarrassing and unacceptable. Staying would be the same as admitting I belonged there. I knew where I didn't belong. Didn't I have that part all figured out?

On my last night, I was sitting at a large table in the common area with a group of other patients. My roommate was there. Lorena, Cheryl, and Mikey too. I can't say for certain if Lorena's grandmother was there, but I'd like to imagine she was. My three-day evaluation period was over and I was free to check out the next day. It was late in the evening, almost time for the hospital staff to check our vitals, which they did every few hours. The conversation at the table had an almost intervention-like feel to it. I remember each person trying to convince me to stay. "We like having you here," one of them said. Their faces were bright and inviting, with warm smiles. I felt wanted by peers in a way I had never felt before, not in eleven years of school. These were people I knew for only a fraction of a second, people I would never see again. They had nothing to gain from the effort they were making, nothing except my company.

CHAPTER 9

Pit Stop

CITY GARDENS WAS NOT MUCH to look at: a brick box on a sprawling asphalt lot flanked by two sidewalks, a moat of brown weeds, the urban blight of a dying city in one of its most neglected neighborhoods. Trenton had little by way of cultural advantages for a discerning teenager of the 1980s, but there was something fortuitous about its location—wedged halfway between New York City and Philadelphia—that made it an irresistible pit stop on the independent music circuit. Every punk or hard-core band that toured the Northeast at that time found its way to this tiny rock club on the asphalt lot: Bad Brains. Black Flag. Sonic Youth. The Ramones could be counted on to show up at least every other month. There was a frenetic and unpredictable energy to the place that imbued my hometown with a spark of life, especially on the weekends.

For a while I couldn't get enough of it. Each weekend, my brothers and I would pile into Lazer's car with as many people as it would fit. We'd stop off at the little Irish pub that never carded anyone, then we'd head to City Gardens. You could see four bands for ten dollars, which I always managed to scrounge up by doing sporadic jobs, like delivering telephone books or selling fanzines. Our social circle was now punctuated by people with names like Lunkhead and Ratbones and Dave Disgusting, the last of whom shot his own teeth out with a BB gun. When the music started, I'd squeeze my way into the sweaty mosh pits, surrounded by teenage boys with biker jackets and liberty spikes and flannel shirts tied around their waists. Arms and legs would flail about as young bodies twisted themselves into an assortment of impossible positions. Fists would thrust in all directions, in sync with the driving beats—maybe Ween or Butthole Surfers with their flaming cymbals and that lady who danced around onstage naked. Occasionally, you'd fall down and take a few boots to the head before someone reached under your armpits and hoisted you back to relative safety. Shyness and self-judgment couldn't touch you here. You could leave those problems in the parking lot, toss them in the bushes with the empty beer cans.

Six months had passed since the mental institution. No one asked me if I was a threat to myself anymore. Ice Cream Cones cereal was fast on its way to becoming a faded memory. I can't imagine who at General Mills ever thought that was a good idea.

My parents and the school district did try one last time to salvage what was left of my high-school career. Together, they set up what they called an IEP, or individualized education program. "Chris' educational needs would be best met in a small, structured classroom setting, out-of-district, for students with emotional/behavioral difficulties," they wrote in what would be my final school evaluation. "Mainstreaming is not recommended."

They also decided on an official label for what I was: *emotionally disturbed*. That was, and still is, a notoriously slippery term in the wonky worlds of special-education and disability law. Broadly speaking, it meant I had learning difficulties that couldn't be explained by other intellectual, sensory, or health problems. Emotionally disturbed people are noted for their lack of close friends, chronic depression, and "inappropriate types of behavior or feelings under normal circumstances," or so says the official definition in federal legislation. According to a 2002 report from the Department of Education, of all the disability categories in special education, students classified as emotionally disturbed had the highest drop-out rate.

At least I was finally classifiable. With my new label, I was entitled by law to attend a special school, courtesy of the short bus that would show up at my house every morning and ferry me to a far-flung district. Debates about disciplinary exclusion and the exceedingly low graduation rates for emotionally disturbed students were, I assume, not yet in vogue.

"A warm, supportive environment is important as Chris feels so negatively about himself," my evaluators wrote. In practice, the environment was neither warm nor supportive. Perhaps no one thought to ask what would happen if you took every kid who got kicked out of a regular school and packed them all in the same room together. If the intent of the federal special-education law was to ensure equal access, the lived experience was very different.

I have only vague memories of what they actually tried to teach us at the special school, but I remember vividly looking over my shoulder at every turn through the crowded halls and stairways, enduring random threats and dodging small objects that were hurled in my direction on a regular basis.

It was horrendous, suffice it to say, and the short bus was a form of public shaming that I was not willing to endure for very long. Within a month, I had stopped going.

Weirdly, I can't recall anyone objecting to my decision or even asking me how I planned to get through life without a high-school diploma. It was as if everyone who was supposed to be invested in my future, most of all me, had given up. There are no brochures or infomercials aimed at helping you make the very important decision to become a dropout. My mom, who once wrote letters demanding that my third-grade teacher stop embarrassing me by trying to make me learn cursive, who once successfully petitioned the school district not to hold back Fred a second time because it would devastate his confidence, who once reamed out a nun for picking on Joe, seemed uncharacteristically oblivious to the fact that her three sons were staying out all night and spending their weekends at City Gardens. She had gone from fierce advocate to absent parent, distant and unobservant in a way that let us act on our teenage impulses with near impunity. I was perfectly content to do so, too wrapped up in my fractious little world to notice the slowly building emotional discord that had been pushing her away from us for years. That is, until the night it all played out in front of me.

I don't remember how late it was. Let's just say late. Well past midnight but before dawn. After passing out on the living-room sofa earlier in the night,

I woke to the muffled sound of voices from my parents' bedroom down the hall. They hadn't slept together in there for a while, so I suspected something was up. Whatever I'd done for recreation that evening was already a blur. Beers and bands at City Gardens, and now friends were crashing in my bedroom upstairs. Oh, right, that's why I was on the living-room sofa.

I lay there on my back in the dark, legs dangling over the arm of the sofa. I tilted my ear toward the hallway to try to hear what was being said. My mother's voice grew louder and more distressed. She was crying. Through the crack of their door, I could make out only bits and pieces of what was clearly a litany of grievances, a monologue from a wife and mother who had reached a breaking point after twenty-three years of an unequal partnership. She accused him of being in denial about his kids, of refusing to take an active role in managing the household. She wondered why he would not acknowledge that there was something seriously wrong with the way his three sons ran wild without supervision or guidance. "You have kids who are sick and you won't do anything," she said through tears. She was tired of being diminished, tired of insensitive comments about her weight. She needed to grow, to find herself, to figure out who she was. Our family was not one for admitting vulnerability. I understood, in what limited capacity I had to understand anything at that point in my life, that what she was saying must have come from a place of last resort.

I don't know if my mom knew I was lying there, darkened by the shadows on the sofa, when she walked through the living room with a garbage bag full of clothes in tow and fled into the night. It made sense that she wouldn't have a proper suitcase. We never went anywhere.

The house was quiet for several moments after she left. Part of me refused to process what had happened, even though I knew they would be better off without each other. They'd never seemed happy. There was no proper gauge to measure whether the slow fracturing of their relationship had come at the worst possible time for my education. Divorce just made sense. Why did anything need to be more complicated than that?

My dad entered the room, noticed immediately that I was on the sofa, and realized that I had heard the whole thing. As we looked at each other, he scratched the side of his undershirt and straightened a crooked book on the shelf. "I just want you to know that had nothing to do with you guys," he said.

Mike Muir, the lead singer of Suicidal Tendencies, was furious.

"Who did this to our bus?" he yelled, pointing at a crowd of skinheads in the parking lot of City Gardens. "Was it you? Was it you?"

He was wearing his trademark bandanna and a sleeveless shirt that showed off his giant arms, looking exactly like he did in music videos. Only now he was surrounded by a team of bodyguards—each more gargantuan than the next—and the rest of his bandmates, some holding baseball bats and pipes. Apparently, showing up at City Gardens in a professional tour bus makes you a sellout in the punk world, so some skinheads thought that was reason enough to hurl a rock through one of its tinted windows, perhaps not taking into account that Mike Muir and his crew were widely known to be associated with gangs back in Venice, California.

The skinheads, too, were in a gang, which they loosely called "the Family," and now it looked as if this clash of gangs was going to come to a head right before my eyes. I had no skin in this game, but would anyone know that? I remember looking at my brother Joe on the opposite end of the parking lot as the whole thing felt ready to explode into a riot. I thought back to one Easter weekend when I was in kindergarten and the kid who lived next door threw my candy-filled plastic bunny rabbit in the sewer. Joe chased him down the sidewalk, and the kid ran home crying like a seal. Joe was always sticking up for me like that, protecting me. But he couldn't protect me now. *Fuck*, I thought. *I just want to see Suicidal Tendencies play a show. They're one of my favorite bands. I hope the singer doesn't hit me with a bat.*

Such scenes of imminent peril had become all too common by the time I reached my seventeenth birthday. The intoxicating energy that drew me to City Gardens, the spirit of discovery and self-expression, was being swallowed up by a dark force. Now there seemed to be skinheads for every kind of ideology you could think of. White-power skinheads. Anti-racist skinheads. Straight-edge skinheads who wanted to fight you if they saw you with a beer in your hand; anarchist skinheads who didn't need a reason. The skinheads who associated with our particular group called themselves American skinheads, meaning they saw themselves as patriots and liked to talk about how America had been built on the backs of the working class. When the Exploited, who had a song that included the lyrics "Fuck the USA," came to City Gardens in early 1988, the American skinheads in the audience unfurled a giant American flag and took turns spitting all over the lead singer.

One by one, people I knew and respected as individuals shaved their heads and strapped on identical pairs of suspenders. They went out and bought the same Fred Perry polo shirts, the same green flight jackets, the same oxblood Doc Martens. Even their shoelaces had to be the right color. Here was all the conformity and group behavior that I had tried to escape in high school repackaged as antiestablishment rebellion, uncorked by testosterone. Through the social circle that my brothers and I had cultivated, we were so close to all this that denouncing it didn't feel like an option. Part of it was a basic survival instinct. The Family was growing more infamous for the random acts of violence they perpetrated at shows — beating up a kid for wearing the wrong laces or looking at someone's girlfriend the wrong way. Through mutual friends, we knew the gang's most dangerous members, and it was better to be in with them than to be their targets.

I guess at some point, if you want to get technical, I was in the gang myself. One Sunday afternoon as I was waiting outside to get into the club, some members of the Family were making their way up and down the line. I watched as they yanked some kid out of the line, punched him in the face, and threw him to the ground. I'm not sure why. Maybe for mouthing off. Maybe just because they wanted to. A skinhead named DJ, who acted like one of the gang's leaders, began yelling at the spectators. "Anyone else got a problem with the Family?"

Silence followed. No problem here.

DJ had thick eyebrows and a fierce stare. He wasn't especially big, but as he stood there shirtless in the parking lot, his spiderweb tattoos catching the reddish glow of the late-afternoon sun, he looked like he had nothing to lose. Clearly, no one was going to risk being the next person to get yanked out of line. I could feel a rush of ice cold flooding into my bones, one of those moments when you realize that physical safety is an illusion. *This could really be it,* I thought as I watched the gang pace the lot with the confidence of full impunity. They could do whatever they wanted, and who would stop them?

DJ continued: "You're all in the fuckin' Family now! Understand?" Then he started pointing to people individually, demanding their loyalty. "Are you in the Family? Are you in the Family?" When he came to me, I nodded obediently. *Yes. Yes, I'm in the Family.*

I sometimes wonder about the extent to which social contagion plays a role in academic failure. During my days at City Gardens, I was hardly the only person in the scene who had dropped out of high school or been kicked out or, in my case, both. There were lots of us. Kids who left school and ran away from home. Kids who thought it would be funny to phone in a bomb threat. But most of the dropouts had totally unremarkable stories. They just stopped going.

My younger brother, Fred, didn't even make it past ninth grade, in part because his problems with reading had worsened but also because my own disciplinary problems in high school left him tarred. When teachers learned his last name, they threw up their hands and clucked. *Another one?* When they saw his leather jacket and combat boots and the way his bangs were cut into a pointy devil lock that covered one side of his face, they made up their minds about him pretty quickly.

The limbo of post high school was looking increasingly bleak. My parents were newly split up. I had no diploma and no plan for how to get by without one. Punk rock had given my brothers and me a sense of belonging, except now I was growing disillusioned with the scene I was supposed to love. The violence. The skinheads. Factions with even narrower codes of conduct. All of this came to a particular boil one night in the City Gardens parking lot as the crowd was shuffling out after a show, the energy still buzzing. My ears were buzzing too. The smell of sweat and beer filled the air. Over the exuberant conversations of the crowd, I heard a voice in the distance yell, "Get that motherfucker! Get that son of a bitch!"

I turned to see a thinly built kid darting across the lot as fast as he could. A small gang of skinheads was chasing him. I don't know what he did—maybe he admitted to liking Depeche Mode—but whatever his perceived transgression, it had stoked the ire of the Family. "Get that motherfucker" became a rallying cry, and once directed to do so, that's what people did. The gang in pursuit grew larger until a good percentage of the entire crowd was on his tail, emboldened by numbers, riled up by the certitude of being on the right side of whatever this was.

The kid was fast but not that fast. It took only one skinhead to grab a fistful of the back of his jacket to slow him down; two or three others grabbed his arms and threw him to the ground. Then the kicking started, Doc Martens flying in every direction, a splash of blood on the pavement. I caught only a small glimpse of the nauseating encounter before the mob obscured my view, but vivid descriptions from people who were close enough to the action told me what I needed to know.

"Eww, his eyeball fell out of the socket," one person said.

"That's what he gets," said another. "That's what he fucking gets."

There was jubilance in the air, a palpable sense of accomplishment, the feeling of being at the biggest party of the year as a person now lay motionless on the ground. He'd barely made it a hundred yards from the club.

The crowd began to disperse as quickly as it had assembled. Some people in it I knew, including Lazer, who had a wild glare in his eye as he walked by me in the parking lot heading toward his car. "I kicked him," Lazer said, chuckling gleefully. "I got a good one in." I don't know if he was serious or not—with Lazer, you never knew. But I couldn't get the memory of it out of my head. Was my friend, the person who first inspired me to think like an individual, swept up in the thrill of mob behavior? Or did he just think mob behavior was so hilarious that it warranted a joke at the expense of someone who might now be dead? Which was worse?

Not long after that night, another person I knew from City Gardens, a fellow dropout, told me about something called a General Educational Development test. "You take it through the State of New Jersey," he said.

"Then you get a certificate that's like a high-school diploma except without the high school." The guy was working in construction, something you couldn't do without a diploma, so he seemed to know what he was talking about.

It hit me at that moment how many months had passed since the altercation with Mrs. Dower that got me kicked out of school. Actually, it had been almost a year. When I did the math, I realized that I would have been graduating that spring had I stayed the course. Spring was just a few months away. I started studying immediately and managed to pass the GED by the end of June. I wish I could say it was about academic ambition. The truth is, I just wanted to win one last fight with my high school.

CHAPTER 10

That Old College Try

WHEN I WAS TWENTY-ONE, I fell in love twice in one night.

It was early spring in 1992, and I piled into a car with a group of friends for a nighttime excursion up to New York City, which by then had become something of a regular activity for us. City Gardens was boring now, a violent circus of meatheads and posers. I knew I was getting too old to be a punk rocker, but I had no idea what was supposed to come next.

New York offered a more elevated kind of stimulation. I'd always known the city was important because basically every movie said so, but I was beginning to understand how its relative adjacency to Trenton made my hometown a winning ticket in the lottery of birthplaces. One of the first things we ever did there, naturally, was go to the Hotel Chelsea and ask to see the room where Sid and Nancy stayed. "It doesn't exist anymore," the cranky desk clerk told us.

Driving in on a Friday night felt like entering a giant concrete theme park. We'd watch excitedly as the Twin Towers rose up from behind the horizon, followed by a sea of skyscrapers and haze. We'd pay four dollars for the Holland Tunnel—round trip, because no sane person would pay to get back into New Jersey—and then suddenly we were on Canal Street, swarmed by squeegee men, horns blasting, our noses assaulted by the odor of car fumes, pretzel carts, urine. On the bustling sidewalks and crosswalks, people yelled at each other in a million different languages.

I was usually content with drinking beer during these trips. Bodegas charged about two bucks for a forty and then shoved the bottle into a paper bag. You could roam around all night that way. Maybe once I was drunk enough, I'd take a few hits off a joint if it was passed around. I had tried lots of hard drugs during those years—acid, PCP, whatever was floating around our scene—but none of them ever stuck. You go through a phase and then you lose interest.

That night was different. We made a stop-off in Alphabet City and a few of my friends bought heroin from some guys on the corner. It came in little waxed bags stamped with logos, brand names like Always Good or King Kong. They were ten bucks each. The stuff was white and flaky, harmless-looking, not at all like the gooey tar you saw in those old junkie movies from the seventies. "You just snort it," one of my friends said. "China white—wanna try?"

I carried the bag around with me for a few hours as we wandered the streets of Lower Manhattan doing nothing in particular, as was consistent with our lack of agenda. Once I was sufficiently boozed up, I hacked off a piece of my bodega straw with a house key and snorted the bag's flaky contents. I was expecting nothing and at first that's what it felt like. There was just this weird chemical aftertaste that kept dripping from my nasal passages. *Not sure what people see in this,* I thought.

We turned up MacDougal Street, which was narrow and lined with charming old tenement buildings on either side. I was talking to a girl in our group, Enid, who had a semi-shaved head and long, thin bangs that flopped around in the wind. She kept talking about how much she loved learning the guitar, her hands in fingerless leather gloves strumming the air, motioning along a nonexistent neck of frets. "Music is my savior," she said. I felt myself becoming unexpectedly absorbed by her pantomimic demonstration, transported. Her face was emitting beams of light. Behind her, the whole city was filling up with a warm glow. "You should keep at that guitar," I told her. "You're so good now. Soooo good." This nonsensical conversation was more or less identical to a million others I'd had, except now I was a different person, a better person, suddenly freed from a lifelong burden of self-loathing. Every single thing I'd ever disliked about myself just floated away as if carried off by helium, leaving purity and giddiness in their place.

At first it didn't register that I was high because I had nothing to compare the feeling to. Maybe it was the beer, I thought, or just the old-world energy of this street, or the pulse of this amazing city. *I could live here,* I decided that night. *I must live here.* By the time we made it to the bottom of Washington Square Park, it hit me: *Heroin did this. It turned me into the person I've always wanted to be. This must be what normal people feel like all the time.*

Dave Disgusting found me a job working in a kennel. He lived out in the sticks and had somehow heard about this "pet motel" off Route 1 that was looking for help. The manager was a Russian fellow named Oleg who drank a lot of vodka during his shift and didn't seem all that affected by the suffering and barking, incessant and desperate, a cacophony of high-pitched yaps and deep woofs and scary growls. He spoke mostly in two-word sentences: "Fill water." "Clean cages." And I basically just did what he told me to do. I had a sense while I was working for Oleg that it would be the worst job I ever had.

But it paid for dope. In the two years or so since my transcendent experience on MacDougal Street, I had developed an increasingly expensive habit, easily a few hundred a week, definitely more than I could sustain by hocking random items at the pawnshop in downtown Trenton. It's not like you wake up one day and realize you're officially addicted. It happens slowly, one bag at a time, starting on weekends and at parties when you want that extra juice to become a social superman, albeit one who nods off in the middle of conversations. Before I knew it, weekend trips to the city with friends became twice-a-week trips by myself. Then I couldn't work without it. Or sleep. Or function. I'd drive my dad's Chevy Celebrity, park somewhere near Houston, and walk up and down Ludlow or Norfolk or Avenue A until I heard someone call out one of the brand names. "No Joke! No Joke! No Joke!" The dope sellers were surprisingly upstanding businessmen. I'd hear stories about people getting beat, but that never happened to me. Mostly I'd tell them a number, hand them the cash, and get what I paid for. In return, they'd get my repeat business. Sometimes, they'd aggressively ask if I was a cop, to which I would answer no and then quietly wonder who in his right mind would answer yes to that question.

* * *

Nothing about my lifestyle during those years was conducive to learning. Community college was a washout, a series of fits and false starts. I'd enrolled in my first classes at seventeen, right after getting my GED, mainly as a way of proving to myself that I didn't need those assholes at my high school who kicked me out. But when classes got too challenging, I dropped them or stopped going, and there was no one around to notice or care. I flunked so many that the Federal Pell Grant people eventually cut me off, saying something to the effect of *Sorry, kid, but you're obviously not serious about this.*

Six years after I'd gotten my GED, still going nowhere, I thought I could rewrite that script. I had a new job working in the warehouse of a mail-order company that sold music merchandise. It paid only five dollars and five cents an hour, but it was much better than the kennel—Soundgarden T-shirts don't bark when you lock them up—and my bosses, a husband and wife named Jasper and Joy, took an unusual shine to me. Jasper and Joy definitely suspected that I was a functional heroin addict, but they were live-and-let-live kind of people and chose to focus on the functional part. Only once did Joy have to pull me aside and politely ask if I wouldn't mind "coming to work more sober."

I asked Jasper and Joy to write a letter on my behalf to the Pell Grant people, maybe explaining to them that I had matured, that I was gainfully employed now and clearly ready to take school seriously. I thought I was. Heroin addiction doesn't move in only one direction. I'd gone through many cycles of quitting or reining it in to a manageable few bags a week, only to slowly work back up to an unsustainable frequency. When I was twenty-four, I stopped for two whole months, and I truly thought I had beaten it. I thought if I worked really hard, I could have an associate's degree by twenty-six.

Jasper and Joy were all too happy to write the letter. They said they had faith in me, that I was one of the best employees they'd ever had. Their glowing endorsement got me another shot with the Pell Grant people, and I was approved for a full year, one disbursement for each semester. I received the first half and was back in classes at Mercer County Community College in the fall of 1995.

One class I was especially eager to take was public speaking. I had it in my head that if I could just confront my biggest fear of all—making a fool of myself in public—doors would open. For our main project, we each had to deliver one oral presentation to the class. This was a terrifying prospect, but at least we each got to choose our own topic. I decided to give a speech on a topic I knew: how I was able to *finally* quit doing heroin. After all, it had been several weeks since I'd touched the stuff. I figured that counted as quitting and thus I must have valuable perspective on the matter. Plus, this was the nineties, and heroin was quite topical. The problem was, heroin was also my go-to crutch for social situations, and the closer I came to presentation day, the more I started to freak out. I'd watch other classmates stumble and sweat through their speeches and knew I was in for the most spectacular embarrassment of my life.

Just one bag to get me through it, I told myself. *That's all I need.*

The day of the presentation, I darted up to the city early in the morning. I picked up three bags—*Might as well get a few extra while I'm here*—and was back on campus in time for class. I don't know if my classmates suspected that I was high on heroin as I was delivering my speech about how I quit heroin. In my mind, I aced it, but that's how it always is. Sloppiness feels smooth. You are the king. In the weeks that followed, I realized what a mistake I'd made, that I was only ever one bag away from being right back where I'd started. Trips to the city got more frequent, and trips to class stopped altogether. You can't half-ass this addiction thing.

Lazer had changed since his high-school days as a wacky, trendsetting creative spirit who laughed at his own jokes and decorated his jacked-up Nova with masking tape. Now in his mid-twenties, he was more partial to Yankee caps than floppy trench coats, and he always seemed to have some mysterious job with the state that didn't involve actual work. His creative impulses had given way to cruelty, a preview of which I'd spotted in the parking lot of City Gardens that time. Maybe it had always been there. He'd make an unnecessarily mean remark about my appearance and then not let up when he saw that my feelings were hurt. He'd keep digging so the open wound from his insults would stay good and fresh. Just as he'd been in high school, Lazer was more concerned with amusing himself than others, but somehow him telling me I looked like Kojak and then cracking up for ten minutes was less funny than the inventive prankster-ism I remembered from the old days. And yet I still saw in him a piece of that spark, that I-don't-give-a-shit quality that I so admired. We'd found new common ground in heroin, both of us addicted and in need of drug buddies. We both loved being in the city and pretending we lived there, as if we could live there. We loved getting our fixes and losing ourselves in shared rituals, like nodding off in Karavas or grabbing a slice at one of those pizza places with the stand-up tables.

Our regular dope spots got less reliable in the Giuliani era. The deal-ers were more careful and the cops more visible. It used to be you'd see one or two, but now blue uniforms and badges were everywhere. One night I was parked in one of those angled parking spots on the Lower East Side, waiting for Lazer to return with our stuff. He seemed to be taking forever and I was getting increasingly worried that he'd come back empty-handed and we'd have to drive all the way up to East Harlem. Not fun when you're jonesing. It was an unusually quiet night, chilly and damp. Or maybe I was too dope-sick to stay warm. I kept turning on the heat, waving my hands in front of the dashboard vents, and then turning it off when it got too hot. This was always the most unbearable part, waiting for the one thing that could take this horrible feeling away, the one thing that could make you human again. You took solace in knowing that it would all be better soon.

Finally, I saw Lazer emerge from the corner, walking with his head down, the flat brim of his Yankee cap nearly obscuring his eyes. I could tell just by his strut that he had scored. *Thank you, thank you, universe.* He hopped in the front seat and I started the engine, but after I pulled out of the parking spot, I saw a set of flashing red lights behind me. Then another set in front of me. The abbreviated whir of a siren rang out. At first I assumed these cops were chasing someone and just wanted me out of the way, but no—we were their target.

"Drive away! Drive away!" Lazer yelled. "What are you doing?"

In a panic, I listened to him, or tried to. I pumped the pedal for a split second before realizing there was no physical way to drive around an NYPD vehicle and evade a bunch of cops on a tiny street in one of the densest neighborhoods in New York City. My revving the engine only served to infuriate the cops, who were now out of their cars and banging on the hood of my dad's Celebrity. "Turn it off," one of them yelled. My door opened and I felt a forceful tug on the collar of my coat and suddenly I was up against the car with my hands on the roof, the cop patting me down and asking me why I tried to drive away. "I panicked, I'm sorry," I might have said or definitely should have said. I looked across the car and there was Lazer, hands on the roof same as me, pale as a ghost as the cops were pulling his pockets inside out. They kept saying they knew why we were there, that our Jersey plates were a dead giveaway. They said we should just make this easy and tell them where we were hiding the stash. Then they started rummaging through the car, which I assumed they had a right to do since I'd basically tried to flee the scene like a fugitive. They pointed their flashlights at every possible hiding space. The glove compartment. The sun visors. The floor mats. Under the seats.

"If we find drugs in this car, you're going to Rikers tonight," one of the cops said.

All I could do in that moment of helplessness was look to Lazer for some kind of nonverbal sign of what we should do. I knew I hadn't seen him toss anything out the window. Should we just fess up? He gave me nothing, just a blank stare as we stood there surrounded, awaiting our fates in the face of four very determined law-enforcement officers.

They turned the car upside down and grew even more frustrated when that turned up nothing. They told us to get the fuck out of there and go back to New Jersey. As we were getting in the car, one of the cops pointed to a can of beer in a brown paper bag that Lazer had left on the sidewalk. "Is that your beer?" he said angrily, as if he might settle for charging us with littering.

Lazer nodded.

"Take your fuckin' beer with you."

I started the car and we drove off, my hands still shaking as I clutched the steering wheel and turned onto Houston. We headed west toward the tunnel. I couldn't believe we were out of there, that we had so narrowly escaped. At first I was grateful and relieved, but those feelings were quickly replaced by a primal sense of dread, the realization that Lazer must have discarded the drugs and that we would not be getting high that night. The idea of going home sick, the thought of fighting off cold sweats, convulsing in my bed all night with no way to get to sleep, produced an even darker hole than the imminent threat of getting locked up. I looked over at Lazer, who was still exhaling deep sighs.

"What happened to it?"

"It's in here," he said, holding up the beer can in the paper bag. Somehow, it was in the one place they hadn't looked, maybe the most obvious place. "New York's Finest." Lazer cackled. They'd put us through hell and then returned our dope to us as a parting gift.

We stopped off at Karavas, snorted our bags from the safety of the restroom, and had a celebratory drink at the bar, watching with zero investment as some of the regulars complained about the Knicks. You couldn't really hear their conversation anyway; "Cannonball" by the Breeders was blaring over the sound system.

I knew there would be more close calls like that if I didn't stop. For a long time, I sought any and all credible scapegoats on whom to blame the untenability of my chosen lifestyle. It was Giuliani's fault, I once decided. Why was he trying to tame this great city that was better off lawless? Why did society get to arbitrarily decide which drugs were legal and which weren't? Why couldn't I choose to live this way if I wanted to? The more obvious conclusion was that I was not choosing to live at all. It was hard to admit to myself that I wasn't ready for New York, that my only hope for breaking the cycle of addiction was leaving the city behind.

Around this time, a friend of mine asked if I wanted to move in with her and her roommates in Orlando, Florida. There was no temptation there, she said, no dope men on the street corners. It sounded like the perfect solution—a healing refuge with a built-in social network—except I had no money to make the transition. Every cent I earned at Jasper and Joy's warehouse went to support my habit. I couldn't move with no money.

And I couldn't save money under these circumstances. It was a catch-22, with an overdose or jail as the only possible outcomes.

Then one day the answer appeared in my mailbox as if by magic: a check for the second half of my Pell Grant disbursement. It was supposed to be for the spring 1996 semester, but I never enrolled. Jasper and Joy had written that letter of endorsement as an act of dual faith. They didn't just believe in the promise of an education. They believed in me as a person. I'd botched the first part, but that didn't mean I needed to squander the second part.

I did my last bag of dope somewhere in Virginia, heading south on I-95, excited for the promise of freedom as the warm rush of euphoria flooded my bloodstream one final time. I tried not to think about the Manhattan skyline shrinking in the distance behind me. It made me too sad to consider the possibility that I might never find my way back.

PART II

CHAPTER 11

Welcome Aboard

THE BLARNEY STONE HAD A smell that defied description. To call it unpleasant would be accurate enough, but it would hardly do justice to the admixture of beer and broth and mold and stew that gave rise to the powerful stench of this dark Irish pub on Third Avenue between Forty-Fourth and Forty-Fifth Streets, a block from the *Show Business Weekly* office. What it lacked in pleasant fragrances, it made up for with chipper young bartenders and happy-hour prices that attracted a diverse range of after-work drinkers, from UN interns to JPMorgan Chase executives.

It was here that I had my first conversation as a professional editor. It was April 2006, exactly ten years after I had fled the Northeast to get clean. Surprisingly little had happened in that time. Six years in Orlando. Three in Seattle. The humility that comes with a decade in retail. Now, after a five-month internship in New York City, I felt like I was getting the opportunity of a lifetime.

Mr. Chieftain had invited me out for a drink to discuss my new role as his editorial assistant, a title that belied the reality that I would be responsible for the newspaper's entire editorial department, just as Kevin had been. News, features, casting, listings, layout. It was all on my plate now. The pay was twenty-six thousand dollars a year, which sounded low even to me, although the idea of negotiating for a higher salary did not enter my mind. There would be no health insurance. "I figured Kevin didn't need it," Mr. Chieftain said. "He's so young, what the hell could happen to him?" To me it was enough that I was not being paid by the hour for the first time in my life.

My drink with Mr. Chieftain was the kind of get-to-know-you meeting that I was sure would invite questions about my past, a prospect that terrified me. He knew I had been working in a picture-frame shop, but that's about it. He had never seen my résumé and did not know I had no office experience, no background in journalism, and no formal education. He didn't know I'd gotten kicked out of high school, or about special education or the mental institution, or about City Gardens or heroin.

Would any of these details be deal-breakers? Could they be? He'd already offered me the job, after all. Who knew how these things worked. My plan was to deflect, to meet whatever questions he asked about my credentials and qualifications with vagueness and omission. I would emphasize my late start, my "unconventional" path to journalism. Putting it that way almost made me sound interesting.

Except none of it came up. Mr. Chieftain spent the entire evening talking about himself, a topic that fascinated him greatly. And, boy, did I learn a lot about him. He was only a few years older than me, about forty, and unmarried, although he frequently mentioned how much he loved women. As it turned out, he hadn't inherited the newspaper from his grandfather like I'd assumed he had. He'd relaunched it from scratch after the original *Show Business* went out of business. Mr. Chieftain had apparently been squeezed out of the family enterprise when his grandfather, a cantankerous old publisher named Leo Shull, sold *Show Business* to an outside buyer in the late eighties. Mr. Chieftain was crushed. He had fond boyhood memories of the old *Show Business* offices in Times Square and saw himself as the most obvious heir apparent.

The decades-old trade paper had a rich legacy. It had been launched single-handedly by Mr. Chieftain's grandfather out of a Walgreens basement at the dawn of the Second World War. Leo Shull's idea to print audition notices on mimeographed sheets and distribute them around the theater district was simple but revolutionary, giving hungry young actors direct access to the opportunities they desperately sought. Lauren Bacall was an early fan of the paper; she sold copies of it outside Sardi's as a teenager before landing her big break. A young Al Pacino worked for *Show Business* as a deliveryman in the 1960s. Characters in the 1980 movie *Fame* read it religiously.

But Leo held on to his baby for too long, refusing to retire in his later years and letting the quality of the paper suffer as a result. When he finally sold it, its reputation had deteriorated. In a bittersweet twist for Mr. Chieftain, the paper didn't survive very long under its new owner. The original *Show Business* folded in bankruptcy in 1991, leaving *Back Stage* as the only game in town for audition notices. In yet another ironic twist, that magazine had been founded back in 1960 by two *Show Business* defectors, which made Mr. Chieftain hate it even more.

Although Mr. Chieftain had studied journalism and had a degree from Boston University, publishing was not his first love. Acting was. He spent part of his twenties working on soap operas and in TV commercials, but he was unable to find bigger success. As he got older, he grew to despise the audition process, the constant disappointment of losing gigs, the sting of rejection at the hands of casting directors he had contempt for, the indignity of trying out for bit parts. A breaking point came when a theater producer at one audition instructed him to make sounds like a farm animal, leaving Mr. Chieftain in the humiliating position of mooing like a cow and reevaluating his life choices. Through it all, Mr. Chieftain believed that he and his fellow struggling actors were being patronized and talked down to by *Back Stage,* which had a tendency to publish unhelpful career advice on topics like how to get an agent, even though no one really knew how to get an agent. "Actors who can't find agents hate that shit," Mr. Chieftain ranted. "They just want jobs."

With his family connection, knowledge of publishing, hatred of *Back Stage,* and firsthand experience as an actor who couldn't make the big time, Mr. Chieftain came up with the idea to relaunch *Show Business,* returning it to newsstands in 1999. "It was a no-brainer," he told me. "We have only one competitor and they suck."

For Mr. Chieftain, running *Show Business Weekly* seemed to come with the fringe benefit of getting revenge on everyone who had wronged him. He resented his family for selling the paper out from under him, yet he loathed *Back Stage* for dethroning his family's newspaper and capturing the market. He also held a grudge against the entire entertainment industry for not giving him an easier path to an acting career. At the Blarney Stone that night, when he talked about how he was showing them all up, running the newspaper he'd always wanted, his face glowed with a strange mix of joy and self-gratification. I was uncomfortable, particularly as a new employee in an industry I was unfamiliar with, watching someone I worked for speak so frankly about the demons that motivated him. And yet part of me could relate to the way he seemed to draw strength from his anger. I admired his willingness to fight, even if our styles of fighting were very different. Our demons, too, for that matter.

What I know is that I left the meeting that night not wanting to let him down. I was determined to fight right there alongside him, whatever form that would take. By the time I joined the bankers and diplomats and other assorted drunken characters spilling onto Third Avenue, I was already used to the smell of the Blarney Stone. It's weird how that happens.

CHAPTER 12

Life Lesson

FROM THE MOMENT HE FIRST hired me for the internship, Kevin had been a guiding presence in the *Show Business Weekly* office, a role model, a template for the kind of editor and manager I wanted to be. Now I was on my own. Although Kevin was originally supposed to stay on and train me for the first two weeks, Mr. Chieftain apparently couldn't stand the sight of him after he gave his notice. "We won't be needing you anymore," he told Kevin on my first day. "Zara knows what he's doing."

I didn't.

With Kevin out of the picture, the gulf between what I thought I knew about putting the weekly newspaper together and what I actually knew grew fiftyfold. Suddenly, nothing looked familiar—*Is that the right key? What's the e-mail password again?*—and Mr. Chieftain was no help. He came in to sell ads and complain about things not getting done, and that's about it. The more he saw me struggling with the details, the more snappy and impatient he became, as if my inability to instantly learn the ropes reflected poorly on his own judgment. Was I a bad hire? Even I didn't know. "I can already tell you have a problem following directions," he said one morning as I fumbled with a stack of smudged-up manila folders, looking for invoices or proofs or something. But directions are a two-way street, and Mr. Chieftain didn't seem to understand that they had to be given before they could be followed.

"Call the distributor and make sure they got the bundles!"

"Where do I find the phone number?"

"Don't ask me such questions."

The interns were helpful when they could be, but they also required direction, direction from me, and how could I give them any when I didn't know what I was doing myself? The webmaster, sweet as could be, was from Thailand, and he did not notice or fix typos when they made their way onto the website. Those were my problem too. Phone calls interrupted me at every turn. One was from a reader who wanted to cancel her subscription. Easy enough, except Mr. Chieftain had explicitly said, "Never let them cancel," so what could have been a one-minute phone call turned into an hour-long one. She canceled anyway. Another was a film-festival publicist with a thick Irish brogue: "Did ya get the Word doc fer the program guide?" That was an easy one because Mr. Chieftain said publicists were always the lowest priority. I checked my e-mail. "Got it—thanks for sending."

Our deadline for putting the paper to bed each week was Monday afternoon—it hit newsstands on Tuesday morning—but when Friday rolled around at the end of my first week, none of the layout was done. All the mad Quark skills I thought I had were far less impressive when I was up against the clock. Mercifully, the weekend was coming up, and since I wouldn't have phones or publicists or interns or salespeople or angry subscribers to deal with, I could actually work. A full day on Saturday and another one on Sunday should be just enough.

Or so I thought. Right before I left the office that Friday, the publicist with the Irish brogue called back. The film festival she worked for wasn't just any festival. It actually had a partnership with *Show Business Weekly*. That meant we were supposed to lay out the program guide. That meant *I* was supposed to lay out the program guide. When was it due? "Tonight," the Irish publicist said. "I sent ya the Word doc, didn't I?"

Mr. Chieftain lost it when he heard I'd dropped the ball. He said maybe publishing wasn't my thing and maybe I'd be better off in a job that didn't require organizational skills. "You're just like Kevin," he said. "Kevin wanted to be managing editor—he couldn't manage shit." I apologized for screwing up and asked how I was supposed to lay out the newspaper and produce an entire film-festival program in one weekend. I mean, how could I even do that?

"Don't ask me such questions."

There went my Sunday night. When I crawled in on Monday morning, I had just enough time to tie up the remaining details. With a few minutes to spare, I uploaded the boards to the printer and exhaled after the longest eight days of my life.

Then I took a deep breath and the weekly cycle started all over again. A new issue, new stories, new ads, invoices, phone calls, and chaos. I blinked and it was Friday, and again the layout was not done. The only saving grace was that there was no film-festival program this time, so maybe I could finish by Saturday and get Sunday off, which would be my first day off in two weeks, except on Saturday the production computer didn't want to boot up, and DiskWarrior wasn't helping, and Mr. Chieftain was at his house in Connecticut and not answering his cell phone, and he'd probably just tell me not to ask such questions anyway. It took me the entire day to figure out that you can bring a dead Power Macintosh G3 back to life by punching it. When it finally started working again, it was almost midnight. Saturday was gone. Sunday would be another workday. And on Monday I'd have just enough time to tie up the remaining details and upload the boards.

Then I took a deep breath and the weekly cycle started all over again.

Day sixteen of a twenty-day working stretch. I was on my way to pass out in my bedroom when Gus Gary intercepted me in the hall. "We need to have a talk," he said in a manner that you never want to hear from your nonromantic roommate. I had just gotten home and could barely think straight, my brain overflowing with deadlines and typos and existential thoughts about me maybe being a terrible editor. But it was his apartment and his rules, and so I didn't feel like refusing to have a talk was an option. Gus Gary sat me down on the sofa and took a seat across from me. As I waited for him to start, I deliberately averted my eyes and stared up at the picture of Huey P. Newton because I needed something to look at as I was pretending not to deliberately avert my eyes. Thanks to me and my old job, the picture was now nicely framed. *Pretty good corners,* I thought to myself. Gus Gary took a sip from his Che Guevara mug and finally got to explaining that he was disappointed in the living arrangement, that I was distant and antisocial and not at all what he'd signed up for. He wanted me to try harder, to make time for him once in a while. I knew he had a valid grievance, but how could I make time? How could anyone make time? If I could just magically make time, would I not have had more of it? Did he not notice that I'd been working for sixteen days or that my eyes were a frightening shade of oxblood red or that I was hunched over with the posture of a wilted scarecrow?

"Look, I'm paying my rent," I snapped. "What more do you want?"

"I'm not in this for the money," he snapped back.

For a maddening second I wondered what exactly he thought "this" was, except I already knew: Gus Gary had always been up-front about what he wanted from our living arrangement, expressing his hope that it would be a springboard into a true friendship, but I'd refused to take that at face value from the outset. I was a newcomer desperate to get a foothold in the city. And now that I had even more to lose—a new job that I was frantically trying to wrap my arms around—I was desperate to hold on to it.

I told Gus Gary that I understood his concerns and would try harder to be more open, or at least less closed off. But by that point our mutual bitterness had already spread like a bad infection. It festered and chafed over the next few weeks, and before we knew it, we'd gone from merely being annoyed by each other to actually detesting each other. He chastised me for every infraction, whether it was leaving a dish unwashed or forgetting to lock the front door when I came home. "That's a serious breach!" he said. With the promise of a friendship no longer on the table, Gus Gary had no interest in politeness or pleasantries. He was done with me. In turn, I did everything possible to avoid him altogether. I worked as late as I could at the office during the week and hopped the NJ Transit to Trenton on weekends, spending them on my dad's dirty sofa, right underneath the decorative Frank Sinatra plate that used to play "My Way" when it had batteries a long time before. My dad lived alone in a small apartment now. He'd never remarried after my mom walked out, nineteen years earlier, so he was happy for the company. Those Friday nights on his

dirty sofa gave me brief moments of precious reflection, but the conclu-
sions I was coming to were self-defeating: everything about my life in New
York was beginning to feel unsustainable.

Spring was giving way to summer. On the NJ Transit to Trenton one
humid Friday evening, I watched the sun disappear behind the blur of a
fast-moving North Jersey horizon. It changed from factories to fields to
strip malls, the sky behind it vast with plumes of pink and orange clouds.
My home state is not the prettiest, but it has its moments. Another long
week had ended, and Mr. Chieftain had just reamed me out for—I don't
know, you name it. I remember convincing myself that my stint as a professional newspaper editor was doomed and that the humiliation of having
to return to a frame shop or an ice cream stand would be the worst thing
in the world. What would I tell people? *Oh, well, you know—I guess I just
couldn't cut it.* I was entertaining the most morbid of worst-case scenarios
when my silver Motorola cell phone chirped in my pants pocket. It was Joe
calling from Seattle. My older brother loved to call randomly and for no
good reason. At the time, he was playing guitar in an alt-country band
called the WhiteTrash WhipLash, bartending to support himself, and
spending a lot of time on MySpace, which is to say he kept odd hours. Joe
asked how the new job was going. Did I like it?

As I explained the particulars of my workplace situation—the crazy
boss, the mountain of responsibilities, the lack of confidence in my own
competence—he slipped into his role as the family philosopher, just like
he had when we were kids being mercilessly teased over our bright red
hair. He talked about why he believed we three Zara brothers had struggled for so long to realize our creative ambitions. We all had the same
problem, Joe said, and it had nothing to do with money or credentials or
education. We'd simply never been able to bridge our creative pursuits
with commercial practicalities. We all sat around for way too long waiting
for something to happen. Waiting to be shown the way out. Growing up in
Trenton with its hollowed-out streets and angry faces had that effect on
people. He said the path forward starts with unlearning the Trenton
mindset, ridding yourself of the belief that a creative activity and a

full-time job must be mutually exclusive. Mindsets can be changed, Joe insisted. "You're the first one of us who has achieved that," he said.

A classic Joe life lesson: an unpolished, big-picture appraisal of a complex and fraught situation, perhaps overly simplistic but also containing a deeper insight. Objectively speaking, I had achieved nothing. My newly attained professional status was fleeting and my job security nonexistent. But Joe's suggestion that my taste of the professional world, even if it was temporary, would somehow free me from the mental feedback loops that had tethered me to low-wage service jobs felt like a revelation. I could be fired, but there was something in the experience I was gaining that couldn't be taken away.

CHAPTER 13

The Ivy League Mafia

I HAD NO PALPABLE SENSE of being outnumbered by people with college degrees when I stepped inside a Broadway theater for the first time, nor would I have cared if someone told me that was the case. I was far too enthralled with the magic, the glittering lights, the gorgeous ornamentation of the archways, the eager buzz of the crowd. It all felt like the kind of important cultural thing that I'd always imagined real New Yorkers did in their leisure time, and here I was doing it for work at the Jacobs Theatre on West Forty-Fifth Street, marveling at the lights and the archways and the crowd. The play was *Rock 'n' Roll* by Tom Stoppard and I was there to review it as a member of the New York press. Granted, my plus-one was empty—it was always empty in those days—but I had great seats, center orchestra, that I hadn't had to pay for, easily close enough to see the spit fly out of Brian Cox's mouth as he verbally jousted with Rufus Sewell about the fall of Communism against the tumultuous backdrop of Czechoslovakia's 1989 Velvet Revolution. Did I mention it was a Tom Stoppard play? I had never seen a play on Broadway before. In that moment, I was the luckiest person in the world.

Which is to say that the last thing on my mind was the demographic breakdown of the audience. Those questions would come later, when I learned to see theater as a stand-in for all the ills that perpetuate the education divide, after I had grown more familiar with its insularity, its power structures, the close-knit theater communities driven by access and status and the right connections. They all led like spider veins back to a handful of top drama schools.

Open a Broadway playbill on any given night and you'll see cast and crew bios peppered with the same three names: Juilliard, NYU Tisch, Yale School of Drama. An out-of-work actor once told me that he and his friends bitterly referred to this trio as the "Ivy League Mafia," which I thought was weird because only one of them is actually an Ivy League school. But I understood the sentiment. In my early days covering theater in New York City, I was quite jarred by the importance of drama-school pedigrees. Actors and playwrights I interviewed often told similar origin stories, with higher education placed firmly in the catalyzing role. They'd honed their skills in college. They'd met their future collaborators in college. They owed their entire careers to their alma maters.

At the time, my idea of the typical path to a Broadway career was steeped in naive show-business folklore: The teenage runaway who arrives by bus at Port Authority and waits tables or sells newspapers outside of Sardi's until he or she is discovered. Isn't that how Lauren Bacall broke in? Isn't that how they all broke in? Tom Stoppard, it's worth noting, left school at seventeen because he was "thoroughly bored." But while we can all enjoy the ironic tingle of discovering that the world's cleverest playwright does not have a college degree, stories like his travel farther than their rareness should permit. When I learned about the central role of higher education in the performing arts, I realized something that should have been obvious: The vast majority of people who make the magic on Broadway do not have backstories like Stoppard's or like mine. The people who make the magic do not arrive by accident.

During my first few months as the editor of *Show Business Weekly*, I vowed to take advantage of my newfound access and give myself an education in theater. I saw every restaged classic I was invited to—Ibsen, Chekhov, Wilde, Beckett. Some were thrilling, others boring, and a few made me want to jump into the nearest vat of chemicals. But at least now I had an opinion based on seeing the works live. More important, or so I thought at the time, I could now discuss theater with *them*—the smart, cultured, educated people whose world I was slowly beginning to infiltrate as a member of the theater press. Hell, maybe I could even occasionally sound like I knew what I was talking about.

Summer was ending and I was nearly six months into the job. The clumsiness, uncertainty, and dread of my first few weeks as editor had slowly given way to rhythm, process, and proficiency. Occasional glimmers of confidence poked through as I corrected a writer's grammar or reamed out a salesperson who'd promised editorial coverage to an advertiser. I was no expert in anything, but I knew enough about journalism to understand that church and state must always remain separate. "Lester, what the hell are you doing?" I scolded. "We're not pay-to-play around here!" The guy was six foot two and a former bouncer but fortunately respected my authority.

The more proficient I became in my role as editor, the less Mr. Chieftain tried to micromanage every single thing I did. His easing up made our working relationship tolerable. He would still have freak-outs, sometimes daily ones, about my perceived incompetence, but I began to notice subtle patterns that helped me better navigate his otherwise unpredictable mood swings. For one thing, he always seemed much more worked up in the mornings or early afternoons or whenever he first came into work. He'd barrel through the door, neck veins bulging, panting in short bursts and ranting about five or six things that needed to be done right now. Like immediately or else. But as the hours progressed, he seemed not to care if most of the supposedly urgent tasks went uncompleted. By the time six o'clock rolled around, he was telling jokes, doing magic tricks in front of the interns, or inviting me out for a drink at the Blarney Stone.

I suspected this progression of moods, from enraged to relaxed, might have had something to do with the bottle of antianxiety meds his doctor had prescribed that he kept in his desk drawer. But the more I got to know him, the more I believed his mood swings were a symptom of deeper issues. He'd confided to me that his parents, especially his father, a successful New York City physician, had been disappointed in his choice to pursue acting. Mr. Chieftain described his father as some combination of manly, worldly, and cruel—an adventurer who liked to travel to exotic places, lose himself in the Sunday *Times,* and verbally cut his son down to size at every opportunity. When Mr. Chieftain spoke of him, his eyes would narrow as if he'd just bitten into a lemon. I wondered if that was better or worse than growing up in a family with no expectations for you at all.

I walked into the office on what was one of our busiest days yet. New ads were coming in left and right. Back-to-school features were due. Mr. Chieftain, who was there early that day, immediately started rattling off a million chores that needed to be completed. Like immediately or else. I explained that I would need just a moment to find a proper container for my tooth, which had fallen out during my subway commute as I was biting into a Bazzini nut with the density of a cast-iron sprocket. I had managed to save it before it was lost to the void of the A train.

Mr. Chieftain's focus instantly shifted away from the busyness of work and toward the small emergency unfolding inside my mouth. What happened? he wanted to know.

"Almond accident," I said.

"Is there pain?"

"Not that much. The tooth has already been root-canaled twice."

Interesting fact about root canals. They fail anywhere between 2 and 14 percent of the time. This particular tooth had required a second root canal a few years earlier, and I couldn't afford to resize the crown so I just left it on there, ill-fitting, until it inevitably fell off.

Mr. Chieftain insisted that this dental snafu be prioritized above all else. He called his personal dentist on the Upper East Side and demanded that I be seen that day. He told the dentist to bill his account and sent me on my way. "Go take care of your tooth," he said. "You can't walk around like this. I need you at full speed."

I would later learn not to expect these bursts of empathy from Mr. Chieftain, but when they happened, they were astounding. When he discovered that my bedroom had no air conditioner during one particularly scorching heat wave, he bought me a new one and came over to my apartment and installed it himself. When he learned that I was sleeping on old sheets, he took me to the Bed Bath and Beyond on East Sixty-First Street to pick out new ones. "You need a high thread count," he said. "Anything under five hundred is bullshit!" Three hours earlier he was berating me over a typo, and now here we were picking out sheets at Bed Bath and Beyond. I didn't know if I should feel grateful or weirded out.

CHAPTER 14

Deep Shame, Sweet Relief

Navigating Mr. Chieftain's personality from day to day was not easy. Would he be the asshole Mr. Chieftain who demanded that we stop everything and rework a feature story that was finished weeks before because he'd suddenly decided he hated it? Or would he be the cool Mr. Chieftain who took me out for sushi and paid for my cab ride home after a few too many sakes? My stress level on any given workday was often wholly dependent on which Mr. Chieftain I got, but the more I learned to resist my instinct to fight or flee, to bite my tongue and weather the dysfunction, the more I convinced myself there would be a big payoff in the end for doing so. He had such an unrelenting desire to beat *Back Stage* and restore *Show Business Weekly* to its former grandeur that I was starting to buy into his obsession. I thought of my mom, who decades earlier had been absent during my first year of high school in service of the war between the *Trenton Times* and the *Trentonian*. Her having a stake in the outcome furthered her career, let her advance from data processing to computers, and ultimately gave her the freedom to break out of an unhappy marriage. I saw fighting and winning my own newspaper war as a virtue.

Just as I was getting the hang of things at work, my life at home in Washington Heights reached its inevitable breaking point. Gus Gary and I now avoided each other at all costs when we were in the apartment together. For me as the sublessee, that meant entering my bedroom as soon as I got home and waiting until he went to sleep before doing anything outside of my bedroom. The waiting was sometimes unbearable. The sound of him rattling around the living room or making a sandwich or getting up from a chair would grate on my last nerve. How easily every-day sounds become noise pollution when they are produced by an adversary. I'm sure my chair usage got on his nerves too.

The situation was made worse by the design of the apartment. My bedroom connected to the living room, which connected to a hallway, which led to the bathroom. This lack of adjacency proved especially problematic because a trip to the bathroom meant that I had to pass Gus Gary on the sofa, and that would send my anxiety levels through the roof. And then my worst nightmare came true: My paruresis returned. The phobia that haunted me in childhood, the one that goes by the dismissive euphemism "shy bladder syndrome." After years of avoidance tactics — urinating behind dumpsters or in dark alleys, going a full day without water before airplane trips — I thought I had beaten this thing a long time ago. Public bathrooms were no longer an issue for me, even in New York City. But much to my dismay and discouragement, the phobia of my youth had tracked me down. Worse — it found me in my own home. When Gus Gary was awake and in the living room, I was unable to go, no matter how long I stood there, no matter how much I tried to relax, no matter how much I told myself I had control.

Why now? Did I subconsciously care what Gus Gary thought of me? There was no point in trying to make sense of it, because social phobias are irrational, but irrational doesn't mean not real. Inevitably, one night I faced a serious problem. I had to use the bathroom and he wouldn't go to sleep. I stared endlessly at the toilet, breathing, trying to focus, trying to stop the snowball of anxiety, the point at which worrying about worry becomes indistinguishable from the thing that made you worry in the first place. It was no use. Paruresis had trapped me in a corner. I went back to my bedroom to devise a plan B, avoiding eye contact with Gus Gary as I passed him on the sofa. Could I run a few blocks down to Columbia-Presbyterian? This was technically an emergency, but I didn't think an ER nurse would buy that. Cafés or restaurants at this hour? Forget it. The pressure on my bladder was intensifying with every moment, my muscles locked in place, the desire to urinate drowning out all other concerns. *Damn it, Gus Gary, go to sleep.*

And then I saw the solution clear as day. The Che Guevara mug, staring at me from the top of my dresser, empty. I had borrowed it from the kitchen cupboard days ago. The particulars of why I could pee in a cup in my bedroom and not in the bathroom with Gus Gary awake in the next room are not something I fully understand, but they cut to the core of a wretched self-consciousness that has plagued me for longer than I can remember. Being watched is being judged, the worst possible fate for a self-conscious brain. There was something about his knowing I was in the bathroom that triggered my anxiety and froze my bladder muscles, and there was something about being safe in my bedroom — where I could be doing anything — that flipped off the switch. If I could control that switch myself, I knew I would be a better human being, or at least a better-functioning one. But that goal has always eluded me.

After I was done peeing, I placed the mug deep in the bottom of my closet and buried it under some clothes. I felt a wave of deep shame and sweet relief. It was an odd mix.

I came home the next night to find Gus Gary had searched the entire apartment, including my room, for the Che mug. He demanded to know where it had gone. I was furious that he had searched my room without asking me — who does that? — but also relieved that he did not find it filled with pee, hidden in my closet under some clothes. That would have been impossible to explain. The thing about paruresis is it doesn't make sense to anyone who doesn't have it. I told Gus Gary to leave me alone, that I had not seen his damn mug, but he didn't believe me. "This apartment is not that big, and you're the only other person here," he said.

Faultless logic. I knew I needed a diversionary tactic, so I told him I'd look again for the mug in my room if he'd just give me a second. Closing the door behind me, I waited and waited until the coast was clear, then grabbed the mug from its hiding place and made a dash for the kitchen. I scrubbed it clean with all my might, drowning it in dish soap, a dash of bleach, rinsing, scouring. Once. Twice. A third time. Would I drink out of this now? Sure. Later that night, I announced that I'd found the mug in my room. "It was in here the whole time," I said. "You must've missed it."

He never accepted that explanation, and I can't say I blame him. Days and weeks went by, and he would keep bringing it up, saying he was sure he had checked my room thoroughly for the mug. How could it just reappear? Had I been planning to steal it? I felt awful for gaslighting him and shameful for the condition that led me to do it, but I didn't think the truth would help salvage what was obviously an irreconcilable living situation. Gus Gary seemed to agree, and one day when we passed each other in the hallway, he said, "I want you out of here by the end of the month."

CHAPTER 15

Be Strong

AFTER MY FALLING-OUT WITH GUS Gary, I ended up back on the Upper West Side, a neighborhood I loved, living alone in a rent-stabilized apartment on West 100th Street. It was one room with a leaky ceiling and an air mattress and roaches, but it was mine. Sweet moments of precious alone time—the roaches didn't count—were once again within reach.

Work was going better than it had ever gone before, not just for me but for the company. *Show Business Weekly* was coming off what Mr. Chieftain described as its best year ever. Our recent back-to-school issues had generated record advertising revenue, some from the very same drama schools that made out-of-work actors insane with resentment. Mr. Chieftain credited my steady steering of the editorial department, saying it freed him up to sell more ads. Somehow, despite his mood swings and my inexperience, despite our frequent arguments, we made a good team. Something was clicking. The newspaper could even afford to start paying for my health insurance, Mr. Chieftain informed me. My title was bumped up to managing editor and I had the business cards to prove it.

Slowly I was beginning to tie my job to my identity, which to me was the very definition of being professional. I had always wanted to *be* what I did. Now I finally was. At after-work mixers and press events, I could clip on one of those little plastic badges and mingle with people from ABC News and the *Wall Street Journal* who were wearing the same little plastic badges. We were all colleagues. Little plastic badges don't lie. For the first time in my life, the question *What do you do?* did not turn me into a stammering over-explainer. "I'm the managing editor of *Show Business Weekly*," I'd say, trying to maintain a matter-of-fact tone that would make the title sound natural and well earned.

My newly emerging professional identity also gave me the confidence to forge new social connections—or at least try to—with people outside of work, people who hadn't known me before. I had a clean slate; I was not tethered to being a high-school dropout or an ex-junkie or a failed what-ever. Or so I thought, until dating became the next logical step. Then I quickly discovered that some parts were easier to hide than others.

The late aughts were a boom time for dating platforms. Early websites like Match and eHarmony were well established, and the maturing social web was fueling the rise of dynamic new options like Plenty of Fish and OkCu-pid. The latter was especially addictive. Once your profile was set up, you could spend hours answering questions on a range of topics to feed the site's matchmaking algorithm. Some of the questions were benign and obvious (Are you a cat person or a dog person?), others darkly bizarre (Would the world be a better place if people with low IQs were not allowed to reproduce?). I never had much faith that answering these questions would actually produce better matches, but it was a fun way to spend time on a lonely Friday or Saturday night.

Less fun but more telling was discovering the wish list of characteristics that women said they wanted in a potential partner. I had never used a dat-ing website before and I was not quite prepared for the raw honesty. "Please have 80 percent of your hair," one profile demanded. "I'm attractive and I expect the same," said another. Pet peeves from past relationships seemed to frequently rear their heads. "I want someone who cuts his toenails because it's time, not because he's told to," explained one user. A reasonable request. I recall being far more anxious about the many women who wanted their dates to be "well traveled." Except for a day trip to Canada when I was a kid, I'd never been outside the country. By my mid-thirties, that was such a source of embarrassment that I would sometimes just lie in casual conversa-tion and tell people I'd been to Luxembourg, which I figured sounded believable because who would lie about going to Luxembourg?

Despite the expectations and stated deal-breakers, a good percentage of women on dating sites seemed to want the same things I wanted, and I found that encouraging. *Nice, smart, funny.* Don't we all believe that these traits describe us?

But another desired characteristic kept coming up too, an adjective that would not so easily bend to the will of subjective self-appraisal: *educated*. I knew my lack of a college degree would count against me in job searches, but I had not considered that it would be a disadvantage in the dating pool. My dating life up until that point had largely involved meeting people through mutual friends, people who moved in the same non-degreed circles.

After reading so many variations of *must be educated* on dating profiles, I began to see the light, and it hurt. Of course, it made perfect sense that a woman who'd spent years of her life and hundreds of thousands of dollars to obtain a degree would prize that same achievement in a partner. And yet I had to see these professed desires for educated mates rendered in pixels on my laptop screen before I faced the reality that I wouldn't measure up, even with my cool new job in media.

Fortunately for me, OkCupid was more forgiving than, say, LinkedIn. You could leave education details blank and it didn't constantly hound you to fill them in. That meant I could at least try the same purposeful-omission strategy that I'd used on my résumé when Kevin hired me as an intern. What I hadn't anticipated was the uncanny sameness of every conversation on every first date in history. College always comes up. It's a mathematical certainty. If your date hasn't mentioned an alma mater by the time the starters arrive, you can bet it's because he or she is waiting for you to mention yours first. And don't even think about trying to small-talk your way out of it. You absolutely will discuss this topic before dessert.

Granted, these rules might be very New York–specific. But I quickly learned in those days that college was the most natural topic there was for two New York professionals seeking to make a potentially romantic connection to discuss. It was up there with music preferences and the weather, a shared experience with which to jump-start any number of conversations. That made for some awkward first-date segues after I said I hadn't gone to college. "I kind of fell into journalism," I would say, employing one of my favorite cryptic metaphors. "That's cool," some would reply. "I thought you needed a degree for that."

A common reaction was for my date to downplay her own academic credentials. "Good on you for not wasting your money," some would say, or "I have a master's and it hasn't done shit for me." I was never sure how to take those kinds of comments. Were they genuinely conflicted about the value of their own education? At the time, I had so little experience inter-acting with women in the white-collar world that I could not see the more obvious explanation — that they were sensitive about having outshined me and perhaps felt pressured to appear less intimidating on a first date. Of course, that could be reading too much into the gender politics. It's also possible that they were just looking for the least awkward thing to say.

CHAPTER 16

But I Just Got Here

MY HEART SANK WHEN SHE told me the number: 10 percent. I asked her to repeat it, as if that would somehow change the outcome, but no dice — 10 percent, the representative from our largest distributor told me a second time. That was the percentage of copies of our newspaper that were actually selling on newsstands. A good sell-through rate was 40 percent, 35 maybe, but we weren't even coming close. She had called the office that day to inform us — inform me, since I'd answered the phone — that the distributor would be reducing its *Show Business Weekly* order by thousands of copies a week. *Sorry, but people just aren't buying your paper.* She didn't say that exact thing, but that's what I heard.

I knew Mr. Chieftain would be devastated by this news, or furious, or both, and I didn't know quite how to tell him. As much as I'd been involved in the day-to-day operations of the newspaper, there were certain numbers he didn't like to discuss, and circulation numbers — real ones, at least — were heavily guarded. Oh, sure, we had a "readership" figure that we cited to advertisers: *We reach twenty-six thousand actors in the New York City area.* But that number was achievable only through the uniquely aspirational calculations of newsstand math. First of all, our entire print run was barely ten thousand copies. But let's say you took that number, assumed every single copy sold, further assumed that each reader would pass his or her copy on to an average of one and a half friends, then added an extra thousand readers just because round numbers looked fake — well, you could get there. Or so the logic went. As inflated as our readership number was, Mr. Chieftain sometimes inflated it even further in conversations with advertisers on the phone. He'd jump to twenty-eight or even thirty-two thousand readers. I once asked him why he exaggerated, pointing out the obvious fact that any advertiser could simply check our media kit and see the actual number clear as day. Mr. Chieftain seemed genuinely unaware that he was doing it. "What are you talking about?" he said defensively, his eyes dodging back and forth like Ping-Pong balls. "I don't exaggerate. I don't *have to* exaggerate."

The disconnect between verifiable reality and some of the things he told advertisers as he was trying to close a deal was at once perplexing and fascinating. When a sale was on the line, when the phone call was do-or-die, Mr. Chieftain seemed to have an automatic pilot that steered him toward superlatives and hyperbole. "We're the *best-read* trade paper in the city...*youngest* readership...*most* affluent...We run circles around *Back Stage*." I often wondered if this instinct was narcissism? Blind pride in his own company? Maybe good salesmanship takes a little of both.

I knew after the phone call from the distributor that morning that the value of the company I worked for was not based on any objective metric. It wasn't because thousands of actors relied on us for jobs each week. It wasn't because of our decades-long lineage or the fact that the New York Public Library for the Performing Arts microfilmed us and considered us the trade paper of record. It certainly wasn't because of my talent. Our value came entirely from Mr. Chieftain's ability to convince advertisers that we had value. The business was a house of cards ready to collapse under an eroding circulation that would eventually be too small to be seen with the naked eye.

I had already suspected for some time that the paper's circulation was not what it had been in its heyday. All you had to do was walk through the theater district on a Saturday night and see all the extra copies of *Show Business Weekly* cluttering up the newsstands. Fresh issues of *Back Stage* would be prominently displayed while unopened bundles of our paper were buried under cases of bottled water and Arizona iced tea. The contrast felt like a punch in the gut. My newspaper war was over before I'd even enlisted. By the end of the 2000s, there was a new problem: the ashes of a banking crisis that had thrown the global financial system into chaos were making the winners and losers of old-school media wars more obvious, even as they hastened the disruptive forces that would soon make them moot. *Back Stage,* which was owned by the Nielsen Company, could weather the economic downturn easier than we could, but it couldn't outrun history forever. Newsrooms from the *Los Angeles Times* to the Newark *Star-Ledger* were being gutted. Magazines were slashing frequencies, laying off staff, or folding altogether. Print was talked about almost entirely in the past tense. *Old media. Dinosaurs.* "Let the hedge funds have their way with them," some said unceremoniously. "Sell them for parts." Some commentators, usually journalism professors with what I imagined were nice offices on leafy college campuses, cheered on the demise. They said newspaper executives were getting what they deserved because they hadn't prepared for the internet in the nineties when there was still time to build a proper business model. Newspapers gave their stories away for free online, and, well, what did they expect? The Great Recession—that's what they were calling it now—was only exposing vulnerabilities that were already there.

This economic flash point came smack in the middle of a technical one. A year before the crash, Steve Jobs introduced the first iPhone at the Macworld conference in San Francisco, an event Mr. Chieftain and I watched on a dusty computer screen from the office. We were both initially bemused but dismissive of the device. So it's a computer, a music player, *and* a phone? Surely it must be a crappy version of all three. Two months after Jobs's presentation, Twitter had its big coming-out at the South by Southwest conference in Austin, Texas, and suddenly everyone was talking about how easy it was to instantly broadcast short messages to the entire world. Even my mom was smitten. She predicted this short-message thing would be useful for journalists and suggested I start an account. "Yeah, I'll get right on that, Ma." It was a lot of innovation for one year, but 2007 wasn't over yet. Just before the start of the holiday-shopping season, Amazon released the first Kindle, a slab of plastic that let you download books, magazines, and newspapers and read them on a white screen that mimicked the look of newsprint. Analysts predicted even more pain for the publishing industry.

Each innovation, each new announcement from Silicon Valley—a place I'd barely heard of before that year—felt like a personal attack on the media career I was hoping to build for myself.

As for Mr. Chieftain, he never cared much for the internet. He saw it mostly as it was captured in the early aughts by the writers of *Avenue Q*—a way to look at porn—and seemed to have little interest in updating his idea of what it could be used for. In terms of distributing useful information like casting and audition notices, Mr. Chieftain thought the internet was a fad, a Wild West that could never be tamed, and he was sure that readers who were migrating to casting websites would one day realize the folly of their ways and return to the superior experience of ink and paper. "You can't bring a computer into the bathroom," he liked to say.

I admired him for his love for print, the way he kept meticulous track of new periodical launches and collected the ones that he knew would fail, like *Trump* magazine, as if to remind himself that *Show Business Weekly* was beating the odds in a ruthless marketplace. But as time went on, I couldn't share Mr. Chieftain's willingness to deny the obvious. Tech was unleashing forces on the world that would make the disruption caused by the early internet look like child's play. As a lover of newspapers, I didn't like what was happening, but it was impossible not to see it.

At some point I developed the rather masochistic habit of counting the iPhone-to-paper-products ratio during my subway commutes. A lot of people will tell you that the personalities of New Yorkers can be sussed out by what they read on the subway. *How* they read is equally important. Early on, the ratio was maybe one electronic device for every twenty paper products. Books were plentiful. Daily rags like the *Post* and *AM New York* were still the rule, not the exception. But the balance was shifting so rapidly that by the end of 2008, I could see only one outcome. Mr. Chieftain was wrong. If you could bring a computer onto the subway, surely you could bring one into the bathroom.

The realization that print was not going to make some kind of glorious comeback after the recession was tough to accept, and it was hard for me not to wallow in my unfortunate timing. After decades of working low-wage service jobs, I'd thought I had finally found a calling, a brave new world in which I could build a future.

* * *

I arrived at the office early to greet Dorothy, our new production assistant, on her first day. We rarely hired new employees, and I was excited for the help. Dorothy had been an intern, but in the few months she worked at the office, she'd made a huge impression on both Mr. Chieftain and me. She wasn't a kid just out of college but a refugee from the world of TV news who was looking to change careers. She wanted to learn everything there was to know about page layout, design, production—things I could surely use help with. Her being there full-time was going to make my life a thousand times easier. That's why I'd pushed for Mr. Chieftain to bring her on as an employee.

But Dorothy never showed up. Instead, I found a small envelope addressed to me slipped under the office door when I arrived, a nice one, like the kind you might give a doorman on Christmas. In her handwritten note, Dorothy thanked me for the opportunity but explained that she had reconsidered. She just couldn't work for Mr. Chieftain. His arrogance and lack of composure, his tendency toward belittling comments, were beyond inappropriate. She mentioned one comment in particular: "I can help *you* more than you can help me," Mr. Chieftain had said to her. I didn't recall him saying it, but yeah, that sounded about right. Dorothy insisted that this was not about her being thin-skinned. She'd worked for lots of tough bosses in the past and could handle them fine. This was about Mr. Chieftain, she wrote. He didn't understand the basic concept of the employer-worker contract. He saw hiring her as a favor, and she had too much self-worth to let that fly. Finally, Dorothy concluded her note with what she believed to be his worst transgression: *I don't like the way he treats you.*

It wasn't the first time someone who worked at *Show Business Weekly* had made that comment on the way out the door. Some called Mr. Chieftain a bully or suggested I suffered from a form of Stockholm syndrome. "Find another job," one intern urged on his last day. "That man is unstable." I vacillated between being flattered and being insulted by these nuggets of unsolicited advice. The truth was, I had been in self-preservation mode, tuning out the noise of Mr. Chieftain's personality to protect myself. On days when he tested my last nerve—and there were lots of days like that—I repeated mantras to stop myself from turning a moment of weakness into an error in judgment with permanent consequences.

If I quit, he wins.

If I say fuck you, he wins.

If I walk out, he wins.

I never showed Mr. Chieftain the note Dorothy wrote to me, but I tried to be honest about why she'd turned down the job, even if I softened her critiques a bit. At the very least, I figured her acknowledgment of his office behavior might inspire a pinch of soul-searching on Mr. Chieftain's part. Instead, he just laughed. "If she can't handle me, she's not going to get very far in this business," he said before biting into a sandwich from Chirping Chicken. I laughed too. Then I nodded in agreement.

In the spring of 1946, Leo Shull wrote an impassioned op-ed for *New Masses,* a magazine of Marxist cultural commentary, arguing that politically progressive playwrights and theater directors had a moral duty to push the bounds of their influence and reach bigger audiences. It was five years after he'd launched *Actors Cues,* the newspaper that would become *Show Business,* and the young publisher was growing increasingly influential himself, particularly with the left-wing intelligentsia of New York theater. In the article, Leo made a persuasive case for the untapped potential of summer stock—small shows that were typically produced out of town but adjacent to the city—as a natural incubator for bold ideas. Writers and directors could use these shows to explore culturally urgent themes, such as racism or anti-Semitism, that major producers tended to shy away from, Leo argued. Summer-stock shows were cheap, easy to produce, and, most of all, offered a direct pipeline into mainstream American culture. "For these summer theaters are assiduously scouted by film companies and Broadway producers," Leo wrote. "There is no better way of breaking through the iron wall of indifference and neglect."

Leo's outspoken support for the arts as an organ of political influence was not without consequences. Years later, he was among the many entertainment professionals whose careers were jeopardized after they were identified as Communists or Communist Party sympathizers, and he was subpoenaed to testify before the House Un-American Activities Committee in 1958. But as a self-employed newspaperman, Leo couldn't be quietly relegated to a blacklist, and as his publishing operation grew, he continued to unapologetically advocate for progressive causes. In 1963, when a group of Black performers, including Ray Charles and Nina Simone, joined Martin Luther King Jr. in Birmingham, Alabama, for a benefit concert to desegregate the entertainment industry, Leo used the pages of *Show Business* to publicly cheer them on. He even flew down on a specially chartered flight to cover the event, facing civil unrest upon his arrival and a bomb threat against the plane on his way home. "Neither heat, bombs, nor Birmingham cops shall stop the show," Leo wrote. "It must go on." Proceeds from the concert went to help transport attendees to the March on Washington, which took place just a few weeks later.

These images of Leo Shull as a civic-minded champion of inclusion and social justice stand in stark contrast to the stories Mr. Chieftain told me about his grandfather as an older man in the 1980s. The picture he painted was of a vindictive, spiteful, and endlessly litigious holder of grudges, an irascible sod with streaks of thin silver hair who spent his golden years hunched over a typewriter wielding the power of print like a bayonet on a battlefield. Leo gave himself his own column in *Show Business*, a weekly mouthpiece through which he would air petty grievances against his many perceived enemies. He referred to *Back Stage* as "Backstab" and once called its two founders "bow-legged orangutans." Apparently, he also wore a camera around his neck wherever he went and sometimes snapped photos of his targets himself. "Smile, I'm gonna make ya famous," he would say, according to Mr. Chieftain.

Mr. Chieftain's descriptions of Leo were so outrageous that they bordered on caricature, but they were corroborated by older actors and other theater types who sometimes randomly called the office for no apparent reason. "That Leo, he was a mean son of a bitch," they'd say. "He sued everybody." Indeed, his legal tussles were the stuff of legends, whether he was going to court with the producers of the Tony Awards for kicking him out of a press conference or squeezing Hugh Hefner over the naming rights of a short-lived magazine called *Show Business Illustrated*. It seemed as if no foe could escape the targeted wrath of his lawyers. Liz Smith, the *Daily News* gossip columnist, summed it up best in a 1985 column: "Leo Shull, who runs *Show Business,* the entertainment weekly, is not a popular guy and he is always suing or being sued or feuding with one or another of the Broadway big shots."

It was this insatiable lust for conflict that Mr. Chieftain seemed most interested in emulating. Even though Leo was not his biological grandfather (Mr. Chieftain entered the Shull family by way of his father's marriage to Leo's daughter), Mr. Chieftain clearly saw the late founder of *Show Business* as a role model, the kind of bygone, iron-fisted, fear-inspiring newspaper mogul he wanted to be. But because *Show Business Weekly* was a much smaller operation now, the legal fights tended to be smaller too. Mr. Chieftain once battled a classified advertiser in small-claims court over what couldn't have been more than a few hundred dollars; the process took many months and multiple trips to 111 Centre Street. He'd sometimes tell me to put on a tie and then send me down to the courthouse in his place. When the case was called, I'd raise my hand, yell, "Application," and request an adjournment. Anything to drag out the proceedings. Mr. Chieftain enjoyed wasting his opponents' time and didn't seem to mind that my time was also being wasted. To be honest, I found these small insights into the legal bureaucracy of New York County courts intriguing.

But lawsuits were also a distraction from the failing business, a fact I learned after that earth-rattling phone call from our distributor. When Mr. Chieftain discovered that our circulation would be dramatically shrinking overnight, his instinct was not to brainstorm ways to increase readership but to sue the distributor. He pored over piles of single-copy sales invoices, which were comically arcane, determined to discover where we had been shorted over the years. And because newsstand distribution is an inherently crooked business, he was able to discover enough — maybe a thousand or fifteen hundred bucks — that he believed it was worth going to court.

These distractions sucked up more and more of our time and energy in the years after the recession. As the newspaper spiraled down and the rise of mobile technology made the viability of our business model look increasingly bleak, Mr. Chieftain became more consumed with winning petty battles. One attempt to upgrade our website—coded in the late nineties by an unpaid intern and left to erode under the unsentimental forces of link rot—ended with Mr. Chieftain firing the web developer halfway through the job because he thought it was taking too long. I remember him going on an extended rant about how the developer's ponytail should've been a red flag. "Who the fuck has a ponytail?"

Throughout this period, as stories of media bloodbaths proliferated and the news cycle was dominated by somber tales of young people graduating from their master's programs into the worst job market since the 1930s, I got the message that I was lucky to be working at all loud and clear. "Tell Zara he's going to be shoveling snow," I overheard one of Mr. Chieftain's associates say when the two of them were discussing some grim advertising numbers in his office. I can't say if the comment was meant to be funny, but I'm certain my overhearing it was no accident. The walls in our office were paper-thin. Like our margins.

CHAPTER 17

How to Avoid a Slush Pile

As I was soaring through the air over the corner of Forty-Seventh and Third, I realized that I had misjudged the size of the slush pile. Or maybe I'd misjudged my ability to leap over it. Slush piles and the puddles that form around them are weirdly deceptive. You never really know how deep they are until your foot plunges into one.

I could hear the office phone ringing from the hallway, so I picked up the pace, trying to ignore the fact that my foot was still partially numb from the frozen puddle. I was already a few minutes late, and you never knew who was calling that early. Sometimes it was Mr. Chieftain—I swear he just wanted to make sure I'd shown up on time—or an advertiser looking to pay an invoice after receiving one of our infamous dunning letters.

But this was definitely not a call I was expecting. The young woman on the line identified herself as Stephanie, an editor from HarperCollins. She loved the book proposal I'd sent. "We could really see this as a trade paperback," she said, her crisp voice brimming with enthusiasm.

I could hardly believe what I'd just heard. This was Harper fucking Collins, one of the biggest publishers in the world. Writing a book was not something I had even considered until a few months earlier, when I'd attended my first book-release party, at a dive bar in the East Village. That night, as I observed the author, a journalist, clinking cocktails with colleagues and offering free copies of his nonfiction work from a pyramid-shaped stack on a back table, it occurred to me that in the journalism world, books served a very specific function. They were not works of art.

They were not even necessarily works of journalism. They were résumé items. Credentials, really. For a journalist, publishing a book seemed to be a way of demonstrating one's expertise in a competitive marketplace of ideas. The reward was a point system meted out in cable news segments, radio hits, possible job offers, and, if you were lucky, royalty checks. Being a book author meant something similar to being a college graduate. It meant options.

I had been obsessing about the sorry state of the newspaper business for many months. The bloodbaths I'd read about at other newsrooms and *Show Business Weekly*'s spiraling toward inevitable obsolescence kept me awake most nights. I asked my doctor to prescribe me Ambien, a drug I had tried a few years earlier when I was living in Florida and struggling with an especially long wave of depression and insomnia. I knew it worked like a charm in that it knocked you out but didn't leave you feeling groggy the next day the way NyQuil did, plus no weird aftertaste. My doctor hesitated when I asked for it by name, perhaps sensing the addict in me. "Have you tried melatonin or deep-breathing exercises?" he asked. Who did he think he was talking to? He finally gave in after I explained that I worked in the newspaper business.

My biggest fear was ending up jobless, right back where I started. That helplessness I'd felt when I was finishing up my internship and no one would even look at my résumé was seared into my recent memory. Sure, I now had a few years as a professional editor under my belt, but as far as résumés went, that was just a single item. I dreaded the idea of competing with people ten or fifteen years younger than me who had twice as much experience and master's degrees from the Columbia J-school or Annenberg or Berkeley. Working twelve hours a day at *Show Business Weekly* meant that I couldn't feasibly get a degree on the side. That would take years, and who knew if the job would last that long? My existence felt like a race against time, especially because Mr. Chieftain was running out of people to blame for the newspaper's decline. First it was the distributor. Then the web developer. I knew he would eventually get around to me.

So, college was off the table for now, but a book? I mean, maybe I could pound something out on the weekends, something light and airy.

For the chance to be able to put *published author* next to my name, something I was sure would make me more employable, it was at least worth considering.

The day after the party in the East Village, I went to the Borders bookstore at Columbus Circle and picked up a book on how to write book proposals. The process was surprisingly uncomplicated—apparently, they all follow pretty much the same format. According to the book I'd purchased, the proposal had to accomplish three things: explain the idea, explain why there was a market for it, and explain why you were the person to write it. I thought back to Seattle, to that first magazine pitch I ever sent out, how it got me my first paying job as a writer. That might have been beginner's luck, but it had also been the exact omen I needed to keep pitching stories, despite how many editors said no after that. Getting a no is always discouraging, but I realized that if I sent out enough pitches for articles, I'd get the occasional yes. Every yes is worth a thousand noes. Pitching a book did not seem to be that much different. The scale was different, maybe, but the process was basically the same. You just needed an idea and someone to say yes. All it takes is one yes.

As for the idea, that came as so many of my ideas did—during a philosophically tinged phone conversation with my brother Joe. During our extended calls, he loved to randomly reminisce about our old punk-rock days. He commented on why he thought punk rock was an especially vital art form, how its practitioners drew from negative experiences—alienation, anger, despair—and turned those things into something positive. Isn't that what the best art does? I took it a step further, riffing as Joe and I do: Maybe that's not unique to punk rock. Maybe *all* great art comes from pain and suffering. Hell, Bobby McFerrin probably didn't write "Don't Worry, Be Happy" because he *was* happy. We both agreed that this was a universal truth about why artists create art—songs, poems, paintings, movies. All artists want to communicate something. It's their struggle that makes what they're trying to communicate worth listening to.

When I got off the phone with Joe, I googled the phrase *tortured artists* and couldn't believe no one had written a book with that title.

Over the next few weeks, I spent my nights and weekends working on a book proposal, racing against the clock in my head that kept reminding me our newspaper's days were numbered. I wrote it and rewrote it, tidied it up, stuck it in a drawer, pulled it out a few days later, and rewrote it again. Eventually, the proposal seemed to include all three goals that my how-to book said it should. The idea? An irreverent pop-culture book that explores the relationship between creativity and suffering. Is there a market for it? Um, have you been to Urban Outfitters? Why was I the person to write it? This was the tricky part. I was a high-school dropout with no practical experience writing a nonfiction book, but I did work for an entertainment trade paper in New York City, which was tangentially related to the topic, and it wasn't like I was proposing a book about the Iraq War. Screw it. We could gloss over that part.

With the proposal complete, I had a new problem. Whom did I send it to? I knew nothing about book publishing, but every blog post on the topic essentially said you had to get an agent to sell a book. No publisher was going to read an unsolicited book proposal. Forget the slush pile; unsolicited proposals were destined to be tossed into a crate, never to see the light of day again. I had no doubt that this was true — the blog writers seemed so sure of themselves, after all — but I also thought the law of averages could work in my favor. If every aspiring author got the same advice about not sending unsolicited proposals, maybe publishers weren't getting that many of them. Wouldn't it make sense that mine would stand out? Backed by this bulletproof logic, I went to FedEx, printed out six copies of my proposal, and sent them to the six major publishers.

Stephanie sounded young. Not teenager-young, but definitely not old enough to be high on the HarperCollins org chart and able to green-light a book project on her own. At the same time, she seemed to really believe in the book I was proposing. She told me her vision for where she thought a trade paperback about tortured artists could live in the marketplace — Urban Outfitters was not far off — and she was eager to move the idea up the chain of command. It was late December and all of publishing was about to shut down for the holidays, but Stephanie said she would share the proposal with some colleagues and reconnect with me in January after she returned from vacation. "That's exciting," I remember saying. "I do hope you're going somewhere warm and slush-free."

I was on cloud nine for the entire day after that phone call. I had recently moved to a tenement building on the Upper East Side, a studio apartment that Mr. Chieftain had gotten me through his connections. My commute home from the office was now just a one-mile walk up Second Avenue to East Sixty-Fourth Street. No subways. No cabs. As far as commutes went, you couldn't beat it. The rent was way more than I could afford, although I was fortunate in that I didn't have to pay for internet, thanks to my downstairs neighbor's reliably accessible Wi-Fi. Sometimes I needed a pasta strainer to boost the signal, but I could live with that.

I walked giddily up the avenue that afternoon, slush piles be damned, fantasizing about becoming a book author. The process seemed so easy. I had sent my proposal to HarperCollins only two weeks earlier, and I already had an ally in Stephanie, a hungry young editor who was ready to go to bat for me. That feeling of accomplishment got me through a rough couple of weeks at work.

By the time the beginning of 2009 rolled around, Mr. Chieftain had completed his annual financial review and was able to better assess how poorly the newspaper was doing. Things were bad. Classified revenue was now practically nonexistent, and display was not bouncing back like he'd anticipated, a huge contrast from just a few years earlier when advertising from the drama schools propelled us to record revenue. Performing-arts programs do not fare well in a recession. Schools scale them back or cut them altogether. Parents may encourage their college-age kids to pursue more practical majors. Everyone was still shell-shocked from the financial crisis. The last thing anyone was thinking about was studying theater, or so it seemed to us.

Mr. Chieftain's reaction was to keep making cuts wherever he could. We moved across the hall into a smaller office, this one with no windows or cubicles. There was barely enough room for the round wooden table where we held editorial meetings. The space, on the spectrum of feng shui, was somewhere between a wine cellar and a nursery school. He also switched us to a cheaper health plan, one with no prescription coverage.

The sticker shock of having to pay for Ambien out of pocket pretty much canceled out any benefit from the pills. Every arrow in the business was pointing in the wrong direction. My salary, just north of thirty thousand dollars, was now the only substantial expense left. If you put it on a pie chart, it would look like Pac-Man.

"How dare you not pay?" So began the latest angry response to our Craigslist ad seeking interns. The author of said response was an experienced journalist who had recently been laid off, a desperate job seeker, incensed that we were asking people to work for free in such a horrendous job market. He was likely a casualty of one of the many newsroom bloodbaths I'd been reading about. Maybe he had a wife and kids or a mortgage. I pictured him in his fifties and pudgy. In an e-mailed response to our ad, he went on and on about how the job duties we had listed described the work of an employee. Our unpaid internship clearly violated labor laws, he said, and we should consider ourselves lucky if we didn't get sued.

It didn't use to be like this. Before the recession, our ads for interns would typically attract fifty to a hundred enthusiastic responses, often from the types of people you'd expect: college students or recent graduates who were all too eager to pay a few more dues on top of the hundred thousand dollars their parents had just shelled out. Occasionally, you would get an older person—by *older,* I mean twenty-eight—who was looking to make a career change and willing to start at the bottom. But job candidates never openly questioned the unpaid-internship model, just as I hadn't questioned it when I saw the ad in the *Village Voice* three years earlier.

Now we were getting more resistance, and I couldn't figure out why. At first, I thought it might have been another consequence of our newspaper's diminishing influence. "How dare you not pay?" is a perfectly valid question when no one's heard of you. But there was also Dorothy, whose note I couldn't get out of my mind. *Was* she thin-skinned, despite what she'd said, or did she just expect more? Where is the line between expectation and entitlement?

* * *

January passed and no word from Stephanie. I kept resisting the urge to follow up with her, in part because I didn't want to come off as too eager but also because I always prefer no news to bad news. In my mind, I was building up the idea of a book deal as the perfect escape hatch, and now I very much cherished the part of my brain that could cling to that. Each day that went by with no news made the possibility of a yes from Harper-Collins feel slightly less realistic, but I was holding out hope. I knew hearing the words *Sorry, they passed* coming from Stephanie's mouth would hurt far more than it should, especially considering how truly shocked I was by her interest in the first place. *Give it another day,* I thought. *Maybe the top brass are discussing the size of my advance this very minute.*

Mr. Chieftain was becoming obsessed with the mail. "Any checks?" he'd say each day when he walked in. His mood for the rest of the day would often depend on my answer. We had so little advertising coming in by that point that each check mattered. On a good day, we might get two or three, and Mr. Chieftain would cheer up and tell me I'd lucked out that week, as if to remind me that these checks paid my salary. Then there would be the dry spells, two or three days or even a week with no checks, and Mr. Chieftain would lose his ability to focus, often disappearing to the Blarney Stone. Sometimes he'd return later in the afternoon, and I'd have to explain to the interns why he suddenly wanted to take everyone out for burritos.

The easiest thing in the world would have been for him to shut the newspaper down, but his ego was too tied up in it. *Show Business Weekly,* Leo's legacy, the brand he'd brought back from the grave, the multi-tentacled revenge fantasy of being a publisher—he couldn't let these things die. Mr. Chieftain and I had a tacit understanding that his ego was the only thing stopping him from pulling the plug. "I keep telling you it's gonna be over," he'd say. "I keep saying it. You're not listening."

Around the third week of February, I decided that it was appropriate to send a follow-up e-mail to Stephanie asking if she'd heard any news from her colleagues. The waiting was becoming unbearable. I picked a

Tuesday morning to send the e-mail. Based on my experience as a free-lancer who used to pitch magazine editors, I had a sense of how to maximize the rhythmic correspondence of a workweek: Mondays are terrible. Nobody wants to hear from you on a Monday. Wednesdays are bad because the week's work has begun to pile up and most people are already falling behind. Fridays? Forget it. People are already checked out for the weekend. And Thursdays are basically Fridays. So, by process of elimination, Tuesday is the only appropriate day of the week to send an e-mail.

At eight a.m. on a Tuesday I wrote a quick one-sentence e-mail to Stephanie, pushed Send, and held my breath. I decided I was going to close my browser and avoid my in-box for the rest of the day. I wanted to give myself that one last day to hope. Except I didn't have time. A response came back almost instantly, an automatic out-of-office reply. It was not from Stephanie but from HarperCollins corporate. She was no longer with the company.

A Google search quickly brought me the answer. Exactly one week earlier, HarperCollins announced a major restructuring. It was shutting down its entire Collins division, with layoffs across the board, from sales and marketing to longtime editors. The second half of 2008 had apparently been disastrous for the publishing giant, the *New York Times* reporting a 75 percent drop in operating income for the period. Until that point it had been one of the few major publishing houses to escape the recession without massive cuts, but now that had changed. The bloodbaths were coming for the book industry too. It seemed to me in that moment that they were coming for all of us.

CHAPTER 18

Must Be Educated

EXACTLY TWO YEARS AFTER I received the out-of-office reply from Harper-Collins—two years to the day, in fact—a different kind of automated message showed up in my in-box. This one was from OkCupid, the dating website, informing me that I had a new message from a potential match. Weird. I had stopped updating my OkCupid profile years before. It was pretty much dormant aside from the occasional ping I received from a random oddball or prostitute. The fact that this particular message came in at two o'clock in the morning suggested that the sender could be one or both of those things. The typos and the general lack of enthusiasm on the part of the author made me additionally suspicious. She wrote that she had scoped out my profile but confessed to being only mildly impressed with my "hight and looks." Apparently, my theater references bumped me up a few extra points. She seemed especially excited that I had mentioned Tom Stoppard as a favorite playwright. In reality, I had seen only the one play, but whatever.

I went to check out her profile. It was long, with extensive descriptions of her favorite books, paintings, music, theater, and cinema—mostly arthouse stuff like Truffaut and Lars von Trier and Almodóvar. Her pictures were a collage of exotic travel shots, her posing in front of a Buddhist temple in Southeast Asia or drinking champagne at a sidewalk café. Paris, Varanasi, Kathmandu, Bangkok, and Rangoon were among her favorite cities. She loved the Met Opera, *Monocle* magazine, and espresso.

Was it all a bit pretentious? It would have been if not for the execution, a zesty writing style laced with profanity, inappropriate jokes, haphazard em dashes, and exclamation points. So many exclamation points. She said online dating made her feel like a "sad slag," and her whole reason for using OkCupid was to meet someone and be done with it. "I want to get off this stupid merry-go-round," she wrote. "It's making me sick." Notably, she had no qualms about stating her deal-breakers up-front. Men who lied about their height were an obvious sore spot: "I think y'all need to get with a damn measuring stick."

The mix of highbrow and lowbrow in her profile was intriguing, but I was not in a position to date anyone. Between the Upper East Side apartment I couldn't afford and the mounting debt from the credit cards I was using to supplement my lifestyle—or, more accurately, to supplement living—my financial situation was beyond untenable. Mr. Chieftain hadn't given me a raise in three years. Although the economy had improved since the worst days of the recession, our situation at *Show Business Weekly* had not. It technically wasn't even *Show Business Weekly* anymore. Newsstand sales had deteriorated to such an extent that printing a paper every week no longer made sense. We turned it into a monthly. Mr. Chieftain abruptly decided he wanted to focus on controlled circulation, distributing the paper for free to drama students in high schools and colleges. A pivot, they might call it nowadays. Never mind that pivots rarely succeed. My job by that point was simply to execute his whims with the appearance of trying to keep the brand alive. I hadn't given up hope on a book deal—an escape hatch—but after I'd gotten turned down by almost every respectable imprint in the world of trade paperbacks, that dream looked less and less likely.

All of which is to say, injecting a dating life into this septic brew did not feel viable. The idea of compounding my precarious financial circumstances with the added stressors of small talk and dinners at nice restaurants made me nauseated. Still, there was something so compelling about this OkCupid profile, the refreshing candor, the brashness. Her penultimate line really got to me: "Oh, and by the way, if you listed *Eat, Pray, Love* as a favorite book, please kill yourself this instant."

That settles it. I have to meet this woman.

I was just about to doze off in front of my thirteen-inch TV when I heard a thump outside my bedroom window. At first it was easy to let it blend in with the everyday din of East Sixty-Fourth Street late on a Thursday evening, but then a second noise came, even louder, this one clanking against the fire escape. Someone was throwing things at my apartment. Before I could get up to see what was going on, I heard my name. "Zara! Get down here!" It was Mr. Chieftain out there on the cold sidewalk, wearing his coat and Yankee cap.

I threw open the window. "Wait, I'll buzz you up."

A moment later he was in my apartment, frantic, sweating, demanding to know why I had stolen his cell phone from the office. He accused me of trying to sabotage him, trying to destroy what was left of the business. "You're not gonna be happy until we have to shut the whole fucker down," he said. He had a wild look in his eye, one I had never seen before. I'd thought I was used to his wild looks, but this was different. Of course I had not taken his phone, but my telling him that did not seem to convince him of my innocence. He went on and on about how he had turned the office upside down and there was no trace of it. He had important phone calls to make, numbers to retrieve. Why had I done this to him?

"Look, it has to be there," I insisted, throwing on a hat and coat. "Let's go find it."

The twenty-block walk to the office was an uncomfortable blur. Taking a cab would've been easier, but pocket money was tight for both of us. I don't remember what we said to each other along the way, aside from me reiterating that I hadn't taken his phone. The more I thought about the absurdity of what was happening, the angrier I got. Mr. Chieftain had never been one for workplace boundaries. Over the past five years, I had grown accustomed to Sunday-night phone calls, mandatory brainstorming sessions at odd hours, invitations to spend weekends at his house in Connecticut (which I always politely declined). But showing up at my apartment? Armed with rocks? This was a new level of boundary-crossing. And yet he was still my boss, still the person who could cut off my income and possibly end my New York life. I was too far underwater to contemplate what would happen if the paychecks stopped. Throughout those twenty blocks, I seethed in the manner I was used to — in silence. *If I quit, he wins.*

Once we got to the office, it took me all of three minutes to find his phone. It was under a stack of papers on the floor by his desk. The second he saw it, his face changed. His eyebrows sank and his jaw unclenched. A beat or two passed before he extended his hand in a show of full contrition. "Man, I'm sorry."

But I was too worked up to switch gears, and with Mr. Chieftain's anger having dissolved into a pool of remorse, I was now free to express my own. My seething would no longer stay silent. And so I laid into him, verbalizing every character flaw, every instance of poor leadership that came to me in that moment. I told him that he was delusional, that he was allowing himself to be blinded by petty grudges. I told him that when he yelled and screamed at me in front of the interns, he undermined my ability to manage them. I told him that he spent too much energy fighting the wrong battles. "Your anger is what's sabotaging the business," I said, "not me." Finally, after the two of us calmed down, I offered him one last piece of advice: "Get some help."

Mr. Chieftain stared at me for a few moments, somewhat taken aback. Sure, I'd yelled back at him before when he screamed at me, but this was less symmetrical. It was me chastising my boss and him having no good retort. For once, Mr. Chieftain didn't argue. He just sighed and said we should both go home and get some sleep. Thankfully, we took a cab.

Work remained remarkably unchanged after that day. The cycles of Mr. Chieftain's moods and my accommodating them as best I could fell back into their normal patterns, at once arrhythmic and totally predictable. There were far more bad days than good now, but that degenerative process had been happening for a while. In my mind, his accusing me of willful sabotage was the moment when the picture that Dorothy and others had tried to paint for me came into focus. In her note two years earlier, Dorothy had insisted that she wasn't thin-skinned, that that wasn't why she refused to work for him. Now I felt shame for the part of me that hadn't believed her, even though part of me still didn't.

She was exactly like her profile: Cultured, well traveled, proudly snobbish about cinema and the performing arts but with an unapologetically puerile sense of humor. Mouth like a sailor. Head like an encyclopedia. If you had told me a person's essence could be so perfectly rendered in the blue-and-white pixels of OkCupid, I would not have believed it.

Christina and I met for drinks at a wine bar on East Thirtieth Street about a week after she'd sent me that late-night message—which she'd done when she was completely drunk, I was not surprised to learn. The neighborhood had a wisp of douchiness about it, but the place she picked was very cozy, with exposed ceiling beams, a little bar area in the front, and rows of wine bottles along the walls. I was so nervous before the date that my heart wouldn't stop racing, a symptom that had been with me for a while but that seemed to be getting worse as I got older. Worried that the sight of my pulsing neck vessels would be a turnoff, I broke off a small piece of an Ambien pill and swallowed it an hour before the date. I figured it would be just enough to slow down my heart without robbing me of the wits I would surely need to keep up with her.

During our first few glasses of sparkling wine, we talked about the usual things: movies, music, and food—especially food. She had a vast knowledge of world cuisines and was an adamant believer that meals should be enjoyed and food devoured, preferably with friends or lovers. She rattled off something about the Greek philosopher Epicurus. Dining should be a social experience, she said, a transcendent one. I was still harboring the scars of various eating disorders from the years of my early adulthood when I was trying to avoid falling victim to the "tendency." For a long time, my strategy for staying thin was a bastardized version of vegetarianism in which I allowed myself simple pleasures like canned tuna and anchovies but stayed away from most meat. In my mind, this reduced my choices and therefore temptation. As I grew older, I saw the obvious flaws in this reasoning, but I never really learned how to eat like a normal person. I was willing to try, though. When Christina asked me what kind of food I liked, she was just happy that the word *vegetarian* applied to my past. "Thank God," she said. "Portobello burgers make me gag."

I had never met anyone so sure of who she was. Tall, with dark hair and strong features, she filled the space around her barstool with the authority of someone who had fought hard for her right to exist. She could crack an obscene joke one minute, launch into a clichéd platitude the next, and both would come off as completely natural. "I work to live, I don't live to work," she said in a way that somehow didn't sound cheesy. She was forty-five, five years older than me, but listed thirty-seven on her profile because she wanted to throw off the search filters, which I thought was clever and hilarious. I studied her mannerisms for any trace of doubt, a hint of fear, and found none. Was this an act or just adulthood? As we worked our way through bottle number two that night, I thought back to various people I'd known, the tenuous social connections I'd made throughout the different stages of my life: the carefully crafted artifice of my punk-rock friends, the shallowness of my drug buddies, the wishy-washy soul-searching of the drifters I crossed paths with in bohemian Florida. None of this had prepared me for coming face-to-face with actual self-actualization.

I kept waiting for the topic of college to come up, but it didn't. Not the entire night. That might have been a first-date first. Christina worked around the corner at an Italian restaurant, where she was the general manager, but she didn't seem interested in talking about work or career or any of the normal small-talky things that New York professionals clung to in moments of dead air. Her identity was tied up in lived experiences, thirty-two countries and counting, plus an endless cache of cultural references. That I'd never been outside the country seemed to give her serious pause, but she loved theater and Broadway as much as I did, and that provided much fuel for the conversation. I shamelessly played up my access. A revival of Tom Stoppard's *Arcadia* was opening at the Ethel Barrymore in just a few weeks. "Oh, yeah, I'll be going," I said. "I'm interviewing Noah Robbins."

I e-mailed Noah's PR people the next day.

It struck me as no small irony that I was shocked to learn that Christina had not gone to college. Here I was, nursing an endless chip on my shoulder, stewing about the disadvantage of trying to build a career in journalism as a high-school dropout, and yet I'd immediately fallen into the same preconceived notions that I hoped people wouldn't make about me. I was equating being worldly with being educated. When I told her about my GED and my checkered academic past, she just chuckled. "Finally, somebody with an education even I can make fun of." We laughed at ourselves together. I was used to being the least educated person in the room, always having something to learn, but now I was tasked with a new lesson, confronted by a student of a different kind. Christina had learned art history in an antique poster gallery in Chicago, where she worked as a salesclerk in the nineties, devouring books on art nouveau and the Vienna Secession movement. She became a cinephile in the back aisles of video stores, renting Ingmar Bergman and Fellini flicks instead of Steven Spielberg. She'd learned world geography not by studying places on maps but by actually going to them. She said she had no regrets about the way she lived her life, outside of a classroom, and I had no reason not to believe her.

We stumbled out of the wine bar and into a cab. It must have been close to eleven, a bone-chilling February night. I wasn't used to staying out so late or drinking so much or spending that much money on anything. I couldn't afford this night out, but I was glad to have a break from the grind. After five years in New York, working nonstop, connecting on a deep personal level with almost no one, I was suddenly very much aware of what I had been missing. As we were shooting up Third Avenue, Christina's physical aura changed. Gone was the tough, authoritative, sarcastic commander of rooms. She sank into the leather of the seat. "Wanna make out?" Her voice was pitched an octave higher, her face suddenly girlish. "I'll give it a shot," I said.

CHAPTER 19

They Call Me Mr. Gates

WHEN HE WAS NOT AT his weekend house in Connecticut, Mr. Chieftain lived in a cramped one-bedroom apartment on the far East Side. It technically overlooked York Avenue, although you could barely see out the window because of all the construction netting. He had been living there since his acting days in the nineties, and he often half joked that he would have been banished to an even smaller apartment in Queens or New Jersey if it weren't for the miracle of rent stabilization. He was proud of the carpeting, though. Monday through Friday, when I showed up at ten in the morning, he would make me take my shoes off at the front door and leave them in the hall. He'd offer me a beverage and we would adjourn to his tiny living room, where we would work at two Mac computers at opposite ends of the space.

By the beginning of 2012, this was all that was left of *Show Business Weekly:* two men in their socks, working from a third-floor walkup on the far East Side. We were both battling waves of depression at that point, both going through the motions, cobbling together bits and pieces from the newspaper's archives to put out special issues in the hope that a few drama schools would keep advertising. Almost every name on the masthead was either fake or belonged to someone who no longer worked there. When I was laying it out, I always saved room for Tim House, our trusty "account executive," the person whose ad in the *Village Voice* I'd thought I was answering six years earlier.

With the help of a very tenacious literary agent, I finally did get that book deal. A small specialty publisher, an imprint of F+W Media, best

134

known for *Writer's Digest* magazine and the Everything book series, agreed to buy the proposal. It wasn't HarperCollins but I was thrilled to have it. The advance they offered me was small, so small that it would not float me for more than a few weeks. If writing a book was an escape hatch, it wasn't a very promising one. Also, I didn't know how to tell Mr. Chieftain. *Leave of absence* was not in his vocabulary, and the newspaper had been in survival mode for so long that I did not think he would accept anything less than a perpetual state of red alert. Any break in my attention, even a temporary hiatus to focus on an outside project, would be perceived as an act of betrayal.

So petrified was I of broaching the subject that I kept the book deal to myself for several weeks. When the pressure became too much, I finally blurted "I'm leaving!" into the phone receiver as he was reaming me out for the millionth time over some administrative task that hadn't gotten done. That was it. I'd said it. There was no going back.

"What the hell are you talking about?" Mr. Chieftain said after a pause. "Leaving where?"

I explained the situation: I'd been offered a chance to write a book, I thought it would be good for my career, and I needed a few months to write it. I left out the part about how I secretly saw the title of published author as a credential equivalent to a college education. In all the time we'd worked together, as close as we were in some ways, we never discussed my educational background. I suspect he figured out the truth at some point, and maybe that's why he never asked, although that didn't stop him from making snide comments about *those people* when the topic of the less educated came up. He used to laugh his ass off at the intern hopefuls who sent in résumés that didn't mention a four-year degree. "Right in the garbage," he'd say.

The first time Mr. Chieftain instructed me to toss an applicant's résumé in the garbage because it lacked a four-year degree was a blunt reminder of how close I'd come to not getting the job. Had he been the gatekeeper when I applied instead of Kevin, the outcome would have been different. And yet even though I knew his biases might be robbing us of promising intern candidates, I tossed those résumés anyway. I did what I was told. That was easier than having to confront him, having to risk uncomfortable conversations about my own background. I hated gatekeepers until I became one. What's truly frightening is how easy it is to be a bad one.

So here I was, grateful he'd never seen my résumé, grateful for the six years, trying to explain in the most delicate manner possible that I needed a little time to achieve a career stepping-stone that did not involve *Show Business Weekly*, his baby.

Mr. Chieftain congratulated me on the book deal and said I should take as much time as I needed. I should not, however, expect my job to be waiting for me when I was finished writing.

Before I worked in media, I didn't think about the fact that the vast majority of media gatekeepers are, unlike me, college-educated. When I had my first meeting with my literary agent, for example, she naturally assumed I had gone to college, leading to some awkward exchanges when she learned the truth. "Wow, but your proposal is so well written," she said. And okay, maybe that stung a little bit. But what ultimately mattered wasn't that she hurt my feelings; it was that she was willing to look past my background and represent me anyway. A gatekeeper's role is defined by choices, and when she makes one that challenges her own biases, consequential things can happen. At least in my case, they did. She got me the book deal and I got the résumé-boosting credential of *published author,* even if it wasn't the escape hatch I'd thought it would be.

CHAPTER 20

Diseased Corpses

I TRULLI ON A WEEKEND night was a whirlwind of carbohydrate-induced merriment. A popular spot for fine Italian dining, it sat between Park and Lex on East Twenty-Seventh Street, one of those busy slices of Manhattan that seem to exist outside the boundaries of any official neighborhood. Wine flowed freely, dishware clanked with melodious rigor, and you could often hear the faint sounds of Sinatra or the theme from *The Godfather* over the giddy voices of patrons slurping up generous portions of orecchiette in rabbit ragù or cavatelli and broccoli rabe with abandon. The place was a well-oiled machine, with plenty of oil to spare.

Christina was the grand conductor of it all. Her job as the general manager was to tame the chaotic components of a busy restaurant—drunken cooks, late busboys, cranky customers—and somehow will a pleasant dining experience into existence. I'd visit her there a few nights a week and enjoy complimentary flutes of prosecco and the royal treatment that went along with being the boss's boyfriend. Our relationship was moving quickly. Within two months of our first date at the wine bar, I had moved into her large apartment in Inwood, at the northern tip of Manhattan. The location was not ideal, but at least I could sublet my closet-size place on the Upper East Side and stop watching the zeros turn over on my credit card accounts. I think Christina and I were already calling each other Bird by that point, a habit that developed after we realized, pretty early on, that we both hated dating someone with the same name. *Christina and Christopher* sounded like a pastry shop. It was too precious. Identical nicknames derived from the word *lovebird* were much easier to stomach.

What impressed me most about seeing the Bird in action at I Trulli was her natural skill as a manager of people. She'd glide through the dining room in a black pleated skirt and knee-high boots, poised and fearless, chatting up guests and directing coworkers while simultaneously solving every random problem that came to the fore. It could be a misplaced cork on a table or a waiter who needed to be told to put away his phone. The details mattered, and everyone who worked for her seemed to understand how they affected the whole. In my years in the service industry, I'd had many bad managers, more than I can remember. Customer service seemed to breed them.

In the white-collar world, I was discovering, people seemed to place much more of an emphasis on Leadership, with a capital *L*. It was seen as a teachable skill, and in fact entire cottage industries were built around the idea that great leaders were made, not born. There were leadership seminars and books and retreats. People flocked to leadership-focused fireside chats, even though no one seemed to know what a fireside chat was. I didn't have a strong opinion about leadership either way, but watching the Bird manage a large restaurant staff with such a keen mix of authority and empathy made me think intently about how nature-versus-nurture played into it. Maybe it's true that good leaders can be made. Good managers, I'm not so sure about.

Then again, she also had a fetish for etiquette and rules that I probably would've found difficult to navigate—okay, intolerable—if I'd had to work for her. The meticulously trained staff rarely faltered. If you walked by a busboy on your way to the restroom, he'd step aside and slowly extend his right hand, always the right, and wave you through as if he had just unhooked a velvet rope in an exclusive nightclub. And if you thanked a waitress for topping off your wineglass, she'd respond, "My pleasure," not "You're welcome," not "Don't mention it," and never, under any circumstances, "No problem." "Why would you want to introduce a negative?" the Bird said. These were the kinds of customer-centric dictates that I'd quietly resented and often gently flouted during my years in the service industry. It's not that I was obnoxious or rude to customers. But I definitely found subtle ways to rebel, perhaps with an off-color joke or a knowing exchange of winces with a coworker. This was how we told ourselves that we were reclaiming some sense of control from the powerlessness that went along with the job, the grief of having to swallow people's awfulness with a smile. I still recognize these small acts of protest when I see them in service-industry workers today, like when the Duane Reade cashier sings his favorite rap tune as he rings you up. It's either a coping mechanism or a survival tactic, depending on your tolerance level that day.

The Bird's subordinates displayed no such signs of discontent. They seemed all too happy to be working at the restaurant (or at least, they convincingly faked it), despite the Bird's hard-nosed management style and her aggressive enforcement of rules. There was an almost familial bond between her and her crew, which, as someone in a dying industry beset by desperation, competitiveness, and alliances of convenience, I found puzzling. It wasn't until she came home from I Trulli one night and casually told me a story about her evening that I understood her workplace dynamics. She launched into a rant about an older Belgian couple who hadn't left a tip. The waiter who served them was visibly upset but not all that surprised. This kind of tip-dodging is apparently not uncommon, even in nice restaurants, particularly among Europeans, who don't have the same type of tipping culture that we have in the United States.

But the Bird did not just let these tip-dodgers slip away with impunity. Even though the Belgian couple was halfway down the block when she learned they hadn't left a tip, she darted out of the restaurant and chased them down Twenty-Seventh Street. When she caught up with them, she waved the check in front of the husband and explained, politely but firmly, that he must have miscalculated. "It's okay, it happens," she said, trying to allow him to save face. The Belgian husband replied that there was no mistake. Tipping, where he came from, was not a common practice. It was reserved for rare cases of truly excellent service.

"That's great, but you're in America," the Bird countered. "Our wait-staff relies on tips."

"Maybe you need a better system," said the Belgian.

"Maybe we do, but this is the system we have right now."

"Maybe I don't agree with this."

The Bird took no pains to hide her disdain. He didn't have to agree with the system, she said, to understand how his actions penalized the most vulnerable people in it. "You are a guest in this country, sir," she continued. "When I'm a guest in your country, I'll abide by the rules there."

This song and dance went on for some time, and eventually it became clear to the Belgian that there was no way he was getting away with not leaving a tip. Fifteen percent minimum. Twenty preferred.

As the Bird recounted the story to me on the sofa that night, she became noticeably agitated, her facial muscles tensing up. The smallness of the man. The idea that someone who could afford a night of fine dining would punish a waiter in protest of a system the waiter had no control over. It made her blood boil. She went on to vociferously defend the tipping system as a whole. It was no accident, she said, that America had the best restaurant service in the world. She was aware of counterarguments — that tipping enables harassment and favors the powerful — but found them unpersuasive, driven by activists or academics for whom working in restaurants was theoretical. She had waited tables herself for many years and tips had been a vital component in her path to becoming a self-sustaining New Yorker. "There was no other way for me to make enough money here, period," she said.

Living in New York City was not, by any stretch, her birthright. The Bird grew up in Aiken, South Carolina, a small town near the Georgia border where class distinctions were practically etched in stone. There were polo ponies and prep schools but also pickup trucks with gun racks and Confederate-flag bumper stickers. When I learned about the mix of instability and grit that marked her upbringing, I better understood her obsession with manners and the finer things in life. Her mother was always on the edge of being poor, between jobs more often than not. Her father had come from money, but he was abusive and, I gathered, mostly absent from her life. The Bird spent summers in Savannah, Georgia, in the care of her grandmother. "Nana," a cultured member of Southern high society, could be tough and abrasive, but she was confident and comfortable with her privileged lot in life. According to the Bird, she'd reprimand you for not using the proper fork and mock you for saying *who* when the correct word was *whom*. And God help you if you buttered an entire slice of bread. "Break off small pieces," Nana insisted.

These kernels of etiquette were conveyed out of love, though. Nana took the Bird under her wing during those summers, molding her into a kind of high-class protégée, showing her a way of life that she never saw back in Aiken. The Bird took comfort in the rules, the idea that every fork and spoon had its place. It made sense. What kind of rube would butter an entire slice of bread, anyway? She wanted nothing more than to be like Nana, refined, worldly, a contrast to her own mother, who wore cutoff jean shorts and took her to the Waffle House instead of the Oglethorpe Club. At the end of every summer with Nana, the Bird returned to South Carolina in tears. And then she threw up.

Listening to stories of her youth, I thought about what it must have been like to spend your childhood teetering between two vastly different versions of American life — the white-trash bumpkin and the country-club socialite. My worldview had been stunted by Trenton, its empty brick factories and blight. That was all I knew. Unlike people who grew up the way I did, the Bird could make an informed choice about whether it was better to live on the upper or lower end of a stark divide. That mix of snobbishness and scrap that I noticed on her OkCupid profile was not a random quirk. It was the product of dueling perspectives, fully entrenched in her personality yet constantly jostling for dominance. This dichotomy, I suspected, was part of what made her such a good manager, instilling in her both the wisdom to impart strict rules and a kinship with those who had to follow them. No wonder I Trulli was such a high-functioning circus on a weekend night. You want to do the best job possible when you know your boss has your back and that she'd take a bullet for you, or at least chase down a couple of Belgians.

Eight-foot shards of shattered glass dangled from the street-level window frame of the *Show Business* office. According to Leo Shull, some pimps had hurled large wire garbage cans through the windows and trashed the place. Half his staff resigned in terror. He was later attacked on the street, harassed by the crooked NYPD, hospitalized, arrested. All of this, in his telling, was in retribution for his efforts to rid West Forty-Fourth Street of the drugs and prostitution that infested the area. It was the early 1970s, and the Times Square neighborhood where the newspaper was then located had fallen into serious disrepair. Leo was an early proponent of bringing the Broadway district back to its former glory. In interviews, he said he sympathized with the cowering business owners who had to close their restaurants early each night, the young girls who came from small towns and were "forced onto dope" and beaten, who were living in seedy Times Square hotels, "two in a room," and earning three thousand dollars a week that they weren't allowed to keep. He blamed unscrupulous hotel owners who turned a blind eye to it all, and, as was his style, he printed the names of the alleged wrongdoers in *Show Business*. "I started documenting the whore invasion by taking photographs," Leo told one drama critic in 1973. "My camera was smashed to bits. I was in a war zone." His efforts to fight back, to reclaim the area, were not entirely in vain. Around the same time, one of the most infamous hotel brothels of the period, a property on Forty-Fourth owned by the Durst family, was shuttered. To hear Leo tell the story, it was his one-man crusade that made it happen. "I have paid dearly for my battle," he said. "They have called me a madman and a publicity hound and much worse names. But Broadway is now 65 percent cleaned up."

Leo's victory lap was, of course, both overstated and premature; it would be many years before true cleanup efforts changed the fate of Times Square, and it would take a lot more than one sixty-something newsman with a camera to do it. But such was the shamelessly boastful nature of the founder of *Show Business*. I thought about Leo Shull on the morning that Mr. Chieftain called me up and told me that my services at *Show Business Weekly* were no longer needed.

After I finished my book, Mr. Chieftain agreed to bring me back on as an independent contractor. No more health insurance. No more stability. Just the two of us working out of his apartment, humbled. Publicly, I could tell people I had only taken a leave of absence. My title would stay the same and no one had to know the extent to which Mr. Chieftain had whittled things down. Optics still mattered. It was the only common goal we still shared. But now I was fired, he said. Effective immediately.

We'd been heading in this direction for some time, but it was shocking to hear it. Although Mr. Chieftain would continue to produce occasional issues from his apartment, the brand was effectively dead, the final chapter in a seventy-one-year history. I thought about Leo in that Walgreens basement back in 1941, cranking out casting calls on a mimeograph machine for starving actors who just wanted a break. Whatever else you could say about the man, he didn't launch *Show Business* to get rich. He gave it away for free until one enterprising newsstand owner suggested that he charge a nickel for it. In one of his first interviews, eight months after the paper's launch, Leo explained that his true goal was to usurp the existing power structures of the commercial theater industry. "Broadway is a diseased corpse," he told a reporter in 1942. "The men who run the theater don't know what theater is. They are a bunch of penny pinchers who should be in the grocery business."

Funny how that line still holds up.

We used to have a picture of Leo in our office. In it, he was young, debonair, with intense eyes and slicked-back hair. Sometimes late at night, after the newspaper was put to bed and I had a few precious moments of quiet before the weekly cycle began again, I would stare at the picture and wonder about all the wild stories I'd heard about the narcissist who called modesty a "great handicap," the lawsuit-happy asshole, the Communist, the visionary who democratized audition information. Even though he died a decade before I moved to New York, I came to believe through these anecdotes that his resentment of people with power was the one consistency in an otherwise complex and contradictory legacy. Now *Show Business* was the diseased corpse. What did it mean that I would be its last full-time editor?

I had no time to dwell on such philosophical questions. With no job and no income, I was too worried about what the hell I was going to do next. I was in shock, terrified at the thought of being unhirable. How many entertainment newspapers were looking for a forty-one-year-old managing editor? Mostly I was angry—at Mr. Chieftain for throwing me back into the wilderness of unemployment but also at myself for letting him define the terms over our six years together. Why had I never asked for a raise, better insurance, days off? Why did I agree to return as an independent contractor after my book was finished? Why did I not try harder to get a new job? I thought back to Gus Gary, my old roommate, who'd warned me of this very possibility. Should I have let his rants about the value of organized labor sink in?

I decided to do the uncharacteristic thing and ask Mr. Chieftain for severance. Two weeks was fair, I thought. Then he would be rid of me for good. Mr. Chieftain refused, reminding me that I was no longer an employee. True, I said, pushing back, but this is six years we're talking about here. What about all the late nights? All the weekends? All the phone calls of his I took at odd hours? After a bit of hounding, he agreed to think about it.

A few days went by, and I received an e-mail, the last one Mr. Chieftain would ever send me, explaining that there would be no severance and that he regretted my feeling "entitled" to it. He went on to express how "greatly disappointed" he was that I had spent company time pursuing my own outside interests, writing press releases for my book on company letterhead, and collecting the company's PR contacts for my own personal use. He wished me luck in my future endeavors and signed off with "warm regards." It was less an e-mail than the opening salvo of a legal case, a written record of perceived workplace transgressions, a hedge against my trying to collect unemployment. He was Leo Shull's grandson to the end.

The Bird was furious when she heard. She had met Mr. Chieftain at my book-release party, where he'd drunk excessively and hit on my agent, and she disliked him on sight. But she was also a big believer in employees fighting for what they were owed. She told me that restaurant employees were commonly expected to work a five-six—that is, six days a week every other week. This schedule effectively robbed people of two full weekends a month. It was standard practice, but the Bird refused to do it. "The reason restaurants can get away with that is that people agree to it," she said. She insisted that I fight for severance, unemployment, whatever I could get. This was not optional. It was my obligation.

I admired her clear sense of right and wrong and her willingness to do what was necessary to make wrongs right. Mr. Chieftain was the Belgian husband who was trying to dodge a tip, and I should have been livid. But as much as I tried, I couldn't rouse myself to the same level of moral outrage. I had to stay focused on the longer game. I knew Mr. Chieftain would make fighting me in court a full-time job. It wasn't just about being angry but figuring out where to channel it. I had just spent the past six years watching the man quibble with salespeople, sue distributors, and chase down advertisers for unpaid invoices while his business succumbed to larger forces. If there wasn't a lesson there on the danger of fighting the wrong battles, what was it all for?

PART III

CHAPTER 21

Clicks

JUDGING BY THE PUBLICATION'S NAME, you never would have guessed it was tied to a religious cult. *International Business Times*. It had such a spiritless ring to it, almost algorithmic, saying so much while saying nothing at all. The more I repeated it to myself, the more I realized that was what made it so brilliant. This peculiar news website was barely six years old, and yet it projected the authority of a trusted hub for global financial information. Familiarity was baked right into the name. "I used to read that back in college," people would sometimes say. "Do they still have the print version?"

There was no print version. There was barely even a record of where the thing had come from. Just vague rumors about the cult, a growing sect of low-profile Christians. They believed, evidently, that the Second Coming was a sexagenarian pastor from South Korea who wore wide suits and operated a network of biblical colleges. No one mentioned the cult when I applied for the job as a media reporter, and I don't think I would have cared anyway. *International Business Times* was offering me thirty-six thousand dollars a year, not a gold mine but still more money than I'd made after six years working for Mr. Chieftain. I lied and told the Bird it was twice as much. She still grimaced at the number. "Bird, come on, you're worth at least eighty K," she said.

We could agree to disagree there. One unforeseen by-product of my having a girlfriend, especially one with such a clear sense of her own self-worth, was that my salary was suddenly judged against an objective set of expectations that challenged my stunted view of what was acceptable. Up until that point, I had been measuring my take-home pay strictly against my own historical rate of progress, from the perspective of someone who had not made more than seven dollars an hour until he was in his thirties. Enough to squeak by was always enough. I knew the Bird's assessment was more in line with professional standards, but I did not feel like I was in a position to negotiate. In the two weeks since Mr. Chieftain had cut me loose without a safety net, I'd spent every day and night on the job-application carousel, panicked. I was having zero success, unless you counted pleasant responses from HR people who promised to keep my résumé "on file." Does anyone actually do that? Is there even really a file?

That's when I received an e-mail from Ellen, the editor of *IBT*'s media and culture section. *IBT* was looking to expand the section, she explained, and they needed reporters with knowledge of both entertainment and business. She'd read my clips and thought I might be a good fit. *Show Business Weekly* had both in the title, after all.

Yes! I told Ellen. *I'd love to apply.*

She forwarded me the job description, and I immediately went from excited to deflated. A bachelor's degree was required for the reporter position, and a master's was preferred. "MBAs encouraged to apply," the ad said. I quickly googled *MBA* and realized I was not one. What could I do? I knew this was going to be another case of sending my résumé and hoping they didn't notice. Worst came to worst, there was always the Jedi mind trick.

Whatever it was, it worked, because Ellen called me in for an interview, congratulated me on my new book—thank God for that book—gave me a writing test, and offered me a job. *IBT* was apparently growing at lightning speed. It sounded like the polar opposite of the publication I'd just left. The iPhone had been the death blow for *Show Business Weekly*, but this digital-only news outlet seemed to be benefiting from the disruption that had upended newspapers. It needed warm bodies to meet a growing appetite for business news that could be consumed on smartphones. There was no time to worry about minor details like its new media reporter not having an MBA or even knowing what an MBA was.

Walking through the financial district on my first day at *IBT,* whose office was in a burnt-orange building on Hanover Square about a block from Delmonico's, I felt like I was transitioning to a new phase of New York life.

Ellen greeted me at the front desk under a large sign that read INTERNATIONAL BUSINESS TIMES in a stately serif typeface. She was thin and hip, maybe mid-thirties—younger than me, for sure—and professional-looking. She lived in Brooklyn, which, I was discovering, was not a consolation prize but the borough of choice among younger-than-me New Yorkers. They didn't want Manhattan and certainly had no love for uptown. I wore a tie and took a Xanax to calm my nerves for my first day, and I was glad I'd done both. Ellen led me down a long corridor, walking quickly, in short steps, apparently in a hurry. It was a big news day in the media world, she said. Anderson Cooper of CNN had just publicly come out as gay, and now her team was scrambling for angles. I made a joke, a bad one, about that not really being news because, well, didn't everyone already know? Ellen turned her head and looked at me with narrowed eyes, as if I didn't understand the job she'd just hired me for. *Okay, no more jokes until I have a better reading of the audience. Maybe making a crack about a famous cable-news anchor and member of the Vanderbilt family is considered punching down around here.*

The rows of cubicles seemed to stretch on forever. *IBT* had an entire damn floor, complete with executive offices along the perimeter, large white pillars that separated the different departments, a Ping-Pong room, conference rooms, and even a studio area for video production. There was a spread of free bagels every Wednesday with seven different kinds of cream cheese. This was the sprawling newsroom I'd imagined I was calling when I spoke with Kevin about the internship seven years earlier. I couldn't believe I was here. The place buzzed with exactly the kind of life you'd expect to see and hear: the electronic chirps of office phones, the clickety-clack of Dell keyboards, intense conversations about story copy and deadlines and sources. If there was an ad-sales department, it was nowhere near where the journalists sat.

After giving me a quick tour of the floor, Ellen stopped at her desk and motioned to the cubicle next to hers. It had a cardboard sign with my name and title tacked to the wall, a computer, and a phone, already set up like magic. Who'd done all this? At one point later in the day, Ellen caught me messing with the wires behind my monitor and asked me why I didn't just call tech support. At my old job, I *was* tech support, and HR, and accounts receivable, and everything else. Now I felt like a caveman who had just learned how to use a cigarette lighter to start a fire.

The Bird came home exasperated one night. She had just worked an extra-long shift at the restaurant, and her list of annoyances was extra-long as well. "I am so over this," she said, collapsing onto the sofa, almost too exhausted to drink the rosé bubbles I had just poured for her. "Bird, what's wrong?" I asked.

A young woman, let's call her Brittany, had arrived at the restaurant in a limousine along with a couple of friends. Brittany claimed to be a travel writer from Boston and said she was researching an article about a "night on the town" in Manhattan. She was cryptic about where she worked and where this article would appear, but she nevertheless managed to convince the restaurant's PR agency to offer her a complimentary dinner for two. When the Bird heard this, she protested loudly, immediately suspicious that a journalist would ask for a free meal—legitimate news outlets typically frowned on that. And what legitimate news outlet would green-light an article about a Bostonian having a night on the town in Manhattan? How was that even a story? A Google search of Brittany's name deepened the Bird's suspicions. If Brittany was a travel writer, she wasn't a very prolific one. Her only apparent byline was her own blog, on which she had written a few sloppy posts about traveling to Europe. Not *around* Europe, but to one country in Europe. "This person is not a professional, hasn't been anywhere, and can't even write," the Bird told the PR agency. None of that seemed to matter, though. The PR agent, who worked for the restaurant's owner and therefore had veto power over the Bird's decisions, insisted that Brittany be given what she wanted: free dinner for two. Good press is good press.

Brittany was in her twenties, blond, and, in the Bird's telling, spoke at an ear-piercing volume that rose high above the crowded dining room, seeming to defy any conventional understanding of psychoacoustics. Worse than that, she was rude to the staff, ordering them around like servants while reminding them, repeatedly, that she would be writing about her dining experience. At the end of the evening, the Bird pointed out to her that the agreement had been for a complimentary dinner for *two*, and Brittany was in a party of three, and the three of them had consumed enough wine for an Italian wedding. Plus, even if the meal was free, the waiter still needed to be tipped.

"Oh no, you're mistaken," Brittany replied. "I don't pay."

The argument escalated, and Brittany became even more combative, saying she had a limo waiting outside and did not have time to debate such things, night on the town and all. In the end, she reluctantly agreed to pay a portion of the bill, and the standoff concluded with no bloodshed, but it left the Bird so infuriated that she could barely see straight.

As the Bird told me this story, she relived multiple levels of disgust about Brittany's rudeness, her sense of entitlement, and her lack of professionalism. What seemed to get her most upset was the possibility that someone, anyone, might be paying Brittany to write—Brittany was clearly a terrible writer, not to mention a terrible person. "I am so over this," the Bird said again.

It was the first time in all the months we'd been together that I'd heard her express a desire to leave the restaurant business. I had assumed, because she was so sure of herself, so fleshed out as a person, so good at the job, that she was happy working there. And she was. But after two decades of restaurant work, she was also tired. She suddenly felt the pangs of roads not traveled, a feeling spurred by similar forces that had taken root in my own life some years earlier. College was never realistic for the Bird. She'd run away from home at sixteen after a physical altercation with her stepfather, and she left Aiken for Atlanta right after high school, drawn to the allure and possibilities of a big city. The realities of survival meant that many of her most promising creative impulses went undeveloped. I was surprised to learn, for instance, that she was a bit of a pioneer in the theater-blogging space, writing hilarious and highly opinionated reviews of Broadway shows for theater websites back in the mid-nineties, before most people even knew what blogging was. The writing gigs got her into shows for free, but they didn't pay, and she eventually gave it up. Her true passion was graphic design. She could work out complex visual concepts in her head with inventiveness and ease, the opposite of me, the left-hander who relied on numbered streets and talked backward as a kid. But design, too, felt unattainable, especially because she had no formal training, and women designers were relatively rare in the industry at that time.

Listening to the Bird express her lost patience for the restaurant business that night, I thought back to our first few dates, how she'd told me that she'd lived exactly the life she'd wanted to live. She'd traveled the world and regretted nothing, certainly not missing out on college. I believed her, but then, regret is a fuzzy concept. Can you regret not making choices that you didn't have the opportunity to make? That's a tough question to answer even on the best of days, and especially after you've just spent your evening dealing with Brittany.

Somehow, it was already Friday. My first week at *IBT* had flown by in a dizzying procession of news stories about media and culture. We were expected to write three a day, and I wasn't used to the pace or the notion of broadening my definition of what was newsworthy. I wrote about Alec Baldwin quitting Twitter, HBO announcing a new season of *The Newsroom*, and other inconsequential events that would be forgotten within days or hours. I knew I would not be getting the attention of the Pulitzer committee, but I was exhilarated by the simplicity and focus of the job. There was only one thing to do: write.

When I wasn't writing, I quietly wondered how on earth a digital-only news outlet like *International Business Times* sustained itself, knowing what I knew about the supposed elusiveness of online advertising revenue. I'd look around the floor and feel overwhelmed by the size of the operation. We had a business desk and a world desk, entertainment and sports writers, a copy team whose only job was to back-read stories after they went live and fix typos. Each head I could see popping over the tops of the gray cubicle walls represented another salary. I couldn't fathom how banner ads and a couple of sparsely placed auto-play videos were paying for it all. Could it be that all those naysayers who had so glibly written off the profit-making potential of news in the age of the internet were wrong? What was I missing?

Metrics, it turned out.

As I was getting ready to leave for the weekend, Ellen sat me down for a frank discussion about my first week, her assessment of how things were going. She was mostly happy with the stories I picked and how I was executing them, but then she delivered some unpleasant news. Basically, no one was reading them. "I've been looking at your traffic, and your numbers are low," she said. "Your stories should be getting more clicks." The situation was not dire, she assured me. It was just a question of being more conscious of how my stories were performing, paying attention to the metrics.

To be honest, I can't remember if she actually said *not dire* during this conversation, but those are the words I remember repeating to myself in that moment. I liked the sound of them. I was used to feeling like every day at work could be my last. What Ellen was telling me was that there was more to this new job than writing stories in a vacuum. Journalists would be judged by an objective measure: traffic. That seemed reasonable to me. Certainly it was an improvement over being judged by a capricious boss whose opinions changed with the wind.

Ellen showed me a platform called Chartbeat where reporters could log in and see how their stories were performing in real time. The centerpiece of its main dashboard was a giant number that bounced around like it couldn't decide where to land: 4,051 ... 4,028 ... 4,063. It changed from one second to the next. These were called concurrents. They were the number of people on *IBT*'s website at any given moment.

The area below the concurrents section on Chartbeat was where things got really interesting — or depressing, depending on your perspective. You could see the top-performing stories and the names of the top-performing authors. My name was not among these superstars. In fact, when I did a search of all the authors on the *IBT* website, I discovered that I was pretty close to the bottom of the list, and not because my last name started with a Z. It was humbling, to say the least, to see numbers as low as seventy-five next to stories I'd written. This Chartbeat list was a kind of scoreboard. Apparently, everyone at work looked at it, which is to say that everyone at work knew I was a loser.

At the top of the list was some guy named Wilson who wrote endless stories about the iPhone and MacBooks and other Apple products. His stories had hundreds of thousands of views. Again, not dire, Ellen assured me. Tech stories always outperformed others. We were on the media and culture desk—no one was expecting anyone on our team to topple Wilson, the king of traffic. I pictured him as Lex Luthor in Old Navy khakis, clearly my office archnemesis. I'd take him down eventually, I figured, but first things first. My short-term goal was to ensure I was not too close to the bottom of the list.

Over the next few weeks, I wrote feverishly about topics on my beat that I thought would attract more visitors—stories about Justin Bieber and Rihanna and the Kardashians—but they did little to lift my numbers. Then, at the end of my third week on the job, a mass shooting took place in Colorado at a midnight screening of the new Batman movie. Suddenly, our media and culture desk was covering the biggest news story in the world, verifying and reporting a flood of fast-moving facts as they unfolded. If you got something wrong, readers noticed. It was chaotic and high stakes in a way that producing a weekly newspaper for local actors never was.

Our Chartbeat numbers soared that day, higher than I had ever seen them go, concurrents growing exponentially as readers sought any new information they could find about the tragic massacre. *What was the shooter's motive? Did he go to college? Why did he look like the Joker?* they wanted to know—8,000...8,600...9,000. Discussions in the newsroom about our sudden jump in traffic took place in tandem with somber acknowledgments of the tragedy's scale and human toll. Twelve people had been killed, seventy injured. Kids. Entire families. As someone who was completely new to digital news, I had no concept of whether these discussions were normal. Was it appropriate to be mourning mass casualties as we stared at our rising numbers on Chartbeat?

The traffic bump was, of course, short-lived. Over the next few weeks, the news cycle returned to a normal rhythm. Most of the stories we covered had a shelf life of a day or two before the reading public moved on to something else. My numbers, consequently, returned to their previous lackluster levels. I was not at the very bottom of the Chartbeat list, but I was low enough to sweat. I remember one reporter whose numbers were consistently lower than mine, a skinny twenty-something with a crew cut who seemed to have an endless collection of striped polo shirts that accentuated his skinniness. In my mind, he was nicknamed "Slim," although that's only because I can't recall his actual name. *IBT* was hiring so many young reporters at that time that it was easy to lose track. Compared to them, at forty-one, I was downright geriatric.

Slim sat toward the front. Like me, he was quiet and kept to himself. When I passed him each morning on the way to my desk, he was always deep into the vortex of work, diligently typing away to make that three-story quota. We never really spoke, but his being there gave me a sense of comfort, in part because we were hired around the same time, but mostly because his low traffic numbers made mine look good.

Then one day his cubicle was empty. His stuff was gone. No one discussed his disappearance or even seemed to notice. I wasn't friendly enough with anyone who worked in Slim's section to ask what had happened to him, so I just went on with my business. But curious employee disappearances became a somewhat regular thing. They generally happened right before the first of the month and usually to people who were near the bottom of the Chartbeat list, like a slow-moving Rapture for the underperforming.

Ellen had assured me that our team was not held to the same standard as the monster traffic-getters, the Wilsons of the newsroom. But how much control over my fate did she really have? Would she protest very loudly if I was summoned to HR and jettisoned through a trapdoor? So much about this place was still a mystery. I hadn't met the CEO, who apparently rarely came out of his office. I suspected that somebody somewhere on the floor was going over daily spreadsheets with the Chartbeat numbers in one column and payroll in another. *Not dire* was starting to feel pretty dire.

CHAPTER 22

News to Me

WILSON DIDN'T LOOK ANYTHING LIKE Lex Luthor, but he had an intensity about him that suited his status as the king of traffic. Slight, with short hair and a chestnut scruff, he spoke with a radio-ready voice and joked frequently—and loudly—with his many friends around the *IBT* office. He had aggressive mannerisms, walking in hasty bursts up and down the aisles, moving from place to place as if he always had somewhere to be and then somewhere *else* to be. I was still learning the unspoken etiquette of working in a large office, the confounding social norms of coexistence that everyone else seemed to follow by instinct. I didn't know, for example, that you're not supposed to say "Good morning" to every person you pass on the way to your desk in the morning. I mean, it's technically not forbidden, but don't expect an enthusiastic response from the puffy-eyed colleagues on the receiving end of daily salutations. Knowing how and when to make eye contact had always been my Achilles' heel in social situations, but gauging it here was downright impossible. Was I really expected to face forward and not acknowledge other people as I passed them in the hall? Judging by the many unreturned smiles, that seemed to be the case. It takes only two or three painfully awkward exchanges before you realize that it's safer not to engage at all.

I found it disconcerting that a busy newsroom had so perceptibly reignited social phobias that I hadn't had to deal with since high school. I'd thought I was over this crap. It turned out I'd thought that because I'd managed to avoid situations that necessitated prolonged, peer-heavy interaction for the past twenty-five years. The fluorescent lighting of the office, under which I looked like a pasty alien, definitely did not help the situation.

All of these new stimuli forced me to withdraw whenever I encountered the people I had sized up as the workplace alphas, people like Wilson. Needless to say, I was not exactly thrilled to learn that he would be giving the entire newsroom a presentation on best practices for SEO. Traffic-wise, I had barely been treading water this whole time. I was staring constantly at Chartbeat, doing my best to make sure I wasn't at the bottom of the list, terrified that the next mysterious disappearance in the office would be me. Now we were going to be forced into a room with Wilson so he could explain what we were all doing wrong?

SEO was still a foreign concept to me. I knew it stood for "search engine optimization" and that it had something to do with using the right keywords in your articles, but I was not aware of the extent to which digital newsrooms like ours relied on Google for their existence. *IBT* was part of an iteration of online media companies that had launched in the mid-2000s and built audiences on search engines and social media, places like *Huffington Post* and *Mashable* and *Business Insider.* I had no association with most of these brands outside of a hazy awareness that they existed. Some of them I had not even heard of. When I started at *IBT* in 2012, I was surprised to learn that younger reporters there not only read a website called *BuzzFeed* but spoke of it with a doting reverence. One look at the thing gave me motion sickness; it was a dizzying composite of lists, animated GIFs, and cultural references that I was too old to care about. But this was the media landscape that had emerged in the smartphone era while I was working at a weekly newspaper, and it didn't need my approval to flourish. While I was fretting about newsstand sales and print windows, search engines and social media platforms were asserting themselves as the primary method of news distribution. By 2012, they were all but calling the shots.

It was against the backdrop of this unsettling revelation that I watched Wilson give his presentation on SEO. He stood at the head of our main conference room flipping through a slideshow of his most successful articles and explaining the thought process behind his headline construction.

He was in his element, confident, detailing how he had chosen each word with meticulous care. The placement of each word mattered, he said. If a story was about a new iPhone release, the headline should start with the words *Apple iPhone*—a process called frontloading—and should include the words *release* and *date* and anything else that people might plug into a Google search window.

I had loved writing headlines for *Show Business Weekly* because you could be forgiven for making corny puns. Wilson's headlines made no such attempts at cleverness. They were straightforward and dense, pushing the boundaries of logical syntax, words strung together in strategic chunks ("Mac OS X Upgrade News: Apple Scores Developer Specs Before iPhone 5 Event Date"). But there was a sly artfulness to his method. The way Wilson explained it, it was less important for online headlines to resonate emotionally than it was for them to get the best placement in Google's search results. You wanted to be the first story that came up when someone searched for a topic because internet users rarely looked beyond those first few results. Search placement was an automatic process driven by algorithms and page rankings and a million other factors programmed by Google engineers. Then Wilson said something I'll never forget: "You're writing for machines. You have to think like one."

CHAPTER 23

Drinking Games

THEY WERE CALLING IT THE most consequential presidential election in history: Barack Obama versus Mitt Romney. Journalists and pundits were lamenting "post-truth politics" as rapid-fire lies and disinformation made fact-checking feel lonely and futile. Social media was rewriting the rules of engagement, coarsening discourse to the point of decay, exploiting political fissures, spreading crackpot conspiracy theories like wildfire. Memes and tweets were replacing conversations.

It seems so obvious now that the presidential elections to follow would be far worse in every measurable sense, but as a digital journalist covering my first presidential election, I felt like I was looking through a grim window at the beginning of the end of something—at best, civility; at worst, democracy. Keeping up with the news each day did not involve paying attention to the news sources I thought it would. For one thing, Facebook was growing in influence, and not in a good way. Back in 2008, it had been credited with helping the Obama campaign connect with young voters, aided by the golly-gee tenor of dutiful tech journalists: *Look at the cool social network and how it engages the young'ns.* Four years later, the cool social network was a machine of unimaginable scale, a bigger driver of news than television and print combined, and yet it was still flying under the radar as a tool for dangerous propaganda. Could this monstrosity actually tip an election? Mark Zuckerberg, who founded the thing, would famously call that a "crazy idea" in 2016. Perhaps if he had been paying more attention in 2012, he wouldn't have thought it was so crazy. All you had to do was rile up your team with fiery memes about binders full of women, Clint Eastwood talking to an empty chair, the president in a turban.

Everyone was talking about the "white working class," which, as far as I could tell, meant white people without college degrees. Technically, that was me. But I didn't recognize myself in any of the news articles about the white working class written by people who, I presumed, did not consider themselves to be a part of it. They talked about how the white working class was aggrieved, or anxious about the changing demographics of the country, or just plain mad that we had a Black president. They cited polls, studies by academics. Sometimes there were charts. I love a good chart, but this aspect of poll-driven political journalism—still new to me at the time—unnerved me. Why were pollsters so eager to categorize people based on educational attainment? Was this a new thing or had I just not noticed it?

The idea of being demographically bound to a group of people who were seen by political journalists as creatures to be studied took time to process. It gnawed at a growing sense of shame I had about my background, reinforcing my belief that I should keep it under wraps at all costs, at least while I worked in journalism. But in journalism, being white also meant being given the benefit of the doubt in ways that I didn't fully appreciate then. As long as the subject of education didn't come up, I could blend in. Journalists of color, colleagues who were far better educated than me, did not have that luxury. The majority of people in our newsroom, in most newsrooms, still looked like me.

I spent much of 2012 keeping my head down and hoping the focus on educational differences would pass after the election. With luck, I thought, future elections would not trigger such weird preoccupations with the white working class.

My biggest contribution to our 2012 coverage at *IBT* was helping people cope with the election through alcohol. I had discovered that roundups of drinking games were a reliable source of traffic. All you had to do was search the internet for drinking games related to a specific upcoming event, then publish your roundup a few hours before the event started:

"Best Drinking Games for the Oscars." "Best Drinking Games for the World Cup." This formula turned out to be pure Chartbeat gold. Using the SEO tactics that I'd learned from Wilson, I keyworded the hell out of my headlines and watched the concurrents roll in. Seeing my name at the top of Chartbeat as I watched these events live on a TV at home with the Bird became a regular thrill ride. "Look at it go!" I'd say, shoving my laptop in her face. Colleagues would congratulate me the next day. "Dude, your story—amazing."

I no longer worried about being the next person at work to mysteriously disappear. As long as I was hitting those numbers, people left me alone. Ellen was happy. I could find time to report stories I cared about and discover the ins and outs of business journalism as I went along. I learned what EBITDA meant, what IPO stood for, how to make FOIA requests to find out things that companies didn't want you to know. I experienced the unadulterated joy of getting a scoop and the adrenaline rush that went along with it. When I started at *IBT*, I hadn't known what an analyst note was, but now I was devouring them like fanfic. Macquarie. Goldman. Morningstar. It was stimulating, a contrast to anything I'd ever been exposed to while I was growing up. Having to produce drinking-game roundups and other traffic-generating fluff felt like a small compromise if it meant that I got to quietly digest the rules of the craft. Hell, even Shakespeare had to write crowd-pleasers to support his tragedies.

The Bird was sitting across the table from me at Joe Allen, swirling a french fry in the spicy mayonnaise that she loved so much, when her face lit up with surprise. I felt a light kick on my shin under the table. "Bird, look who it is," she said. "God bless 'er."

I looked across the dining room to see a very old woman with a walker being escorted to the exit, moving slowly but surely, taking tiny steps and pausing between each one. She was small and hunched over. It was Lauren Bacall.

Celebrity sightings were not unusual at Joe Allen, an unpretentious restaurant on the ground floor of a townhouse on West Forty-Sixth Street. The place had been a favorite hangout for theatrical royalty for decades and was known for its fatalistic collection of old Broadway posters—all from shows that were commercial flops. Theater celebrities felt at home there; they blended in with the after-theater crowd, tucking themselves away at quiet tables behind the brick archways that made up the interior. On any given night, you might see Stockard Channing or Al Pacino or that lady who's in everything but whose name escapes you. None of the patrons at Joe Allen ever acted starstruck.

Still, there was something emotional for me about seeing Lauren Bacall, once the very epitome of showbiz glamour, enjoying a night out during her final years on this earth. On seeing her, I told the Bird a story she'd probably heard a million times, how a teenage Lauren Bacall sold copies of what became *Show Business Weekly* on the streets of Midtown in the early 1940s, before the newspaper even had a name, and how she mentioned Leo Shull in her autobiography. Maybe it was the transition taking place in my professional life at that time that made this encounter feel so poignant. I'd moved on from thinking about audition notices and theater press releases each day and was now consumed by stock tickers and SEC filings and SEO. This was bittersweet. Part of me wanted to march right up to Lauren Bacall and say hello, but I've never been one to approach celebrities, not even ones with whom I share a workplace lineage. It was enough to know that we'd both moved on from *Show Business Weekly*.

I wasn't the only person at Joe Allen that night who was going through a professional transition. The Bird had been laid off from her job as a restaurant manager, and rather than looking for another job that would have her chasing down Belgians and haggling with fake food writers, she'd decided to pursue graphic design. She saw getting laid off less as a sign— the Bird didn't believe in those—than as a circumstantial impetus with a limited shelf life. "It's now or never," she said.

I taught her the basics of Photoshop. Like me, she was initially intimidated by all the pointers and tools and the busy interface—hurling obscenities at the screen became a regular thing—but the Bird stuck with it, and before long she became obsessed with typefaces and kerning, logos and color theory, watching Paula Scher and Chip Kidd videos on YouTube. As someone who had begun a new career with no formal training, I recognized in the Bird the stages she was now going through. They were defined less by a single aha moment—*I can do this!*—than by a progression of small accomplishments, each one fortifying your confidence against the next inevitable failure.

The Bird and I were going on two years of cohabitation but still rarely talked about money. As long as separate bank accounts were a thing, she needn't know how much—or how little—was showing up by direct deposit each pay period. Nor did I need to know the specifics behind her small savings, which were now dwindling rapidly. I had urged her to pursue design, but what if I was wrong? Was that gamble worth her life savings? We were getting very good at the art of harmonious denial, embracing the things we loved to do as a couple while pretending that anything unpleasant would wither under the force of our refusing to acknowledge it.

I was just about to step away from my desk and grab lunch when the instant message appeared.

Can you come by my office right now?

It was from Jeff, our editor in chief. I'd had only limited interactions with him in the nine months since I'd been there, and he almost never reached out to me directly. Ellen was not at her desk. Getting summoned to his office could not be good, right? Was this going to be the day of my mystery disappearance? I'd never been much of a lunch eater, but now my small appetite was wrecked.

Anxiety in general continued to be an increasingly disruptive force in my life, especially at work and especially around people in authority. It wasn't like Jeff was physically intimidating. He was short and soft-spoken, sixtyish, with a dusty, office-casual style that I imagined he hadn't updated in decades. But he really knew his shit when it came to business and finance, having worked as a national news editor for *Bloomberg News*, and I constantly feared that he would spot me as a phony who didn't know the first thing about business journalism. During our first one-on-one meeting, on my second or third day, Jeff asked me what kind of companies I was interested in covering for *IBT*. I mentioned entertainment and media giants: Disney, Viacom, Time Warner, News Corp. I figured those were on my beat.

"That's great," Jeff said. "We need more coverage of those companies. When do they report?"

Report? Report what? What was he talking about? "Oh, you know, all different times," I said, pushing my palm against my leg to keep my foot from tapping on the carpet tile.

I later learned that he was talking about earnings, that earnings were a thing that all publicly traded companies reported every three months. That I didn't know what an earnings report was during my first meeting with the editor in chief definitely did not look good, but I think I managed to redeem myself after that bad first impression. The more Jeff saw my writing and reporting, the more he seemed to like my approach, especially how I took serious-minded business stories and topped them off with Wilson-style SEO headlines that would ensure they got clicks. In June 2013, Edward Snowden was revealed as the whistleblower who'd leaked details about the NSA's spying program, and Jeff put me on that bombshell story, asking me to find out everything I could about Snowden's background. According to media reports, Snowden had only a GED, and yet he had been working as a government contractor; Jeff seemed astounded by this and wanted me to play up the "loser aspect" of the story. It was right around this time that Jeff promoted me to senior reporter.

As soon as I got the instant message, I went to Jeff's office, and he looked at me with the seriousness of a brain surgeon after a failed operation. "Well, my friend, you drew the short straw," he said. Over the next few very long seconds, I pondered the meaning of *short straw* in this context and ran through every possibility in my head. Finally, Jeff delivered the news. It was an assignment. I was going to interview Etienne Uzac, the CEO of IBT Media, our parent company.

My first reaction was bewilderment. What the hell was the point of interviewing my own boss? *Our* own boss? Jeff explained that IBT Media had been looking to gain more exposure, and that someone—maybe a PR agent—thought it would be a good idea to publish a Q and A with Etienne on the company's flagship website. During the interview, Etienne could talk about the challenges of running a media start-up in the fast-changing landscape of digital news. I was *IBT*'s senior media reporter, so the job naturally fell to me.

I knew almost nothing about Etienne except that he was French, had been educated at the London School of Economics, and rarely interacted with the staff. People around the office whispered about him a lot, but there was little consistency in their descriptions. Some called him awkward and shy, a lurching goofball with square glasses who couldn't speak in public to save his life. Others branded him as ruthless and cold, a sociopath who would unceremoniously fire underperforming executives at the drop of a hat. Rumor had it that Etienne was in the cult—not just in it but involved at a high level, a devout and devoted foot soldier for the Christian sect that was supposedly affiliated with IBT Media. I tried to ignore those rumors. It's not that I didn't wonder who was running the show at the company that paid my salary, but I figured the truth was probably far less interesting than the chattering gossip. Plus, it wasn't like anyone was telling me to write articles about Jesus or the Old Testament.

When word got around that I was going to interview the CEO, I was suddenly the most sought-after reporter on the floor. People I rarely talked to or didn't even know swung by my desk with suggested questions, telling me I should go hard, not hold back. A litany of workplace grievances emerged. "Ask him why we're paid only once a month." "What about those terrible auto-play videos?" "Have you seen our ridiculous Glassdoor reviews?"

All these complaints baffled me, someone who was new to the environment of a large newsroom and still very much in awe of it. Was *International Business Times* really so bad? I understood that we weren't the *Wall Street Journal* or *Bloomberg*, that there was a scrappiness and sort of makeshift manner to how we did things. The bagels, I supposed, could have been fresher. But nobody yelled and I figured Jeff would never show up outside my apartment and throw rocks at my window. I once again thought back to Dorothy and that note she'd left me under our office door, how she couldn't—wouldn't—work at a company that did not meet her expectations. As I was being bombarded by the complaints of coworkers who were eager to see me put the CEO in the hot seat, it suddenly seemed to me that I was working in a whole newsroom of Dorothys. I really struggled to understand what it was they expected work to be.

For the moment, it didn't matter. With my access to Etienne, I was to be the voice of their grievances, and my reputation as a journalist was on the line. If I softballed the interview, I'd fail them. If I pushed too hard, I'd risk pissing off the boss. This must have been what Jeff meant by the short straw.

CHAPTER 24

Point A to Point C

ETIENNE ENTERED THE LARGE CONFERENCE room and I rose to shake his hand. The CEO of IBT Media was tall, at least six three, with a round face and neatly parted brown hair. And he was young, still in his twenties, and he definitely looked it. He apologized for keeping me waiting, complimented my work, then took a seat across from me at the large blond-wood table. It was just the two of us, and the room felt twenty sizes too big, empty even. I was used to being the uncomfortable one in professional settings, but my boss was giving me a run for my money, shifting in his seat and futzing with the crisp collar on his white shirt. When I asked if I could record the interview, he nodded an affirmative but flashed a pained expression that signaled how much he hated the idea. I pressed Record on my little Olympus and placed it on the table.

The voices of my coworkers rang in my head—*Ask him, ask him*—as I pressed Etienne on workplace morale, our endless pages of negative Glassdoor reviews, the auto-play video ads on the *IBT* website, universally despised by employees and readers alike, that blasted at full volume and offered no easy option for turning them off. The damn things followed you down the page as you scrolled, taunting you, robbing you of your agency as a consumer. They were commercial violence. Etienne was unapologetic about them, though. He said video ads were the only path to profitability for a digital publisher, that display banner ads—the old-school kind that had been populating websites since the nineties—were a game of diminishing returns. "Content providers must be proactive in this marketplace," he told me. "That's why we are doing all that we can to stay ahead in video." He had a weird definition of *stay ahead,* but okay.

Listening to Etienne's answers during the interview, the way he spoke in quiet, robotic sentences, and his hard-to-place accent, which was only vaguely French, I got the creeping sense that he had little to no confidence in what he was saying. I wasn't used to such opacity and self-doubt from a person in a major leadership role. The high-level media executives I'd encountered up until that point were usually engaging and forward, salesman types. At the very least, they were *people* people. After spending forty-five minutes with Etienne, I became preoccupied with a burning question: How on earth had this person become the chief executive of one of the fastest-growing online news organizations in the country?

The story he told me — that he'd come up with the idea for *International Business Times* while studying economics at LSE — seemed believable enough, but it didn't explain how he'd gotten from point A to point C. When I was his age, I was slinging scoops of butter pecan ice cream for cranky Florida dads in cargo shorts at Fashion Square Mall. I was living in Orlando with a friend and her roommates, people who were best described as nineties-era neo-hippies, which is to say they never shaved, they flirted with veganism, they smoked a lot of weed, and they embraced a certain style of communal living. "Live with us," they had said, proudly generous in the way that neo-hippies tend to be. "Don't be a junkie."

But you could draw a straight line from my days as an ice cream man to my interview with Etienne that day. While I was working at the Häagen-Dazs cart one afternoon, the Prints Plus manager — a huge cherry vanilla fan who looked like Bill Clinton — asked me if I would be interested in a job at his store. "What the hell are you doing working at an ice cream cart?" he asked. Then he said he could teach me how to do custom picture framing. Prints Plus had this one-hour framing gimmick that was popular with people who didn't care about quality. Pushing thirty and sick to death of ice cream, I took him up on it, and before I knew it, I had learned a trade: miter saws, glass cutters, dry mounting, the whole works. Those skills got me out of the mall and eventually out of Florida. While I was in Seattle, picture framing supported me as I pitched magazines and built my first professional bylines. It also helped me find a job in New York City and earn a paycheck while I was doing the unpaid internship at *Show Business Weekly*. Retracing all of those steps, I shudder to think of where I would've ended up if Prints Plus hadn't been fifteen feet from my ice cream cart.

I found myself wondering if Etienne had had a version of Prints Plus along his own career path, an intermediary that helped propel him from an economics student with an idea to a digital-media entrepreneur. He denied taking lots of VC money, the usual route for a start-up founder, and I didn't doubt that. Based on his personality, I honestly couldn't picture him wowing a roomful of investors in a *Shark Tank*–style pitch meeting. Most of what I'd heard about him — that he was awkward and shy and maybe a walking version of the Peter Principle — appeared at first blush to be spot-on.

And yet I didn't dislike the guy, or couldn't, at least not in the way that everyone else seemed to. There was something oddly sympathetic about him, almost unfinished; I felt as if I were staring into the eyes of a young child on his first day of school. He seemed to desperately want my approval. Or, if not mine, someone's. I knew what it felt like to want approval. I'd been wanting it ever since I'd started working in media, had been walking around with the constant sense that I was pretending to be something I wasn't. That feeling only got more pronounced after Jeff promoted me to senior reporter, which I guess is one of the big contradictions of impostor syndrome, how it can get worse as you advance in your career. Maybe that was Etienne's problem too.

My first thought was that it must be a joke or maybe someone got hacked. Or maybe I just misread it. I was checking Twitter one Saturday evening when a tweet from Etienne zipped through my feed: We acquired Newsweek!!!

Wait, was he kidding? *Newsweek* the magazine? I had just interviewed him six weeks earlier. He talked extensively about his plans to grow IBT Media but said nothing about having a legacy news brand in his sights. Also, who announces a major acquisition on a Saturday evening, literally the worst possible time of the week to announce news? But no, it was real, confirmed by a swell of texts from colleagues and a phone call from Jeff. Our company, out of the blue, had just acquired one of the oldest news-magazines in the world. By the next morning, media circles were abuzz with this unexpected news and I was once again interviewing Etienne, this time along with his business partner Johnathan Davis, the company's chief content officer. *Newsweek*, they told me, would be brought into the IBT Media family in the next thirty to sixty days. As I processed this information, I could think of only one thing: change was coming to our newsroom—and fast.

For anyone who followed the media business in the early 2010s, *Newsweek*'s long history and checkered backstory were sources of endless fascination. Actually, *checkered* doesn't do it justice. It was practically operatic. The magazine was founded in 1933 by a former World War I pilot, Thomas J. C. Martyn, who elbowed his way into journalism as a foreign editor for *Time*, married into a wealthy Connecticut silk family, and decided it would be a good idea to launch a competing newsweekly at the height of the Great Depression. *News-Week*, as it was originally called, barely survived its cha-otic early years in Rockefeller Center's brand-new RKO Building. Read-ership was strong, but the publication was said to have quickly burned through all its start-up cash. By 1937, it was facing the first of many exis-tential crises to come: bankruptcy, a merger with another publication, and Martyn's exit. The magazine found a new lease on life with buckets of cash from Vincent Astor and the editorial leadership of Malcolm Muir— a self-made publishing magnate and president of McGraw-Hill who insti-tuted a fresh strategy that emphasized analysis over digest-style news. Under Muir, *Newsweek* lost the hyphen and got infinitely spicier. "Do Radio Bedtime Stories Give Children Nightmares?" teased one ad for the magazine in 1937, practically daring you to buy a copy.

From there, *Newsweek* rode a wave of popularity during the golden age of newsweeklies, competing fiercely in the postwar decades alongside *Time* and *U.S. News*. The Washington Post Company scooped it up in 1961 and ushered it to the peak of its influence, with a circulation, at one point, of more than three million. *Newsweek* assiduously covered the political tumult of the era nationally and globally, weighing in on geopolitics, the civil rights movement, cinema and literature, and every topic in between.

In the seventies, social change came inside the walls of its own newsroom when forty-six women employees sued the magazine for sex discrimination. In the nineties, rapid-fire news cycles brought on by cable TV and the internet put weekly magazines at an obvious disadvantage. Few people in the news business still thought *news* and *week* were a winning combination. By 2010, when the Post Company put *Newsweek* up for sale, the magazine was hemorrhaging money. Sidney Harman, a ninety-one-year-old audio entrepreneur with no background in journalism, bought it that same year. He paid one dollar, agreeing to take on tens of millions in liabilities. Harman was briefly seen as a savior for the ailing publication before he passed away less than a year later. By then, *Newsweek* had been weirdly merged with the Daily Beast, a website operated by Barry Diller's IAC/InterActiveCorp. Diller's most famous contribution to the magazine was saying, publicly, that he regretted buying it.

In 2011, *Newsweek* was relaunched yet again, this time under the editorial control of the Daily Beast's founder, Tina Brown, who took on the challenge of reviving the brand with gusto. During this period, *Newsweek* was mostly known for its attention-getting covers, like one that used a digitally altered photo of Princess Diana to imagine what she would have looked like at age fifty. But shock value wasn't enough to save *Newsweek* from an unsustainable business model. In December 2012, it published what would be its final print issue.

Or so everyone assumed.

Newsweek barely existed as an actual company when IBT Media bought it in the summer of 2013. But it had something that IBT Media lacked: a recognizable brand. Media people might have been familiar with its history of operatic twists and turns, but everyday news consumers were not. As someone who covered the media business, I knew that general-interest readers were only vaguely interested in what happens inside a news organization, if they were interested at all. To them, *Newsweek* was just a magazine that existed, that still exists. Etienne's gamble, I surmised at the time, was that his young company could buy instant access to the mainstream with a name that still had authority among people who weren't paying that much attention. As far as gambles went, it wasn't a bad one. Maybe he had more business savvy than I'd given him credit for during our interview.

Then again, there was also the timing of that interview, which was probably no accident. After I thought about it, I realized that I had been asked to interview Etienne for a reason. It was much bigger than Etienne and much bigger than the company he pretended to run.

CHAPTER 25

Retrofit

I DON'T REMEMBER WHAT NEIGHBORHOOD the party took place in, but I remember the energy: alive with possibility, exciting in the way that spaces feel when people with a collective sense of purpose gather for free drinks, food, and holiday cheer. I had never been to a big corporate Christmas bash before, and I was very much looking forward to this chance to mingle with my IBT Media colleagues away from the harsh glare of the office lights, aided by booze and a less formal setting. The newsroom had probably doubled in size in the year and a half since I'd started working there. I was growing fond of many of my coworkers, but forging bonds at work was still not my forte. A party atmosphere could be just the catalyst I needed to boost our camaraderie to the next level. I brought the Bird along as my guest, eager to show her this burgeoning new world that I was a part of.

There seemed to be no stopping the company that year. With *Newsweek* in the fold, we were attracting high-caliber journalists at breakneck speed. Seasoned reporters and editors from the *Times, The Atlantic,* and everywhere else were flocking to the company. Jim Impoco, the new editor in chief of *Newsweek,* had come from Reuters. He was cheery and personable and had a stellar reputation. Not long after he started, I worked up the nerve to walk into his office and ask if I could write theater reviews for the magazine. My pitch: "What better way to say '*Newsweek* is back' than to see it quoted on a Broadway marquee?" He told me to go for it.

Between trips to the open bar, I snuck glimpses of the Chartbeat app on my phone—I checked it everywhere now—and saw that one of my stories was insanely blowing up. Earlier that afternoon, a high-level PR executive had tweeted a racist joke before taking off on a long flight, and I happened to be on Twitter just as the controversy was escalating. The internet was out for blood. I wrote up a news post as I fended off the better angels in my head that told me a person's worst moment shouldn't be fodder for rage clicks. This was *newsworthy*, I reasoned. I was one of the first reporters to write about the controversy, and now it was the biggest story in the country as everyone waited for the PR executive's plane to land. My speed was rewarded with the thing that *IBT* cared about most: metrics.

Toward the end of the night, the DJ cut off the music and Etienne took the microphone to give a speech, raising a glass and toasting to what he described as an incredible winning streak for IBT Media. He talked about our growth trajectory, how we were gobbling up talent from legacy news outlets that were three times our size. He made a joke about how the word *Newsweek* autocompleted when he started typing it into his phone. *Who else owns a news brand that does that?* His tall frame lurched awkwardly over the crowd, forehead sweat glistening under the blaze of the lights. He'd never be a great public speaker, I thought, but this was the most animated and engaging I'd ever seen him; it was as if the approval he had sought for so long had finally arrived. I still had my doubts about Etienne's leadership, but I was rooting for him—for us—in that moment.

The Bird was less impressed. "This guy sucks," she said. "He's up there bragging about how much money they're spending, and they can't give y'all a Christmas bonus?"

I responded with a mild shrug, spilling a bit of my house chardonnay on her pitch-black blouse. I couldn't argue, but then, why should I?

Outside the walls of our holiday party that night, there was no doubt far less enthusiasm for our company. Of course I'd heard the grumblings—that *Newsweek*, a once-respected giant among magazines, had been acquired by a mysterious digital-news start-up that everyone said was tied to a cult, that its sale to IBT Media was a darkly poetic fate, given the brand's checkered history. But those complaints came from established people in the media who took for granted that they were allowed to be part of the media, people with pedigrees and connections and college degrees who didn't worry about being outed as unqualified frauds. Those people weren't me. I didn't have the luxury of being cynical about what was happening at our company, especially not when the rules of media seemed to be changing by the minute. The ground was shifting under our industry. When it finally fractured, I knew people like me would be the first to slip through the cracks. *Newsweek* was an opportunity to hedge against that instability. As long as name recognition counted for something, I could affix myself to a mainstream outlet that never would have hired me off the street.

Actress, author, performer, producer—there was nothing Isabel couldn't do. Or at least that's how it seemed to the Bird and me as we were combing through search results on her late one afternoon. This Renaissance lady had written a novel published by Doubleday, produced and starred in a movie alongside Eartha Kitt, performed in her own critically acclaimed one-woman play, and graduated from Yale—summa cum laude, of course. More recently, she had been working on a retro-inspired pop album: Katy Perry meets Ann-Margret meets Bette Midler. She was looking to hire a full-time graphic designer for the album cover and other collateral projects, someone who understood mid-century-modern aesthetics and all the campy cultural references that inspired her work. The Bird responded to an ad that Isabel had placed on Craigslist, sent over some mock-ups, and heard back that same day. She was beside herself with joy. After almost two years of relentless self-study—learning design software, watching tutorials, working pro bono, depleting her life savings—she had her first real job interview for a position in design.

Isabel's office, on the twenty-ninth floor of an art deco high-rise in Tribeca, had sweeping views of the city and was not far from her sprawling home in a prewar doorman building that counted Mariah Carey among its residents. The Bird described Isabel as impressively put together, a redhead in her early forties, and gorgeous. She was also driven, not by the kinds of basic needs that motivate mere mortals—survival, earning a living—but by a quest for recognition and expression. Isabel came from a very prominent New York family and wanted nothing more than to eclipse it with a career in the arts, to forge her own name. No expense was being spared to ensure her path to Grammy glory: backup singers, a top-notch recording studio, a PR team.

During the interview, the two of them hit it off immediately, joking and talking about their favorite music and movies, debating the perfect shade of turquoise. The Bird's natural ease with the well-heeled, a by-product of her summers with Nana and her uniquely Southern attunement to class distinctions, proved especially useful that day. Money never intimidated her. That showed in the way she'd smile and meet people's eyes, pull them in close for a firm handshake, and make herself big, like her favorite president, LBJ. Isabel had probably been expecting a parade of young twenty-somethings to apply for the designer job, but here was a worldly, forty-seven-year-old woman who was self-assured and edgy, someone who could talk at length about the Viennese Secessionists or the Eameses or Saul Bass. As the interview came to a close, the Bird felt that a job offer was inevitable. It was so close, she could taste it. Then came the curveball.

"You went to school for this, right?" Isabel asked.

The Bird responded with an affirmative nod. It was a reflex, the kind of spontaneous social signal that you don't even realize you've communicated until it's too late. "Yes, of course," she said. "I went to the Art Institute of Chicago." *Went to* was technically true, if you counted the many hours she used to spend at the museum. One moment of uncomfortable silence later, the exchange was over, and Isabel offered her the job. When the Bird left Isabel's office, the afternoon sun was high in the sky and she was over the moon. She was a professional graphic designer.

When she told me the story of her knee-jerk embellishment later that evening, she seemed at once confused and disturbed by her own actions, as if she had somehow betrayed her better self. The Bird was proudly self-taught, proud of the life she lived. She didn't walk into a job interview expecting to lie. "It just came out," she said, and she wasn't sure why. Was it money? She needed the job, sure, but much stronger forces were at play. The power of the question, the perception of the person asking it. These elements conspired together to form a barrier that made the truth untellable.

I told the Bird that I understood exactly how she felt. I did, but I was also surprised. I had come to know her as being fearlessly unapologetic—about her background and everything else. I drew inspiration from that quality, selfishly it seems to me now, without really trying to understand the source of it. Being comfortable around people with money meant being able to put yourself in their shoes, being able to relate to them. That's something the Bird did well, but it also meant being able to fully comprehend the harshness with which people in the upper echelons of society can sometimes judge you.

A few months into her new job, the Bird came clean. She and Isabel were riding the elevator up to Isabel's condo where they were going to have lunch, courtesy of Isabel's personal chef, Glen. Somehow the topic of higher education came up and the Bird seized on the opportunity to blurt out her confession. She hadn't studied design. She hadn't gone to college at all. It was a tough thing to admit to her Yale-educated boss, but there it was. "Girl, that's okay," Isabel responded. Then the topic turned to food. Glen was making his famous chicken tagine.

The attention that came with *Newsweek* was double-edged. Lots of top-notch journalists wanted to write for us but others wanted to write *about* us. And did they ever. Cover stories and investigations, weekend reads and hot takes—our company was under the media microscope in a way that felt suffocating. Gone were the days of flying under the radar, hiding behind a vaguely recognizable name that people sometimes confused with the *Financial Times*. Reporters called the office constantly asking for comment, breadcrumbing the latest would-be bombshell. DMs slid into our Twitter in-boxes. *Working on a story—talk off the record?* At journalism mixers and press events, I found myself trying to convince people that, no, we were not being dictated to by an enigmatic religious leader who lurked behind the proverbial curtain.

"For crying out loud, I've written at least a half a dozen stories about atheists," I would say. It was true. As someone who worked at the company, I had no greater window into our supposed cultish connections than anyone else. I just wanted to do good work. As far as I could tell, most of us did. The orbit of a mainstream magazine made that both easier and more difficult.

Over time, a few tenacious investigative journalists who were determined to uncover details about the shadowy company behind *Newsweek* did just that. They wrote about David Jang, the pastor from Korea whose followers allegedly saw him as some sort of Second Coming and who was connected again and again with IBT Media. Jang was not a familiar name in the United States, but he was a hugely controversial religious figure in parts of Asia. According to media reports, he had formerly been affiliated with Sun Myung Moon's Unification Church—Moonies, as they're called, a sect known for its bizarre mass weddings and members who deified Moon as the savior of humanity. Moon, who died in 2012, was well known for his media ventures, including the conservative *Washington Times* newspaper, and for using the veneer of journalistic legitimacy as a means of gaining influence around the world. The more I read about Jang, the more it looked like he had taken a page out of Moon's playbook. His ministries recruited heavily on college and university campuses, often targeting impressionable first-year students. Jang eventually founded his own biblical college, Olivet University. It had a campus in San Francisco and another one in Lower Manhattan, just a few blocks from the *IBT* offices. Etienne was reportedly on its board of trustees. Johnathan Davis, *IBT*'s other founder, had once been affiliated with Olivet's journalism school.

Jang and his followers, referred to as "the Community," were said to be involved in a number of business ventures that funneled money back to Olivet. Those business ventures included online media companies. Conflicted about the digital revolution, Jang reportedly believed that humanity in the twenty-first century was drowning in ungodly information, so he sought to build a "Noah's Ark" of digital-media outlets to save the world from the metaphorical flood. Some of the outlets had generic names, like *Christian Post* and *Gospel Herald,* that could easily be confused with more established publications, a strategy of forced familiarity that reminded me of the first time I'd seen the name *International Business Times.*

Jang's vast business ties were already known in Christian media circles. *Christianity Today* magazine (founded by Billy Graham back in the fifties and not to be confused with Jang's *Christian Today*) published two investigative stories about Jang right around the time I started working at *IBT;* they quoted former Community members who said they had been coerced into working for business ventures under Jang's control. Some said they saw Jang as God, or not the actual God but a version of God, a messianic figure who was here to finish the work that Christ started. Jang always seemed to maintain plausible deniability about these apotheosized views of him. He didn't go around *saying* he was the Second Coming. But if people were going to believe that, well, what could you do?

After *Newsweek* came into the picture, more investigations followed. One extensive deep dive, from *Mother Jones* magazine, quoted sources who claimed that *IBT* itself was Jang's idea. Apparently, Christian media sites weren't enough to create a truly expansive digital Noah's Ark. He needed secular news outlets too. In this telling, Etienne was less the entrepreneurial brains behind *IBT* than a follower of Jang's who had been handpicked to run it, in part because his economics background and LSE education gave the operation credibility.

I read this story with my mouth agape, not knowing what to believe. I thought about my interview with Etienne, about Prints Plus, about the sometimes bizarre ways that people get to where they are. Alone with him in a conference room that day, I didn't have the guts to ask my CEO about what seemed like fantastical rumors, the cult-connected origin story. Now that we had a higher profile, journalists with far more gumption than I had were asking him.

Etienne told them the same story he'd told me: He and Johnathan Davis teamed up in the mid-2000s, begged, borrowed, and stole, and launched *International Business Times* on their own. Case closed. IBT Media did admit to having an internship arrangement with Olivet University, but David Jang had no official relationship with the company, business or otherwise. That was the story they were sticking to, at least for as long as it remained tenable.

Sordid revelations about my workplace didn't change my situation at work. I was still trying to build momentum, still figuring out a career that felt shaky and unstable. The only new element was the crash course I was getting in the power of sticky media narratives. Here I was, the senior media reporter for a news organization that had just become the news, and all I could think about was the deep chasm between what was being written about us (cults! conspiracies! chaos!) and what I could see with my own eyes in the newsroom (people at their desks trying to do good work). Media journalists were uncovering the truth about our company, but they weren't necessarily interested in the whole truth. How interested had I been in the whole truth when I wrote that quick hit about the PR executive, putting her name in a headline and reducing her life to a bad tweet? I suspected that no small number of reporters were equally self-satisfied about the clicks they were now getting on stories about us.

Granted, it didn't help that *Newsweek*'s much-hyped return to print was a scandal in its own right. Its first issue under *IBT* was a cover story that claimed to have unmasked the anonymous creator of Bitcoin; it named a retired software engineer who vehemently denied having any involvement with the cryptocurrency. The story caused a major backlash, with critics calling it reckless, the evidence circumstantial. They clamored for a retraction that never came. The relaunch became a cautionary tale of journalistic folly, immediately erasing any trace of goodwill that the name *Newsweek* might have carried in discerning media circles. Who the hell would give us the benefit of the doubt now?

But the Bitcoin controversy came and went, the chatter about David Jang died down, and IBT Media continued to grow at a dizzying pace, defying the odds at a time when much of the news business was still contracting.

Only occasionally would I be reminded of our pariah status among the more respected media outlets, and all I could do was try not to take it personally. I recall the first time I went to cover South by Southwest, the big tech, entertainment, and culture conference in Austin. I was thrilled to be there, intoxicated by the block-party energy as I strutted through the jovial crowds on Congress Avenue at twilight, the dome of the Texas Capitol glowing in the distance. Opening my laptop at a hotel bar and posting news dispatches with a G and T in my hand was next-level knowledge-worker badass in my mind. If only those spoon-sucking parasites at Fashion Square Mall could see me now.

At one of the SXSW sessions, I ran into a semi-familiar face, someone I recognized from Twitter who had just been laid off from a well-known news website. I wanted to help her, in part because I wasn't used to being in a position to help anyone professionally. I'd been in the white-collar world long enough to understand the importance of paying good fortune forward. After the session was over, I approached her and offered my business card. "You should give us a shout," I said. "We're hiring like crazy right now."

She took a second to acknowledge the gesture, then her eyes shifted rapidly from me to the exit. "Thanks, but I don't want to take your business card."

CHAPTER 26

Midseason Replacement

"PETER HAS FULL PERMISSION TO clean house, just so you know."

Matthias, one of our markets reporters, delivered this unpleasant piece of gossip to me at the bagel table. It was late in the morning and most of the cream-cheese containers were already empty. The everything bagels, of course, were gone. I was applying a light slab of butter to an under-cooked plain when I froze to process what he'd just said, feeling a twisting sensation in the pit of my stomach. "Do you think he'll do that?"

Peter was Peter S. Goodman, an accomplished economics journalist and editor who had spent most of his career at the *Washington Post* and the *New York Times*, only to jump ship for digital media in 2010 when Arianna Huffington hired him to help bring journalistic respectability to the *Huffington Post*. He had just been named the new global editor in chief of *International Business Times*, yet another notch in our own quest for legitimacy. Jeff had left a few months earlier—no one knew exactly why—and after a brief period of blissful self-rule, we now had an intimidating new boss.

Through the osmosis of covering the media business, I knew enough about leadership transitions in large newsrooms to realize that they usually spelled trouble for a lot of people, especially people in other leadership positions, because the first thing all new leaders want to do is install their own leadership teams. Actually, that's the second thing they do. The first thing they do is announce to the newsroom how much they're looking forward to working with all the great people they're about to fire. When I heard we had a new boss, I just hoped that I was low enough on the org chart to escape the fate of procedural replacement but high enough on his radar to make a good impression. The uncertainty of the predicament, the loss of control, bred in me the immediate sense that I had to do *something*. I tweeted at Peter on the same day his new position was announced, welcoming him to *IBT*. I tried to be funny about it: Our cafeteria makes pretty good oatmeal raisin cookies. He tweeted back: Who knew? Perks already. It seemed like a nice start. Now all I had to do was prove to the guy that I could do my job.

With *Newsweek* up and running, Etienne and Johnathan wanted fresh blood in the flagship *IBT* newsroom, a break from our scrappy past. In Matthias's telling, Peter was part of an organization-wide push to get IBT Media to the next level, and those of us who had worked the hardest to bring a modicum of professionalism to the place over the past few years would be the ones who paid the price. This was the thanks we got for taking a content farm and building it into a news organization that was impressive enough to attract the likes of Peter S. Goodman.

If you had asked a group of sitcom writers to conjure up a midseason replacement character who was the polar opposite of Jeff, they would've produced Peter S. Goodman. He was tall and imposing with an enviably deep voice and a commanding presence, erudite, with thin glasses and sharp eyebrows but also manly—an intellectual bro, if such a thing existed. Whereas Jeff had always led the newsroom with a sense of soft detachment, Peter came fully energized, ready to put his hard-edged stamp on the brand. He was not youthful exactly, but he had an animated curiosity that seemed almost childlike. He also looked ten times better than I did bald.

During Peter's first all-hands with the staff, he spoke with a blazing sense of mission, wielding a jargon-filled vocabulary and institutional knowledge of the news business that left no question about the direction he wanted to take us. Together, we were going to "hold the powerful to account," he said, "elevate our report," connect the dots that "reshape the global and national economies." His kinetic delivery might have seemed like overconfidence, but he backed it up with demonstrated expertise and talent—stunning prose, the mental agility to steer conversations about topics ranging from geopolitics to sports to Jay-Z.

I could imagine no scenario in which I would not be trying desperately to win Peter's approval. My job depended on it, first of all, but I also hoped that doing so would make me a better journalist. His sacrosanct view of the news-gathering process, his deep knowledge of journalistic norms and conventions—the thought of absorbing tenets of the craft from someone like Peter excited me. Maybe it's because I have always been uncomfortable trying to define what journalism is. It can be a tweet, I'd sometimes argue, or a blog post written by an anonymous whistleblower from a café in Minsk. If something is true, isn't that journalism? And don't we risk shutting out vital points of view the moment we call journalism a profession? Maybe so, but I also wanted to square that anarchic view of the practice with my more visceral desire for acceptance among the people who were paid to do it. I was a professional, technically, but I still didn't feel like one in my core, not in the way that Peter seemed to. He spoke of our profession as if it were a higher calling. I wanted to see it that way too.

SEO tricks and drinking games were not going to be enough to satisfy Peter's ambitions, clearly, but I was fortunate in that I had been working on a few deeply reported stories right around the time he started, stories that seemed to align with his vision. Not coincidentally, these stories were about unpaid internships in the for-profit sector, a practice that was increasingly being challenged in the courts. It had been almost nine years since I walked into the *Show Business Weekly* office in search of an unpaid internship at the age of thirty-five. Since that time, a movement had emerged to ban them. Young people were refusing to accept the status quo, suing employers for lost wages and back pay, especially in so-called glamour industries such as entertainment and media. They were fed up, tired of working for free, passionate about their cause. Attending protest events on college campuses, I met some of the most prominent intern activists, wide-eyed twenty-somethings with impressive social media game, people who introduced me to sources and filled me in on the latest gossip. I managed to break a few legitimate scoops. Law journals and academics began citing my articles, arguing that unpaid internships were inherently exploitative, fueling even more leads. For a while, unpaid internships were my semi-regular beat.

Of course, writing these stories brought some degree of internal conflict, since I had personally benefited from an unpaid internship. I didn't even necessarily believe that there was anything wrong with them. They could be exploitative, sure, but as far as I was concerned, they could also be learning opportunities. I certainly didn't expect to solve some of the thornier legal questions that were best left to lawyers. What I wanted, more than the gratitude that came with exposing routine abuses of workplace power, was to understand the righteous lens through which the young activists I wrote about saw the world. They seemed to have no appetite for gray areas, no room in their arguments for exceptions. Unpaid internships were capital-*B* Bad. I can't say if I envied their sense of absolute right and wrong or if I was trying to convince myself that it didn't scare me. What I knew was that their idealism was connected to something bigger, an evolving sense of what workers were demanding from employers. If I could look past the punk-rock nihilism that I'd grown up with, the Trenton mindset that told you it was not cool to care about anything, I might be able to wrap my head around something vital that was happening in the world of work.

I sent Peter one of my internship stories during his first week on the job, hoping that he would see it as representative of the kind of work I could do—wanted to do—when I wasn't worried about traffic. He asked me to come to his office for a one-on-one meeting. The invitation petrified me, but I also felt lucky for being singled out. I knew he wasn't asking to meet individually with everyone on staff.

The meeting, from what I recall of it, went well. Sitting in a small chair across from his wide desk, I took long, deep breaths and explained my vision for the media beat, trying hard not to stammer or sweat. I suggested big swings, like a series on the proposed mega-merger between Comcast and Time Warner Cable, which was raising all kinds of concerns among antitrust bigwigs at the time. Peter was on board with what I was saying, rapt, focused on my ideas in a way that seemed to fill them with weight. There was something about the cool tone of his responses that made me feel like a colleague on equal footing. The man gave great jargon. I remember at one point he encouraged me to go down to DC for a few days and meet with cable regulators and lobbyists. No agenda, he said. "Source up."

CHAPTER 27

Mousetrap

FRED AND I DIDN'T AGREE about Orlando. When I'd moved down there in the mid-nineties to escape my addiction, I felt immediately smothered by its flat suburban neighborhoods and emerging sprawl. The downtown area was barren and uninviting, rows of oatmeal-colored buildings and tinted windows, car dealerships and banks set against a misshapen Lego set of a skyline. There were maybe two or three cool bars, but the hipster bartenders who staffed them were absurdly mad with power, sometimes refusing to serve you if they didn't like your tone. All the avenues in town were sun-bleached, the snaky side streets poorly planned out, twisting and turning without purpose until they ended abruptly at some highway or lake. I owed my life to this Central Florida town, the healing refuge it offered, but I resented it just the same for six long years.

Where I saw a marriage of convenience, my younger brother saw a home. Fred came to visit Orlando while I was living with the neo-hippies. He loved the vacation vibe, the familiarity of having an Applebee's and a Barnes and Noble at every intersection. What he found even more appealing, I think, was that Orlando wasn't Trenton. It wasn't cold or crumbling or decades past its prime. In fact, it had been growing insanely since Disney first arrived in the early seventies.

The first time Fred came to visit me in Orlando, in 1998, I could already see him plotting out in his head the adult life that he wanted to build for himself. He'd talk about the movie business, how people were calling Florida "Hollywood South." He moved to Orlando permanently and started taking filmmaking classes at Valencia Community College, no small accomplishment after his struggles with dyslexia, being ejected from high school at fifteen, and not fully learning to read until he was an adult. Fred was less interested in trying to salvage an academic career than in learning a craft, and the emerging tools of digital video—accessible but still new at the time—offered the perfect creative medium. Before long, he was shooting and editing his own projects on school equipment, learning how to light scenes, mastering Final Cut Pro. For a while, with both of us in Orlando, we rekindled the effortless collaboration we'd shared as kids. I wrote short scripts for his projects and he directed them. When he needed an actor, I put on a bushy wig and played a character I made up named Skippy Lightfoot. I was cringeworthy on-screen, but you have to admit, it's a catchy name.

During our overlap years in Orlando, Fred and I were doing more than just picking up where we'd left off as kids. We were mending a frayed relationship, one that I'd damaged during my heroin years. Fred took my addiction hard, maybe even personally. It was a weakness, and Zara boys weren't supposed to be weak. Some nights in Trenton when I'd come back from the city in a state of glorious bliss, he'd stare me down with that unflinching Italian-mobster look that he got when he was mad. He'd follow me through the living room and ask me where I'd been, then not believe me when I made something up. I couldn't hide it: pinpoint pupils against my brassy eyes were a dead giveaway. Occasionally, he'd explode, giving in to his temper by punching a wall or hurling books across the room. It scared the hell out of me—my little brother outweighed me by more than forty pounds—but he was the only person in my life at that time who told me the plain truth. "You're digging your own grave," Fred growled one night, pounding my bedroom door. "You look sick, like a fuckin' stick figure."

Collaborating together in Orlando offered us a way forward, not by forcing us to relitigate the past, but by letting Fred and me do what we did best: draw on our shared language of movie references and inside jokes. That's mostly how we communicated anyway. He could cock an eyebrow and mutter, "Gutless punk," and I'd immediately know he was being Sergeant Hulka from *Stripes*, daring Bill Murray to take a swing. In response,

I'd fire back with an angry retort as General Zod from *Superman II:* "Why do you say this to me when you know I will kill you for it?"

In retrospect, it made sense that Fred blew up at me like he did on those nights when I came home high, because the alternative would have been to say nothing at all. One thing he would never do, that neither of my brothers would do, was tell my parents how far gone I really was. I guess that would have violated some brotherly code.

In the summer of 2002, I told Fred that I was leaving Orlando for Seattle, and he tried to convince me that it was the wrong decision. He had ambitions to keep making movies, better ones, and he didn't think he could do that without me. One night over drinks in the backyard of the duplex we were sharing, Fred pulled up a deck chair and made his case for why the two of us were better poised to succeed in a small pond, combining our creative forces. The Florida air was still and thick, the sound of crickets almost deafening. "I just want to say one thing," Fred said. "We gotta do this."

I understood exactly what he meant. That's what we used to say to each other as kids back in the ZTV days, setting up the black-and-white video camera on a Sunday morning, turning the house upside down with lights and props, putting on costumes, filling up hours of VHS tapes with skits and music videos. No one watched those videos except us—it was decades before YouTube—but we took our commitment to them seriously. If a skit was bad, we'd redo and redo it until we got it exactly right. "We gotta do this" became code for our shared delusions of greatness, the secret belief that someone out there cared about what we were creating together.

As adults, we laughed at our hyper-serious tween selves—*What the hell was wrong with us and why did Mom and Dad put up with it?*—but there was a deeper benefit to our partnership that I didn't appreciate until much later. We motivated each other. We had expectations for each other in a family where expectations were few. I still hear *We gotta do this* in my head whenever a bout of laziness starts to get the better of me.

I was about to turn thirty-two and still felt like my life hadn't actually begun. The thought of being trapped in Orlando forever, waking up in a town that I had sought out only as an alternative to death, became more unsettling with each passing year. I was still obsessed with New York. It drove me crazy that I'd grown up an hour outside of the center of the world, this exhilarating alpha city that now seemed farther away than ever. My girlfriend at the time, Sophie, would have been miserable in New York. She had spent a formative part of her childhood on a small island in the North Pacific where her dad worked on weapons systems for a multi-national aerospace company while she lost herself in books and quietly communed with nature. She had a strong affinity for animals big and small and seemed especially drawn to fantasy novels that were populated by anthropomorphic mice.

Sophie's laid-back childhood was upended when her dad relocated the family to New Jersey. She was traumatized by the coldness of the place, the meanness of her classmates. Like me, she ended up in Orlando not by active choice but through a network of mutual friends who had migrated there. She disliked Florida as much as I did, but the thought of returning to the aggressive Northeast—living in a city whose idea of nature is Central Park—made her physically ill. I didn't realize it at the time, but her aversion to New York commingled nicely with my fear of moving there. It was a convenient excuse to push away the lure the city still held for me.

I guess that's why Seattle emerged as an attractive compromise. My brother Joe had recently moved there to play lead guitar in a punk-inspired Beatles cover band called the Speedles. He wore tattered suit jackets and makeup and went by the stage name Lenny Best, all very Joe. I had never been to Seattle, but I was intrigued by what I imagined it was, a quirky mix of creative energy and mountaineering spunk—the polar opposite of Orlando, basically. Two months before my thirty-second birthday, Sophie and I packed up my white Toyota Corolla and drove it three thousand miles, from one corner of the country to another.

Our first sight of the Space Needle as we approached the city filled us with a sense of excitement, the rush of possibilities for a life anew. "I see it, I see it." Sophie pointed, her giant brown eyes alive with wonder. Seattle was a beautiful town, with steep hills and scenic views at every corner, crisp air and a welcoming vibe. Hikers in REI boots, blue-haired baristas, gutter punks, Belltown yuppies—they all seemed to be safely doing their own thing, protected by the Cascade mountains, sophisticated and yet unspoiled by the glare of mainstream society. Sure, grunge had happened ten years earlier, but real Seattleites clicked their pierced tongues at the mention of Kurt Cobain. Here was a place where I could—where anyone could, it seemed—plant a flag of personal identity that was not tied to anyone else's expectations.

Except I still had no idea what my personal identity was and no good plan to find one. In Orlando, I at least had a clear backstory: the recovering junkie in self-imposed exile. Clumsy attempts to start a writing career by sending out screenplays and entering contests were forgivable in that context. But what would my story be now? I mean, outside of being the younger brother of Seattle's own Lenny Best. Some nights early on, I'd go out to clubs or shows against my better judgment, despite having lost nearly all interest in any environment that exceeded seventy decibels. Joe would introduce me to a cast of drunken characters and they would annoyingly call me "Brother" for the rest of the night. It was tenth grade all over again. Watching Joe charm these hip Seattle crowds, seeing him slip his arm around some dude and share a belly laugh as if they'd known each other forever, reminded me why I'd always looked up to him. He had this ability to blend into any social situation and seem like he belonged there.

Maybe that was why he seemed so completely unbothered by the passage of time. It was admirable, at least to me, that Joe still hadn't given up on playing music at thirty-four, that he was perfectly happy jumping up on bar tables, grinding out hundred-mile-an-hour versions of "Twist and Shout" until two in the morning. He had no illusions about the Speedles becoming a serious band, but when you're having such a great time doing the thing you love, why ruin it with pesky questions about your next act? "We'll work it out," Joe liked to say. It was his answer to almost anything.

I appreciated his laissez-faire philosophy probably more than he realized, particularly during our quieter moments alone together. Some nights when we were walking home from a bar in Capitol Hill, the funky neighborhood where we lived, our conversations would veer into the metaphysical, going deep in a way that my conversations with Fred never did. It wasn't that Joe and I had a deeper connection—we wouldn't die laughing over an *Outsiders* reference, for instance—but our relationship was warmer, less competitive. The collaborative dimension I shared with Fred often pushed us into adversarial territory, and maybe some of that junk left over from him being the youngest seeped into our adulthoods. Conversely, Joe never really shed his protective older-brother instincts. It suited his personality, his penchant for doling out life lessons to anyone who would listen, and I was grateful for his nonlinear view of the world. He would talk about weird coincidences, like hearing a familiar song on a dead friend's birthday, as if they were messages from the beyond. I would dutifully remind him, with an eye roll that belied my deep respect for his earnestness, that meaningful coincidences were pseudoscience.

Mostly Joe talked about Seattle, how much he loved the creative energy, the vibe, how he wished he'd discovered the West Coast when he was much younger. "Can you imagine what we could have accomplished if we'd grown up in a place like this?" he said, pointing to the lively cross section at Olive and Denny. The centerpiece of the block was an irreverent espresso joint called Coffee Messiah that proudly declared CAFFEINE SAVES in blue neon letters. Way down the hill, you could see pieces of the towers that shaped the city skyline sparkling like gemstones through the fog. Joe's extended praise for Seattle ran parallel to Fred's feelings about Orlando, the contrast with Trenton being central to what they both found so appealing. I envied the sense of home that my two brothers had discovered.

Within weeks of arriving in Seattle, I settled into a new routine that felt stiflingly similar to my old one. I took the first job I could find, in a sawdusty frame shop at the bottom of Queen Anne Hill. The owner was nice enough, but he had a weird sense of humor that could be belittling. As I was sweeping up one Friday night, he came in and started to hand me my paycheck, then whipped it away in jest. "You missed a spot," he said with a devious smile, pointing at the pile of triangle wood chunks on the floor under the miter saw. *Uh, good one?* Months and months of this went by and now thirty-three was approaching. *How's the writing going?* friends would ask. *What are you up to now?* I had no good answer.

My utter discontent, of course, started to push Sophie away. She was blossoming in Seattle, meeting cool new friends, painting and drawing in her signature whimsical style, and yet she had to navigate my moods. I think she felt responsible for my being there. I'd argue with her if she wanted to go out with friends but then moan if she asked me to come along. "This was why I was afraid to move here," she said one night as we lay in bed. "I knew you would resent me and cling to me at the same time." Sophie was not usually one to criticize so bluntly. I huffed at her comment, offended, clutched my pillow, and turned over on my side. How dare she pick this moment to discover her talent for cutting insight?

It would be almost a year in Seattle before something finally changed. One afternoon in the summer of 2003, I was wandering the aisles of the Elliot Bay bookstore, which was in a charming old section of downtown known as Pioneer Square. The store was glorious: multiple levels, winding corridors of bookcases, wooden floors with scuff marks that looked like they were left over from the Alaska gold rush. The café section had inspired the coffee shop in *Frasier*, or so the rumor went. I couldn't enjoy the splendor of my surroundings, though, knowing where I was, both physically and mentally. Seattle was not my town. It never would be. I was fighting depression, hypochondria brought on by having my own computer and constant access to the internet for the first time in my life. I started googling every random symptom. Halos around lights. Butterfly rash. At one point I became convinced that the paleness of my nail beds was a sign of advanced liver disease — surely a fate I deserved, given my history of drug use. I pored over medical literature and online message boards. I showed up at health clinics only to be turned away by exhausted doctors who looked at me like I was wasting their time. Part of me understood that I was obsessing over my health as a way of ignoring the larger question of what the hell I was doing with my life, but the worst-case scenarios I conjured up felt so real.

I came to the bookstore, I guess, to waste more time with medical texts, but somehow I ended up thumbing through a reference guide about how to write magazine articles that sell. I don't recall if I even bought the book—probably not—but I remember wondering why I had never considered magazine writing before. It had been seven years since I'd left New Jersey, gotten clean, and started what I considered to be my second act. Seven years of sending out query letters to Hollywood agents and mailing out screenplays. Seven years of *No, thank you,* of envelopes being returned unopened. What exactly was I expecting to happen? I rolled my eyes at Joe when he talked about meaningful coincidences, but how was my blind faith in some unlikely opportunity not its own form of magical thinking?

I looked over at the bookstore's magazine rack. There were hundreds of magazines, glossy and fresh, covering every topic imaginable. Culture. Politics. Business. Sewing, for Christ's sake! Each one of these periodicals represented countless editors who had space to fill every month. By contrast, Hollywood production companies bought maybe five or six scripts a year. I'd never been great at math, but the law of averages sure seemed to be on the side of pitching a magazine editor. I went home that afternoon and used my computer for something other than PubMed.

The editor of the first magazine I pitched, *MovieMaker,* e-mailed me back within a day, maybe even a few hours. She loved my idea. I'd proposed a reported story about underground film festivals, how young directors used them to hone their skills. "They're the community theater of the film world," I wrote enthusiastically. She offered one hundred and twenty-five dollars for the article, payable upon completion. I was ecstatic. My first-ever magazine pitch had landed me my first-ever freelance assignment— the proverbial first time I got paid for it.

In the years to come, I often bragged about that moment of beginner's luck, sometimes using it to anchor advice to young people who asked me the best way to break into journalism. *(Three things to know: freelance, freelance, freelance.)* But beginner's luck doesn't really describe what happened that day. What I was doing was more akin to alchemy, experimenting with some new concoction because nothing else in my life was working.

Hearing yes at that moment of desperation transformed my view of what I saw myself doing professionally. Maybe it wasn't technically a meaningful coincidence, but it was a sign.

I owed that idea to my collaboration with Fred or, more specifically, to Skippy Lightfoot. Fred had submitted our short film to an underground film festival in Seattle. It was called—you can't make it up—the Fucking Fabulous Film Festival. We got in. The screening was held at Coffee Messiah, a few blocks from my house. My cringeworthy, wigged performance as Skippy played to a small crowd of bemused indie-film buffs on a bright Saturday afternoon. For a while, a few people around Capitol Hill took to calling me "Skippy" when I walked down the street, which I found hilarious.

Small bits of success followed. The editor at *MovieMaker* liked the article and ended up giving me more assignments, and I used those to get even more freelance work elsewhere. I contributed regularly to *Seattle* magazine, covering local arts and culture. The body of clips I was building up was not objectively impressive—I couldn't quit the frame shop or anything—but at least I could keep a conversation going when someone asked me what I was up to. I started to ask myself if maybe I had been wrong about Seattle.

No. It definitely was not my town. Or even Joe's for that matter. Seattle was Sophie's town. Just as I was starting to claw my way out of a years-long malaise, our relationship came to its inevitable end. My moodiness and lack of direction, it turned out, were not the entire source of our problems. Sophie also needed to find herself, and Seattle was giving her wings to do that. She had a whole new crowd now; she was working at Coffee Messiah, hanging with the coolest people on the hill. She dyed her hair pink. She talked about going back to school, maybe U-Dub, to study health science. I wanted all that for her, truly. But I was fighting off baser instincts, petty possessiveness, circular thought patterns that I could not seem to dislodge from my brain.

That is, until I finally started to see Sophie and me for what we were: an early snapshot of my own parents. Stepping back in time gave me clarity. It let me realize that the most important thing for both of us was space. I tried to imagine my dad as a young man, but a more elevated version, someone who did not see love as a form of control. I imagined a freer version of my mom, someone who'd had the chance to discover what excited her about the world before a husband and three boys made that impossible. I imagined her as a college graduate, a person with options. It seemed to me that Sophie and I were at a crossroads, and we still had a chance to avoid the most oppressive of timelines.

In the weeks after we broke up, my universe felt like it was collapsing. I was living alone for the first time in my life, holed up in a dark studio apartment on Pine Street. Or maybe it was Pike. Damn you, Seattle. There were a lot of desperate nights, serious thoughts of suicide, and tears. Thirty-five was practically here. The more I came to realize that there was nothing left for me in Seattle, the more disgusted with myself I became. What the hell was keeping me from New York now if not fear?

I took small steps to assert my intentions, to prove that I was not one of those people who would fantasize out loud about moving to the big city but never actually make the leap. *You can't live there,* friends would say. *People do,* I would bark back. I sold the white Corolla, even though I was still paying off the car loan at the time. (Spoiler alert: The balance turned into several more years of credit card debt.) I started buying the *Village Voice* each week, looking at apartment listings, jobs. Some of the SROs seemed almost attainable. Then I started to tell people. Everyone. My brothers. Friends. Random people at the frame shop. *I'm moving to New York City.* Once you tell enough people, you have to go through with it. Fear of humiliation will see to that.

On one of my last days in Seattle, I passed by Coffee Messiah and saw Sophie working behind the counter, smiling and mingling with the hipster customers. I lingered just long enough to watch as she pushed her pink bangs away from her eyes and pulled a foamy cup from the espresso machine. I had never seen anyone so weightless.

CHAPTER 28

Bump

THE PETER GOODMAN ERA AT *IBT* was shaping up to be very much the radical overhaul that Matthias had predicted. The firings began soon after his arrival—longtime staffers whose roles didn't align with his newsroom vision or whose salaries were inconvenient barriers to his budgetary ambitions. New hires came just as fast—an international editor, a managing editor, correspondents in Beirut and Moscow, bigger teams in London and Bangalore. Cosmetic changes inside our Lower Manhattan headquarters were no less dramatic. Giant TV screens were fastened to every beam, pumping in live feeds of twenty-four-hour cable news networks. Every other person seemed to have a standing desk now. Over on the other side of the floor, large posters of *Newsweek* covers lined the walls, starting with the Bitcoin one, displayed with pride near the entrance for all to see. The bagel table remained unchanged. I guess no one dared mess with the ultimate office perk.

Ellen, who was still my manager, had survived the transition so far, but she was not exactly embracing the changes. As a senior editor, she was vulnerable—Peter had replaced many of them within the first six months—and she seemed to be facing increasing resistance from the upper rungs of management, in particular the Peter loyalists. She spent lots of time in meetings and would come out looking rattled or just plain irritated. I was worried for both of us. Ellen and I had worked together for more than two years, and I had grown to rely on her counsel as a manager and her perspective as an editor. She had a way of pointing out my blind spots. "I'm not a fan of using *sexy cop* here," she once said of my description of a woman's costume. I had walked over to Zuccotti Park to interview people for the anniversary of Occupy Wall Street, and one of the protesters was dressed in a dark blue onesie, badge, fishnet stockings, and handcuffs. When Ellen and I both failed to come up with a better description, we ended up putting it in quotes—"sexy cop"—a compromise. Our working relationship was seamless that way, or at least it seemed like that to me. I found it frustrating when some of the newer hires would waft by my cubicle to quietly feel me out, hinting they did not get along so famously with her. I wondered if all offices had these types of passive-aggressive troublemakers, people who would dance around words like *difficult* without actually saying them, as if daring you to react. My instinct was not to engage. "We get along great," I'd say, then leave it there, feeling empty, as if I'd just failed a crucial test of loyalty. I'd remind myself that it wasn't a Jedi mind trick that got me this job but Ellen's willingness to overlook the bachelor's requirement. Her open-mindedness as a gatekeeper was the only reason I was there.

I asked Ellen for a few days off to take a last-minute trip to Orlando. Asking was a formality because she typically didn't care about such things, but something was different this time. She was hesitant, clearly working out numbers or schedules in her head. "I guess it's fine," she finally said. I was glad. By some fluke of the calendar, my two brothers, my parents, and I were all able to be in Orlando at the same time. It was October 2014, twelve years after Sophie and I had hightailed it out of the state of Florida in my white Corolla. Fred had never left the place. He now had a wife, two kids, and a ranch-style house at the end of a dead-end street with no sidewalks or sewer system. My leaving Orlando turned out to be the best thing for him, forcing him out of his creative comfort zone. He got involved with the local film scene and wound up landing a job as a video producer for a hip tech start-up, one of those coding schools that were all the rage at the time. Four-day workweeks, no bosses, Lake Tahoe retreats, the whole works. Over in Seattle, Joe and his wife now had a baby girl, which brought out a serious side to Joe's personality that I had never seen before. He'd finally given up on music, although he did find a job that allowed him to continue to indulge his love for nightlife: managing a tiki bar in Lower Queen Anne. Weekends off were rare, but he somehow found a way to swing the twenty-five-hundred-mile flight to Orlando on this occasion. My mom was there, too, living in one of those Florida senior centers. She had retired from the *Trenton Times* just in the nick of time, which is to say she was spared the worst of the newspaper's downward spiral. Not long after she left, its printing plant was shuttered, its corroding office on Perry Street abandoned, and the bulk of its administrative operations outsourced. My mom was lucky in that she got out with a modest pension. And then there was my dad, still in New Jersey, now eighty, reluctant to go anywhere that didn't have slot machines. In the face of my constant badgering, he finally agreed to fly with me to Orlando to see his grandkids, even though traveling made him anxious. At the Newark airport, I remember him being unusually worried that we would accidentally get on the wrong flight and end up in Texas. "Dad, they don't let you just board any plane."

Dealing with our parents in the same space, as we had to that October, was always tricky. In the twenty-seven years since my mom had walked out on my dad, they almost never spoke, or rather, she never spoke to him. She couldn't, lest the patterns of control and submission that had marked their marriage immediately reassert themselves. My dad had a way of always saying just the thing that would get under your skin, which I think must have been some combination of instinct and a reflection of how he grew up—a dozen-plus sweaty Italians in a row house in Chambersburg, all jostling for attention and dominance. He spoke loudly because he had to in a culture where the concept of an internal edit button was unheard of. When I wanted to get my ear pierced at fourteen, he told me it was a bad idea, even though he had let Joe do the same thing at that age. "Joey can get away with it," my dad said. "If you do it, you'll look like a fruit."

These digs weren't uttered with malice. In fact, when we were growing up, he was just as likely to apply his unpolished style to any number of well-intentioned morality lessons. "Never hit somebody unless they hit you first," he'd say. He told us not to judge people based on their skin color, which we knew, from spending time at our friends' houses, was not a universally shared value among Italian American parents in Trenton.

But my dad's cluelessness about the impact of his more thoughtless comments did not blunt their psychological toll. And he couldn't have been clueless about their cumulative effect on my mom, the slow chipping away at her self-esteem that came with cracks about her weight or how she was free to go to marriage counseling by herself if that's what she wanted to do. He'd later say things like "I don't know why your mother left," but none of us ever bought that. Or at least I didn't.

There is a telling piece of eight-millimeter film from their honeymoon in the Poconos in 1964. My dad is thirty, handsome, athletic, with jet-black hair. He's teaching her how to putt on a miniature golf course at the resort. My mom is smiling, holding the club with an awkward grip. She swings, misses, and tries again, willing to learn the game in the spirit of fun but clearly lacking his aptitude for it. I remember watching that choppy, silent footage as a kid, thinking about how cool it was that my parents were once so young and in love. Somehow, I missed the subtle agitation that washed across my mom's face as she threw down the club in defeat.

The Orlando trip was a constant dance; we had to keep our parents in separate rooms, far enough from each other, never alone. We were successful except for one notable lapse. As we were all heading out to Applebee's one afternoon for lunch — scrambling for keys and wallets and whatever else — we found ourselves standing in the middle of Fred's small living room. It was just the five of us. We hadn't been alone like that in decades. Four walls and a few seconds of silence amplified the dissonance between our shared history and the people we were now. There was my dad, gray and wrinkled, tired eyes peering out from behind his red-tinted De Niro glasses. My mom was hunched over, wrapped in a shawl, holding on to the back of the sofa for balance. My brothers and I were all in our forties. New York and the professional identity that I'd been agonizing over for the past nine years suddenly didn't exist, and I was overcome by the unnerving sensation that I had invented that life for the wrong reasons: the subways and the stimulation, the networking events, my weird fascination with office culture. Was I perversely determined to define myself against the standards of a white-collar world because that was preferable to being defined by the four people who stood with me in this room?

It was on Joe, naturally, to remark on the unplanned occasion of our intimate reunion as a family unit. "Whoa, guys," he said. "This is how it all started." Five seconds later, it was over.

I was still unpacking my bag when I saw an e-mail from Ellen with the subject line *Heads up*. She wrote to tell me that she wouldn't be in the office when I returned—or ever again. Oh, and she hoped I had a good time in Florida. I called her immediately to ask what was going on. She and *IBT* were parting ways, she explained, a "semi-amicable" split. Things at work had been too unpleasant for too long. Too many fights with management. Too much drama. She wished me continued success there, although she confessed to not knowing whether my job was secure. What could I say? I told her it was a pleasure working with her and thanked her for taking a chance on me. I don't think I truly appreciated at the time how big of a difference she'd made in my working life, nor did I realize that I would never get the opportunity to tell her.

We hung up and my concern drifted to self-interest. It's weird how scars from past job searches never fully heal. I barely had a few minutes to think about my prospects before Peter called, eager to tell me that Ellen was gone and big changes were afoot. He was handing the media and culture section over to Michael Learmonth, our recently hired tech editor; he would now be in charge of both sections. I was instantly relieved. I'd had a good rapport with Learmonth so far. We were almost the same age, although our backgrounds couldn't have been more different. He struck me as one of those lifer journalists who'd never had a second thought about what he wanted to do for a living. Neatly combed hair, shirts always tucked in, grad degree from UC Berkeley, whip-smart about the media business. He was equally blessed with workplace wile, careful and strategic in his management style. As a newcomer to *IBT*, he seemed to have identified me as someone worth getting on the good side of. Peter suggested that Learmonth was going to need a deputy, running two sections and all, and wondered if I'd consider making the leap to editor. I was flattered, scared, and hesitant all at the same time, wondering if I was ready to manage a big team when I felt that I had just gotten the hang of digital reporting. I told Peter I would have to think about that one.

Either way, Peter said, he wanted to give me a "bump," a show of appreciation for the good work I'd been doing. I quietly suspected that he'd seen how little I was being paid and was just shocked by it. I knew that most of his hires were getting a lot more money, but I was too happy not to be on the chopping block to complain about anything. The number he threw out at me was, in my mind, a significant milestone. For the first time in my life, I was making more than fifty thousand dollars a year. It felt good, even if it was tinged with uncomfortable questions about why it had happened the way it did. Ellen was forced out and I got a raise. Was it a reflection of my abilities or my reward for not being difficult?

CHAPTER 29

Title Change

THE BIRD AND I STARED up in awe at the opulent ceiling of the New York Café in Budapest, a neo-Renaissance wonder with stunning frescoes, glass chandeliers down the center, and twisted marble columns on either side. We lost ourselves in its vastness, took in its history. According to our guidebook, this grand building was once a fertile meeting ground for prominent journalists and literati, dating back to the Austro-Hungarian Empire, when a pulsating café culture defined the city's landscape. We stayed for a quick Hungarian dessert and pressed on, trying to pack as much as we could into a thirty-six-hour visit. St. Stephen's Basilica. The Parliament building. A museum of "terror" that we later learned was a pet project of Viktor Orbán's. We braved the chilly November wind for a nighttime walk along the Danube, keeping ourselves warm with spiced mulled wine. I grabbed the Bird by the wrist and dragged her onto the Budapest Metro. Compared to New York's, it was smaller, older, and more rickety but also more charming. We couldn't figure out how to buy a ticket, so we just walked on and took a seat in the closest car. "Bird, we'll just tell them we didn't know," I said. Then we both laughed as the boxy train rumbled into the tube. At some point, the Bird took my arm and remarked how grateful she was that I hadn't turned out to be a miserable travel companion. "I was a little worried about that," she said.

This was our fourth trip to Europe since we'd started dating, and she probably said that same thing to me on each trip. When we first met, I had never traveled abroad, didn't own a passport, and thought airline points were an utter waste of time—all deal-breakers to the Bird back in her

OkCupid days. She made an exception after going on a few bad dates with well-traveled men who turned out to be insufferable, including one schmucky Wall Street type who hated all the countries she loved. By contrast, I was a blank slate, a travel virgin who expressed an openness to going anywhere she wanted. She had only one rule: no Belgium. That was fine with me. Maybe there's a lesson there about the folly of deal-breakers.

My reasons for not traveling overseas never had anything to do with not wanting to. It's just that as I was stumbling through my twenties and thirties, there always seemed to be a valid excuse for not prioritizing it, whether it was the credit card debt I was carrying around or just my willingness to believe that there'd always be time for it later on, perhaps when I finally reached some hypothetical level of success in some hypothetical career. After I started working in journalism, I began to realize what I'd missed. Colleagues would talk about how they'd studied abroad or took gap years to backpack across Europe or gone on trips with their families when they were kids. They'd yearn for those formative adventures, describing them as vital to their understanding of being connected to a larger world. That such experiences were irreplaceable quickly became obvious to someone who'd missed out on them. I didn't need to see statistics on the correlation between passport ownership and education to appreciate the extent to which they're inextricably linked.

The Bird was an outlier in this sense, a person for whom travel offered a way to buck the ruthless determinism of her past, of growing up without means, of having to quite literally fight for her identity. She didn't like to talk about certain parts of her youth, but she often spoke of the day her first passport arrived in the mail, how she tore open the padded envelope and broke into tears. Here was a document that finally offered the freedom she longed for. "I really thought it would be denied to me for my entire life," she said.

It was also validation for the person she truly was, the result of hard-fought battles to assert her identity as a woman after being raised a boy. When she was growing up in the South, most people she encountered didn't understand what transgender was; she didn't understand it herself. There were no books to read or search engines to use or even family members to talk to about why she felt she was a different gender than the one she had been assigned. Being true to herself meant pushing back against cultural norms, against the expectations of people she loved. It meant challenging assumptions about sex and gender that were rooted in an immutable binary. It meant she had to pick her own name and then navigate a labyrinth of unhelpful bureaucracy to change the one she'd been given, often wondering if the court clerks and medical experts and pencil pushers would cooperate.

Before her doctor would perform her surgery, the Bird needed to provide a document from a mental-health professional stating that she was psychologically fit and that she understood that the procedure was permanent. At the time, changing the gender marker on your passport required a letter acknowledging that you had had gender-reassignment surgery. Without the surgery, there would have been no letter, and without that letter, there would have been no *F* on her passport.

When she finally saw that dark blue booklet in the mail—with both the name she had fought so hard to claim and the *F* officially documented by the U.S. Department of State—she felt empowered for the first time to explore the world as herself. It's something she has never taken for granted.

As profoundly affected as she was by that moment, the Bird could never say exactly when it happened. She was maybe twenty-four or twenty-five when her first passport arrived, not that such details really mattered. Being unable to remember dates was almost a point of pride for the Bird. "I remember places," she liked to say. "I remember stories." To her, travel was a sublime marriage of the two, place and story combined. No wonder it was such a big part of her identity.

So it was perhaps a stroke of good fortune that we traveled well together, so well that I let the effortlessness of our trips blind me to a bigger picture that was undermining our growth as a couple. I didn't stop to ask myself why we were still just boyfriend and girlfriend after almost four years. That's a long time to go without a change in title. At the café in Budapest that day, I didn't notice the wrinkle of disappointment on the Bird's face when she realized that I was not going to seize upon the magical moment to produce a ring. The Bird turned forty-nine on that trip.

She was closing in on a milestone that made the five years between us feel more distant. I took her out for birthday goulash at a funky little restaurant where a band played festive Hungarian folk music and customers randomly leaped from their chairs to join them in singalongs. We loved the place so much that we went back a second time despite only having two nights in town. The Bird thought a ring might appear on that magical night too. For years, in fact, she thought the same thing on every special occasion, every birthday, every anniversary. It finally took her sitting me down one weekend and saying it out loud. We were well into 2015 by that point, months after Budapest, the weeks blurring into each other without distinction as I struggled to keep pace with the growth at *IBT*. The Bird looked at me with a seriousness she reserved for only the most important moments. "I don't want to wake up on my fiftieth birthday as someone's girlfriend."

It suddenly hit me that I was being willfully clueless, pushing off thoughts of marriage in much the same way that I'd pushed off travel and for much the same reason: I thought it could wait until I'd reached some undefined *next level*. My heart broke at the realization that I had been letting her down. She deserved what she was asking for, this one thing, and time was not going to extend its generosity forever. I felt trapped between two competing visions of myself, the version who saw fifty thousand dollars a year as an accomplishment worth celebrating and a more sobering counterpart who knew how far that actually went in New York City. I could not even afford the trips we were taking, let alone a ring to pack for the journey.

Our newest hire at *IBT* was twenty years younger than me and twice as good. He was running circles around me, in fact—landing big scoops and generating the kind of buzz on social media that I could only dream of. He used the bullhorn of Twitter like it was his first language, trading in post-ironic humor and coded self-reference, memes I didn't get and lacked the mental space to learn about. I'd stare dumbfounded at my feed as his indecipherable tweets ricocheted like metal projectiles across the network. Brendan was only a few years out of Skidmore, but he had a natural reporter's instinct that took him wherever a story led, whether that meant DMing a high-profile executive who didn't want to comment or spending all night with liquored-up sources at a dive bar in Brooklyn, the borough where, of course, he lived. Despite the bold streak of fearlessness that made him the hot new star of our team, he never came off as arrogant around the office. The kid was impossible not to like, truth be told. Bearded, with mussy curls and a liking for faded jeans and scuffed-up boots, he'd pace the newsroom with the air of a modern-day Russian revolutionary, eager to engage in debates about politics or culture but quickly turning deferential when things got too heated. He was clearly repulsed by power and had a strong desire to skewer the people who had it, not unlike some of the punks I'd known in my youth. Talking to Brendan often made me wonder how some of them might have turned out had they had the opportunity to channel their anger into a more productive outlet. I thought of Dave Disgusting, who was living under a highway overpass in Philadelphia the last I'd heard, and Lazer, whose only online presence was a mug shot. I knew I was closer to them than I liked to think, closer to them than I was to Brendan.

Learmonth was still pushing me to take the role as his deputy editor. He had been building up our combined tech, media, and culture team with the strategic precision of a military commander, hiring exactly the right person for every role. We had Max, tall, bespectacled, and cerebral, who covered the rapidly evolving music business. Kerry, fresh out of Harvard, was a digital native who wrote about social media and influencer culture. Oriana, who wrote about the TV industry, was still in her twenties, but she had the smart-alecky cynicism of someone who had been in the business for fifty years. She kept a jargon jar on her desk and made Learmonth put a dollar into it every time he said *platform*. Ismat focused on the intersection of religion and business, two of her passions. She'd spend hours on the phone chatting with faith leaders as if they were old friends. We had a person in Los Angeles and another in Silicon Valley, not to mention a guy in the UK.

Brendan rounded out the team and was killing it on the media beat, ruffling feathers among the higher-ups at *Gawker* and *BuzzFeed* and any company he wrote about. The more he outshined me—the more they all outshined me—the less secure I felt as a reporter who essentially shared their rank. Learmonth could sense it. He was too attuned to discord as a manager not to. He'd take me out to lunch in the cafeteria, where we'd get into these guidance-counselor-like discussions. "So...what do you want to do?" he'd ask. It felt nice that someone seemed to be looking out for my career development, but I also understood that he saw me as a well-positioned chess piece. He kept urging me to "show more leadership" in the newsroom, take writers under my wing. The team was so large now that he couldn't handle it on his own.

Here in front of me was more or less an obvious ultimatum. I could wait around for this new crop of younger reporters to make me obsolete, or I could be their boss. Surely I looked the part by now, at almost forty-five. I just hoped that none of my new subordinates asked too many questions. Or looked at my LinkedIn. I took Learmonth up on the deputy editor job, and fifty thousand dollars became seventy thousand overnight.

Dr. R. pressed his fingers forcefully at various points along my neck, looking for swollen glands, not that I have any idea where glands are. "So, how's work going?" he asked. I fixed my gaze on the small window of the examining room that overlooked Third Avenue, thinking about how much I appreciated having a doctor on the Upper East Side. He knew exactly what to expect whenever the subject of work came up. *I have a gazillion deadlines and I'm stressed out.* Dr. R. had known about my anxiety issues ever since we first became acquainted, back when I was working at *Show Business Weekly* and still new to the city. One spring morning, a minor stomach cramp and some Google searches brought me to the irrefutable conclusion that my appendix was about to burst. I rushed to the ER at Lenox Hill Hospital and demanded a CT scan, the results of which were, in doctor-speak, "unremarkable." The pain mysteriously vanished within an hour. Mr. Chieftain wasn't yet paying my health insurance, so my unremarkable CT scan resulted in a very remarkable bill for seven thousand dollars.

I hadn't had a regular doctor since I was a teenager, so the attending

ED physician recommended that I start going to see Dr. R. It worked out. He was quite personable, as far as doctors go, and he cared enough to express some degree of concern whenever I mentioned how nervous I got in social situations and how my anxiety seemed to be getting worse. It was affecting my career, I told him, because ever since I took the deputy editor job at *IBT*, work had become a veritable minefield of anxiety triggers. Peter Goodman's morning editorial meetings were notorious for the fear they instilled. All the section editors and their deputies would shuffle into the main conference room at nine a.m. We'd take turns pitching stories for our sections and await our fates as if we were on some bad spinoff of *The Apprentice*.

When it was your turn to pitch, Peter would lean back in his chair, adjust his square glasses, and stare you down in icy silence. Then, after you presented, he would either shower you with praise or shred you to ribbons, leaving you deflated in front of a table full of your peers. Sometimes he'd grill you for more specifics, which you obviously didn't have because, let's be real, you had only nine minutes to prepare for this damn meeting. If I was pitching a story about, say, China's growing influence over Hollywood, I'd better come armed with a working knowledge of two centuries of globalization. When Peter shot down my idea, I could expect him to toss in a vexingly impressive anecdote about his time as the Shanghai bureau chief for the *Washington Post*.

As nerve-racking as these pitch meetings were, they were also kind of fun. Maybe part of me had just missed the real-time friction I'd had with Mr. Chieftain, but I remember reveling in the challenge of getting Peter's approval on a pitch. I lived for those rare moments when I could school him on a topic I knew more about than he did. He seemed to enjoy being proven wrong, and my one-upping him would instantly lighten the mood of the room. "Get 'em, Zara," I heard a colleague mutter quietly on one such occasion. All of us at the table rooted for one another in that way because no one enjoyed watching what happened when Peter hated an idea.

Anxiety had a stubborn way of not cooperating with my career goals. Try as I would to psych myself up for big meetings—deep breaths, ten-minute meditation sessions—I'd invariably find myself racked with a barrage of physical symptoms: shaking hands, stammering, pulse like a bass drum. As a bonus, time slowed down during those moments, so you really got to experience them to their fullest horrifying extent. I started to wonder if there was something wrong with me beyond run-of-the-mill social anxiety. Shouldn't I be getting better, not worse, the more I forced myself into these social situations?

This is where Dr. R. proved most useful. He prescribed me a beta-blocker, something that musicians sometimes took to help them with stage fright. It wasn't a miracle cure—that is, it didn't make my anxiety go away—but it did help control those bothersome symptoms. And unlike Xanax or some of the self-medicating remedies I'd tried in the past, these little blue pills didn't rob me of my mental reflexes. The more I thought about it, the more it made sense that a treatment for performance anxiety would help me cope with everyday workplace interactions. I often saw them as a kind of performance. From the very first time I set foot in an office, I'd been playing a role that I thought aligned with what my colleagues in journalism expected to see. Now at least I had the proper tool to help make my white-collar cosplay more convincing.

One year after Budapest, the Bird and I set off on a two-week trip to East Africa. It was the farthest we had traveled together, the farthest I had ever been from Trenton. I may have googled the distance a few times, not that I needed to. I brought a ring that I had purchased at one of those window-less jewelry stores in Midtown where they have to buzz you in. The Bird didn't know I had it, and I wasn't sure if it was safe to leave the thing tucked away in my suitcase, so I carried it around with me for much of the trip. I had it as I walked through the streets of Nairobi; I had it with me at an outdoor market where a vendor got mad at me for not wanting to buy one of his T-shirts. I had it with me when we were eyeing gazelles and zebras on safari and as I was interviewing conservationists for a story I was writing about Kenya's tourism industry. I had it with me on the plane during our stopover in Dar es Salaam and then in Stone Town, where we wandered the dark alleys and ancient streets and had drinks at Mercury's, a restaurant named after Freddie Mercury, a hometown hero. I had it with me on our drive across Zanzibar Island as our driver took us through thick forests and over bumpy terrain, paths that were not really roads.

An opportune moment to pop the question — *the* opportune moment — finally presented itself. After dinner one night at the lodge where we were staying on Zanzibar's east coast, we took two flutes of champagne to the edge of the beach and sat down on some wooden stairs that led to the powdery sand below. The sky was clear and black, the moon huge. It was beaming like a spotlight over the vast Indian Ocean, which had the bluest water I'd ever seen. This was nothing at all like the muddy Jersey shoreline I knew from my childhood. It was hard to believe we were even on the same planet. I handed her the ring and we both cried, our sobs of joy barely audible over the roar of the waves. "Just under the wire," I said, placing it on her finger. She was turning fifty at midnight.

It took a fair amount of restraint not to break down and apologize for having waited so long, but I suspected that her terrible recall for dates would eventually be on my side. I was counting on her remembering this place, this story.

CHAPTER 30

Operation New Deal

THERE WERE DAYS WHEN IT felt like everyone was mad at us. The phone would ring and it would be people from Airbnb, unhappy about David Sirota's privacy story. "Utter misrepresentation of our policies," they yapped. An e-mail would appear from Vice Media. Their people were upset that Oriana reported the dismal ratings for their fledgling cable network. Agitation was in the air. Another presidential election was on the horizon—far more contentious than the one four years earlier—poisoning every story, every angle, every conversation with the politics of the moment. Democrats were incensed when Ismat interviewed Muslim Americans who supported Donald Trump, newly emerging as a front-runner candidate. On the other side of the aisle, a flack for Fox News was furious about Brendan's admittedly unflattering profile of Sean Hannity, which went into detail about the TV host's workout regimen ("I hit the heavy bag, I hit the mitts, I do a lot of core").

My job as an editor in this environment, I learned quickly, did not end after a story was published. Fending off demands from quoted sources or PR people who wanted details changed after the fact became a fixture of my routine. They'd home in on the most minor thing, an adjective or a phrase that was open to the slightest interpretation, then whittle around the edges of semantics and context until their argument for why something was incorrect seemed like the only plausible version of reality. They'd appeal to my professional judgment in a way that felt like a referendum on my humanity. "Christopher, I think you know this is wrong," they'd say.

I felt for these PR people because I knew their only mandate was to toe the line of their corporate overlords, and their day hinged on my willingness to cooperate. But I had to balance being fair to them against the more natural impulse of defending my own writers at all costs, often with the actual truth of facts and details getting caught in the middle. I was used to getting pushback from companies on stories I'd written myself—Comcast no doubt had me on speed dial at some point—but I hadn't anticipated how personally I'd take criticism when the byline was someone under me. I'd lie awake at night agonizing over whether I'd made the right call by letting a slick PR person talk me into an update, whether I had let a writer down by conceding to a clarification note.

Or worse—the dreaded correction. I'm not sure why journalists are so averse to admitting that they've gotten something wrong, but somewhere along the line, correction notes became our industry's scarlet letters. The abject shame that goes along with them is unfortunate when you consider they are the end result of accountability and transparency, two things that all news organizations should strive for. But then, who wants to spend days or weeks or months on a story only to have it sullied by an italicized blemish that everyone can see?

Granted, they are often an easy call. If you report that Taylor Swift is sixty years old or Moldova is the name of a landlocked country in Central Asia, well, those things are plainly wrong and you have to suck it up. But what if you say Taylor Swift is *controversial* or Moldova is *ugly?* Working within the permissive parameters of digital media, you can find corroborating details to back up pretty much any value judgment. And very often you're tasked with producing content at a speed that obscures the line between valid perspectives and rants. Writing and reporting a story quickly becomes a battle between confirming your assumptions and arriving at an objective truth. Once those choices are made, you have to live with them forever, out there in the easily searchable, easily screenshot-able abyss of digital history. When you're an editor, writers count on you to help them make the right choices. That's why nothing feels worse than fucking up a story—except fucking up someone else's story.

* * *

Brendan came by my desk one morning and asked if I wanted to have coffee, which was unusual, to say the least. Actually, I don't think we'd ever had a conversation outside the office. When I asked him if something was wrong, he said no, nothing specific. He just wanted to catch up. He picked a coffee shop near Water Street, where we sat on wobbly stools in front of a large window, elbowing our way between the chattering suits of the busy lunch crowd. Brendan was wearing an open blazer and a half-unbuttoned shirt, one of his signature looks.

He took a sip of his coffee and paused, clearly searching for a way to broach a sensitive topic. Then he told me that some of the editorial staffers at *IBT* had been meeting regularly with the NewsGuild. They wanted to form a union, and now they were going around quietly to see how much support they could get. They especially needed buy-in from deputy editors, people at my level, because we were in supervisory roles but not considered full management. The goal was for an expansive union that would include as many *IBT* journalists as possible.

Unions were practically unheard of in digital media. It was one of the things that separated us from our more established counterparts in print and television. Digital was supposed to be nimble, quick to adapt, not hobbled by the work stoppages and contract battles that were all too common at newspapers. But sentiment was changing. A few months earlier, *Gawker* had become the first high-profile all-digital newsroom to unionize its journalists. The headline-grabbing campaign set off a domino effect of organization efforts within the broader industry, emboldening employees and sparking sudden discussions about job security, workplace conditions, stability, better pay. Brendan saw how my expression changed when I realized where the conversation was heading. He reined himself in.

"Do you support unions?" he asked.

"Uh, of course." I mean, how can you not? The labor movement is responsible for so many of the workplace rights we take for granted. Workers have strength in numbers. I'd be a fool not to concede those points, just as I had ten years earlier during those many half-hearted arguments with my old roommate Gus Gary. But that was not the same as saying I wanted to be part of a union myself. Suddenly being presented with that possibility, I was forced to confront a deeper fear of the collectivist mindset that I'd never been able to shake. Unions did make me uncomfortable. My thoughts immediately went back to City Gardens, to those shirtless, tattooed skinheads who demanded that I join "the Family," to the ease with which they could direct obedient mobs of teenagers to beat dissenters to a pulp and leave them bloodied and unconscious in the parking lot. Those memories infected my views about group behavior, and being in the working world had apparently done little to quell my distrust of any institution that required a membership.

With his coffee cup now empty, Brendan asked if I would be interested in coming to a meeting. "No pressure," he said. "Just observe, see what you think." I nodded, fiddling with my barely touched latte, which was now giving me psychosomatic jitters. "I'll always agree to a meeting," I said.

The NewsGuild of New York had an office just off Times Square, tucked away over the top of a Sephora and that obnoxious Starbucks with the glittering sign that's supposed to look like a Broadway marquee. I entered to find about twenty of my *IBT* colleagues gathered around a large conference table, chatting and laughing, munching on pizza that had been supplied by the union reps. There was a strong undercurrent of joviality in the room; it felt like recess. Most of the attendees were younger. Brendan saw me enter and rose to greet me, then led me to an empty chair at the table. "Glad you could make it," he said.

Listening in on their conversations felt almost voyeuristic. They were open and candid, nothing like the guarded small talk that punctuated a typical day at the office. People spoke bluntly about transgressions real and perceived, instances of sexism and microaggressions, our obvious lack of diversity. Peter Goodman's fear-inducing editorial meetings were held up as an example of everything that was wrong with our workplace, forcing me to reexamine how I had seen them. I'd viewed them as just another challenge. It had not occurred to me that some of my colleagues might have been left in tears by his confrontational style or that I had been lucky enough to escape the worst of his impulses.

I was struck by the implicit sense of trust at the meeting, how no one seemed at all concerned that what we were saying might be funneled back to Etienne or Johnathan. I thought of my early days at *IBT,* those mysterious disappearances. If underperforming on traffic was enough to get you fired, what would attending a secret union meeting get you? My young colleagues seemed unfazed. At work I was a manager, but here at this table they were in charge, sure of what they wanted and how to get it. Being included, seeing the passion on their faces, their collective faith in the promise of a better workplace, made me feel electrified and proud.

But those warm feelings gave way to something colder when someone placed a union card in front of me and asked me to sign it. What happened to "no pressure"? The room fell silent as Brendan clicked a pen and handed it to me. I looked around the table, meeting the eyes of some of my coworkers, feeling the urgency of their expectations and suddenly resenting them for what they were asking of me. Where were they when I was cleaning out dog cages or scraping dried chocolate syrup off the ice cream cart? Where were they when I was buried under debt or eating shit from Mr. Chieftain because no other employer would look at my résumé? I fought the urge not to be insulted by their embrace of proletariat language, how they'd spent the meeting talking about solidarity and how they referred to newsrooms as "shops." *Our workplace is not a shop,* I thought, biting my tongue until it nearly bled. *It's an office with air-conditioning and free bagels. It has an HR department and ergonomic chairs and a Ping-Pong table. Shops are dusty and dark. I've worked in shops.*

Later that night, I told the Bird about the meeting and that I'd signed the card. We weren't officially part of the union yet, but we were getting closer to the critical mass of support we needed in the newsroom. Signing cards meant that we were giving the NewsGuild permission to bargain on our behalf once that happened. I suspected the higher-ups at *IBT* had no idea what we were up to.

"Does any of this help you?" she asked.

"I don't know," I said. "I don't think so."

I explained that I just wanted to work, that all of this felt like a distraction at a time when I was just starting to feel like I was gaining momentum in this career. Who knew if IBT Media was even profitable or whether it would exist in two years? Every second we spent on union meetings and committees and contract points was time we could have been spending shoring up our résumés against the next cataclysm.

"Well, if you feel that way, why did you sign it?" the Bird pressed.

It was a good question. Surely it had less to do with having the card shoved in my face than it did my fear of being on the wrong side of history. "I have to support my colleagues, and this is what they want."

When I first arrived in New York City, I'd thought Gus Gary was an oddity. His militant stance on organized labor. His liking for Karl Marx and *The Communist Manifesto*. Relics of a bygone era. He was twenty years older than me, a baby boomer clinging to the idealistic pangs of his youth. Now here in front of me was a younger generation that seemed to be yearning for the same things but in much greater numbers. If anyone was the oddity, it was me, still stuck on the idea that work was about individual achievement, that no one would be there for me when the rug was pulled out. It didn't matter that I didn't fully understand why my colleagues believed otherwise. Their faith in the collective was clearly stronger than my ambivalence toward it. The least I could do was not get in their way.

CHAPTER 31

Cliff Notes

THE WARNING SIGNS WERE THERE if you looked for them. Paychecks not showing up on time. Image-licensing services abruptly cutting *IBT* off because we hadn't paid a bill. But, I told myself, such was life at a fast-growing media start-up. When you're on a constant upward trajectory, lapses and oversights are easy to shrug off as the price of success. Omelets and eggs and all that. In my mind, the first real sign of existential trouble at IBT Media came at the beginning of 2016, when the shadowy people controlling the purse strings—I still didn't know who they were—suddenly scaled back our travel budget. I was lucky that my request to cover SXSW that March was approved just under the wire, but our team in Austin would be only a fraction of the size of the previous year. Oh, and we all had to share the same Airbnb.

In the three and a half years I'd been at the company, everything had been about growth. Buying *Newsweek*. Bringing on Peter to transform *International Business Times*. Sending reporters everywhere from Davos to Comic-Con. For a while, it felt like the spending spree would never end, and even though my curiosity about where the money was coming from always lingered in the background, I let myself ignore such inconvenient questions and enjoy the ride. Deep down I knew the math of online advertising didn't add up. Our business model was an unsustainable arms race between increasingly intrusive auto-play videos, readers with more sophisticated ad blockers, and the finite nature of scale. But as long as Peter was willing to run our newsroom like we were the *New York Times* or the *Wall Street Journal*, I was happy to go along with it, not because I thought it would last forever, but because it was fun. Chasing almost any story I wanted, having the freedom to pursue leads and develop sources, collaborating with a brain trust of fellow truth seekers—this was how I'd always pictured working in the news business would be.

Besides, what did I really know about IBT Media's profit margins and revenue streams? Maybe somebody somewhere had finally figured out how to make this digital thing work. So many cynical old-school media prognosticators had been predicting the collapse of digital media for so long, often from the perch of academia or with an old-school newspaper pension to prop them up. I wanted those people to be wrong.

Now, suddenly, we were being told to tighten our belts, hearing words like *hiring freeze* and *no*. Peter was getting more and more frustrated with the restraints. Back when he started, he had been assured by Etienne and Johnathan that he would have the budget to keep growing the newsroom, but something had changed. The two owners were pumping the brakes and they did not seem interested in communicating why.

Peter called an unexpected meeting of senior editors one morning in late March, not long after I returned from Austin. Attendance was mandatory. We gathered in his office, which could barely contain the large group. That's how big the senior staff was now. Some of my colleagues took seats on the windowsill or the floor as we waited for Peter to deliver what we all correctly assumed was going to be unpleasant news. Once everyone was accounted for, the room packed and anxious, the remote people dialed in, Peter closed the glass doors and took a seat at his desk.

"Guys, things are bad," he said, accentuating the word *bad* as if it were the final note of a German opera. The health of the company, he continued, was far more precarious than he had been led to believe. It wasn't just that we couldn't keep growing. We couldn't sustain our current size. "They're talking layoffs, and they're likely to be significant," Peter added.

His words left silence in their wake, shock. Somehow we had gone from high growth to hiring freezes to layoffs in a matter of weeks. When someone asked Peter which teams would be affected, he said he didn't know. When someone asked when the ax would fall, he didn't know that either. In fact, he wouldn't be around to find out because he had already plotted his escape. He was going back to work for the *New York Times*.

It didn't take long for the bad news to spread. Over the next few days, a palpable thicket of existential dread filled the newsroom as we went through the motions of our daily routines, zombie-like and humbled. Most of us knew deep cuts were coming, but we didn't know when or how deep they would be or what our future would look like without Peter. *IBT* was rudderless, a ship adrift in an ocean of bloat. The only question left was who was expendable and who wasn't.

For some reason, I thought we might have a few weeks to prepare for the worst, but I wasn't nearly as clued in as I thought I was. On Thursday morning of that same week, Brendan came by my desk, walking restlessly, clenching his hands into fists and taking deep breaths as he often did when he was about to break a big story. He looked me in the eye and mouthed a single word as he passed: *Now.* I felt an icy wave shoot down the back of my neck. Of course Brendan would know. Media gossip was his job. Learmonth did not seem to be aware of what was happening, so I sent him a DM on Slack.

Hey, so I think the layoffs are starting now, I wrote.

How do you know that?

Our trusty media reporter seems to know more than most.

An eternity went by as I stared at the screen.

Well, I might be out too then, he finally replied. Nobody told me anything.

Seconds later, I heard the chirps of a desk phone from near the back wall. You always knew when a call was coming from within the office because it had that European-style double ring: *bliiirt-bliiirt.* This particular desk phone belonged to Blake, a reporter who covered diversity and civil rights. He answered and mumbled a few words into the receiver. Then he rose from his desk and walked toward the HR office on the far end of the floor, clearly summoned there. Ten minutes passed, maybe twelve, before he returned, walking with his head down and nodding somberly at colleagues whose eyes followed him along his path of shame.

The look on his face said all we needed to know. Blake was not even back at his seat yet when another desk phone rang: *bliiirt-bliiirt.* This one came from the other side of the floor, maybe the business or world section. I saw another colleague rise from her desk and walk toward HR. By now, the newsroom had fallen completely silent, noticeably devoid of keyboard clicks and other sounds of office work. A few more minutes passed. *Bliiirt-bliiirt.* Our defense reporter this time. "Shit," he yelled out. Silence gave way to incredulous murmurs, vocal acknowledgments of indignity.

So, this is how it's going to be? Picked off one by one, sitting at our desks and waiting for the next phone to ring, wondering if it will be yours? In fact, it wasn't so easy to tell. The ringtones had an unusually high pitch, like crickets, making their origin hard to determine. As soon as one of the phones rang, my heart would stop for a split second. *Bliiirt-bliiirt.* Was that one mine? I felt relieved when it wasn't and then instantly guilty. These were colleagues I'd worked side by side with every day, losing their livelihoods in real time. The perceived disadvantage of my background temporarily vanished, leaving what felt like a bastardized version of the equal opportunity I had always obsessed over. We'd taken different paths to get here, but we were all going out the same way.

Three cubicles away, another phone rang. Then a DM popped up on my screen from one of my closest colleagues. Well, I'm fucked.

I know. I'm sorry.

The phone calls continued all afternoon, and no one knew when they were going to stop. Some of the people who had received a call were now packing up their desks. Others were making the rounds. *Nice working with you . . . good luck.* Loud sobs rose up from cubicles near and far. At one point, I looked across the floor and locked eyes with Matthias, who had bitterly griped about Peter coming on board two years earlier. Against all odds, we had both survived that rocky transition, a stroke of luck that we sometimes joked about. "We're still here!" I liked to say, pretending to raise a bottle like Justin Theroux in *The Leftovers.* Would we still be here after this? Matthias looked at me and shook his head with a sigh, the familiar cynicism about his job replaced by a fear of losing it. We just wanted this day to be over.

* * *

I met the Bird that night at Thai Market, one of our regular places on the Upper West Side. The bartender loved us and was always extra generous with the gin-to-tonic ratio. It's hard to recall a day when I so badly needed a drink. At least fifteen people had been fired, some of our best journalists. I was alternating between sighs of relief and spasms of guilt, sprawling my elbows on the bar, barely supporting the weight of my head. Why them and not me? I had no window into the decision-making process other than later being told about the existence of a nonnegotiable spreadsheet that listed all the people they were cutting. Etienne, I assumed, had signed off on it. Long gone were the days when he would come by my desk with a copy of *Newsweek*, as excited to show me the cover of the latest issue as a kid with a new toy. But I wondered if whatever brief connection we'd shared in those early days had played a role in keeping my name off the list of the damned.

My problems that night were minuscule compared to what the Bird was going through. Her mother had passed away three weeks earlier and she was still in shock, finding moments to grieve between working a new design job at a small clothing brand where her boss didn't offer bereavement days. She excelled at compartmentalizing, but the stress of it all was wearing on her. Her mom was her last connection to the South, a comforting tether to a fraught past. In the Bird's telling, she was vivacious and flirty as a younger woman, hopping from one ill-fated relationship to the next, some more abusive than others but always with men who could take care of her. "She never planned for her next act," the Bird said of her mom. She spent her final years living alone in rural South Carolina, repulsed by the aging process and neglecting her health to the point where it deteriorated. She'd been dead for two days in her small apartment before someone found her.

The shock of her mother's death forced the Bird to reevaluate the class divide that had marked her upbringing and the side with which she thought she aligned. Summers with Nana had shown her a world of refinement, of exclusivity, a lifestyle she aspired to create for herself. The Oglethorpe Club and the beautiful cathedral in Savannah were the curative refuges of her childhood. But later, when it came time for the Bird to express her true gender identity, Nana recoiled, inhibited by the blinders of privilege and the strict cultural dictates she knew. She didn't — or didn't want to — understand what the Bird was going through, at least not for a long time. It was her mother's side of the family, the so-called poorer side, that embraced the Bird without conditions or hesitation. "Mother always accepted me," the Bird said, "even when I was becoming me." Now her mother was gone and it was time to plan a memorial and what would probably be the Bird's final trip to Aiken.

The strong G and Ts were already kicking in when the waitress brought our order of larb gai, a salad made of ground chicken and vegetables. We always got it extra-spicy and then added even more spices from the table caddie, reveling in the mood-boosting quality of the intense heat. Then one of us would remark about how much we loved Thai Market, a place where nothing bad ever happened.

The layoffs didn't dampen efforts to unionize. As the dust was settling, one of the lead organizers sent an e-mail to those of us who had signed union cards explaining how the erratic and random nature of the cuts only reinforced why concerted action was needed and needed quickly. They were planning to regroup at the NewsGuild offices the next day and discuss next steps. More outreach. A mission statement. A list of demands. And ultimately announcing the union to IBT Media ownership.

I made up an excuse for why I wouldn't be at the meeting. "I'll be there in spirit," I told them, but that wasn't really true. To me, the only thing the layoffs reinforced was my sinking belief that we had no real power at the company, collectively or otherwise. I couldn't shake the feeling that we were interchangeable parts in a machine that was indifferent to our existence.

Late one afternoon as I was finishing a story, I received a call at my desk that furthered my spiral of doubt. The person on the other end sounded distraught, his voice weak and cracking. It was a person I'd written about a while back, a lawyer whose firm had been sued by a former unpaid intern. The suit had claimed that aspiring lawyers who worked for him were made to do grunt work for forty-plus hours a week with no pay and for no educational benefit. It was one of any number of stories I'd written about alleged intern mills during that period. Years later, my story and the negative headline were still the first things that came up when you googled this lawyer's name and practice. "I don't know if you realize this, but what you wrote really hurt me," he told me over the phone; it sounded like a lump was forming in his throat. He said his life had fallen apart, that he'd lost business and faced serious financial repercussions, suffered from depression. He was struggling to put the pieces back together, but my story kept following him around like an ankle monitor that wouldn't come off. Finally, he asked if I would consider taking it down. I didn't know what to say. News outlets don't just take down stories at the request of the people mentioned in them, especially not true stories. "I'm sorry, but that would go against our policy," I finally said. "There's nothing I can do."

The phone call haunted me over the following days and weeks as our newsroom adjusted to its smaller size and smaller-scale ambitions. I started to wonder what it was we were supposed to be doing as journalists, whose lives were really being made better by the information we put out in the world. Balancing truth against harm seemed impossible when every story we did lived forever on the internet. David Jang, the rumored puppet master behind the curtain at *IBT*, supposedly believed that the world was drowning in a flood of ungodly digital information. How were we, his Noah's Ark, not part of the very problem that he sought to solve?

We still hadn't heard a thing from Etienne, but Johnathan held an all-hands meeting shortly after the layoffs. *IBT* had gotten too big too fast, he said. We needed to "course-correct." That's all these layoffs were, he insisted. He was still optimistic about the future of the company and where it was heading. In fact, a search for Peter Goodman's replacement was already under way.

CHAPTER 32

Last Call

By THE BEGINNING OF SUMMER that year, a confluence of stabilizing forces made a more sustainable version of work life seem within reach. The Bird and I got married on a warm, cloudless day in May. We said our teary vows under the arch in Washington Square Park, commemorating our love not just for each other but for the city. We were surrounded by about forty friends, my parents and brothers, and a crowd of onlookers who had gathered just because New Yorkers love a guerrilla-style wedding almost as much as they love a pornographic movie shoot, which was also happening nearby. The park was alive with hope and cheer, students and punks and drummers and the same cast of characters who had been populating this pavement since time began. That guy with the snake was there too.

Back at *IBT,* we had a new global editor in chief, Dayan, who was nothing like Peter. He had started his career as a stringer for Reuters in his native Sri Lanka and eventually worked his way up to become the regional editor for the Americas. Dayan spoke in a reserved manner and used lots of corny analogies, like "butter-to-bread ratio," which was his formula for how much substance a piece of journalism actually contained. Unlike Peter, he had no illusions about *IBT* becoming the next *Wall Street Journal*. Rather, he compared online media to a giant cocktail party where some news outlets started conversations and others joined them. He seemed to be content with the idea that we would mostly be joining them. Most important, Dayan said he had no grand plans to revamp the staff. "This newsroom has been through enough trauma," he said.

In ways, it seemed like the best-case scenario, because even though I had grown conflicted about the place, I was still afraid to confront alternatives in a job market that never seemed to improve and with a personal backstory that I still couldn't bring myself to talk about. I had a level of seniority at *IBT* where people—even this new boss—just accepted my being there. I couldn't remember the last time someone asked me where I'd gone to college, and when that topic did come up, I had perfected the art of gentle obfuscation. I no longer worried incessantly about money. I had entered the realm of being on the lower end of a decent salary, still short of the eighty K that the Bird had said I was worth when I first started, but closer than I'd thought I would ever get. Clearly the best option was to follow the company into its next chapter, whatever bizarre form that happened to take.

It turned out to be more bizarre than any of us anticipated. A few short weeks into Dayan's tenure—weeks that we'd spent implementing many of his organizational changes—he called a mandatory meeting of senior editors. We gathered in the same office that Peter had summoned us to just three months earlier. In fact, it was a lot of the same people, many remarking about how the whole thing felt like déjà vu. More layoffs? Was the company sold? No one knew what fresh hell was in store for us. Once everyone was accounted for, the room packed and anxious, and the remote people had dialed in, Dayan closed the glass doors and delivered the news.

IBT Media was being restructured, and our flagship *International Business Times* was going to see significant cuts—again. The gravity of this sudden development produced a haze around whatever he said after that, but I remember hearing Dayan mention three sections: entertainment, sports, and breaking news. Once again, I felt a mix of relief and guilt that was becoming all too familiar at this place. I didn't work for any of those sections. I was safe!

No, Dayan explained. Those were the sections that *weren't* being cut.

What was he talking about? What about the international desk? What about business? What about tech and media and culture? What about the copy team and the data-viz team, personal finance, the managing editors?

"Let me say it again," Dayan continued softly and slowly. "Unless you work for one of the three sections I just mentioned, your team is being cut."

"When is all this happening?"

"Today."

It took another second or two for that to sink in, but there it finally was. I was fired. My entire team was fired. Almost everyone in that room was fired.

Dayan tried to explain that he was just as surprised as we were, that he truly had had big plans to turn the company around. But he was given new marching orders from the top, abruptly and without warning. Or maybe it was more complicated than that. Maybe David Jang or one of his ministries needed a sudden influx of cash or Peter's overspending had left a hole in the budget that was too deep to fill. Or maybe it was a combination of all those things.

What's clear now is that Etienne was always out of his depth, even if my early impression of him as an impotent figurehead with no apparent business acumen was not the whole picture. Shortly after the second round of layoffs, he stepped back from his day-to-day role as CEO, staying on for a while as chairman and seeking less visible ways to help rebuild the company he'd cofounded. He eventually resigned, but only after the Manhattan DA's office raided the newsroom one morning in early 2018 and seized over a dozen computer servers. The raid was part of an expansive fraud investigation into IBT Media—one that laid to rest any lingering questions about whether it had financial ties to David Jang's Olivet University. According to the probe, Etienne and his coconspirators had bilked lenders out of thirty-five million dollars, telling them they were using it to purchase equipment but then laundering it for unrelated purposes, including funding the cash-strapped business.

Back when I was asking myself where all the money was coming from, I'll admit, that was one scenario I hadn't considered. Etienne pleaded guilty to fraud and money laundering and, according to the DA's office, was sentenced to probation and three hundred hours of community service. He served no jail time.

* * *

We spent the afternoon filing into our main conference room, one team at a time, as HR read us the last rites. Severance. NDAs. *Thank you for your service.* After it was over, a crowd of now-former IBT Media employees gathered in a dark basement saloon for one final round of after-work drinks. I can't recall which of our many financial-district watering holes we settled on—happy hours in that neighborhood tended to bleed into each other like tie-dye—but what sticks in my memory is the pureness and joy of it. It's not something I would have expected after a mass layoff. We threw back drinks and laughed heartily, trading war stories and bonding over the absurdity of our shared experiences at IBT Media, a company that no single person ever rooted for. "We always knew it would end this way," I said to Learmonth at one point, recalling the many intense discussions we'd had about the crazy business of media.

I felt an overwhelming sense of gratitude for these people, for having had the chance to learn from them, absorb their collective knowledge about our profession, grow as a professional alongside them. It seems almost too on the nose to compare journalists to mental patients, but it occurs to me that I hadn't felt that raw camaraderie with a group of people since my hospital stay in New Jersey all those years before.

Two drinks became four. I didn't want to leave, so I just kept making the rounds, saying goodbyes, exchanging vows of support, reciprocal acknowledgments of brilliance. "I know you have an amazing career ahead of you," I said to Brendan. We reminisced about when we'd pissed off Sean Hannity. Good times.

He thanked me for being a great editor, but in all honesty, the kid taught me more than I ever taught him. Watching him lead the charge of our unionization efforts, fearless and undeterred by the company's dire instability, forced me to reexamine so many of my personal hang-ups. The union campaign had been in its final days before the layoffs, and it had overwhelming support among the staff. Had it not imploded, *IBT* would have been one of the earliest all-digital newsrooms to unionize its journalists, a practice that is now common throughout the industry.

As was characteristic of Brendan, he did not seem concerned about what he would do next. "Aw, you know, I've been working on this podcast," he said. It was called *Chapo Trap House*, a name that sounded so ridiculous I asked him to repeat it. Months later, I read in *The New Yorker* that Brendan and his fellow podcasters were the leading voices of an anti-capitalist political movement called the "dirtbag left," and it sort of made more sense, but only sort of.

I snaked up the narrow streets toward the Wall Street subway station, taking in the landmarks that had become so familiar to me over the last four years. Fraunces Tavern. Delmonico's. Those little Dutch Revival buildings with the stepped gables. It was a long way back to our apartment at the top of Manhattan, but I was used to that. What I wasn't used to was having nowhere to be the next morning.

The weight of my situation began to seep in as my train rattled slowly up the island, making all local stops, because the express never runs when you really need it. Warm and fuzzy feelings about my ex-coworkers gave way to a creeping realization that they were now my professional competitors, that we'd all be applying for the same precious few jobs that existed in media. Back at the saloon, we'd all promised to look out for one another, to forward leads and have one another's backs when we landed somewhere. But how does that even work? There were so many talented people in that room, so many credentials.

CHAPTER 33

Networks and Networking

THE GOODWILL STARTED ALMOST IMMEDIATELY the next morning. Messages from LinkedIn recruiters. E-mails from former colleagues, fellow journalists, strangers. *Heard about what happened at IBT — sooo fucked up!* The layoffs had been big news in the media world, and sympathy was on our side in a way that caught me by surprise. Even though IBT Media was universally disliked, people seemed to genuinely want to help us find our next opportunities. Severed from a company, stripped of a title, strangely, I felt more connected to the white-collar world of media than I'd ever felt in my life.

"I'm not worried at all," the Bird said, showing the enthusiastic support of a new wife as I googled *How to get on Obamacare for married couples.* "You've never been in a better position to find a better job."

I agreed. This wasn't like last time. This wasn't like when I was tossed to the wolves by a boss who made it clear that I should not bother using him as a reference. I had connections now. Experience. Hell, maybe even wisdom. I scoured my contact list — the last thing I forwarded to myself before the company shut off our e-mails — for leads. I tracked down every editor I'd ever worked for, even my old editor at *MovieMaker*, because you never know. Everyone said the same thing: They're keeping their eyes peeled and happy to help. Some offered freelance, others drinks. I took them up on both. And I kept on looking.

One by one, my former *IBT* colleagues started to land jobs, each fit more perfect than the last. Max got scooped up by Digiday, a fast-growing website that covered the online ad business. Kerry took her deep knowledge of social media to *Mashable*. Oriana did the same with her TV knowledge, landing at *Variety*. I imagined the jargon jar would never be empty at a magazine that used terms like *boffo* and *kudocast* in earnest. Learmonth emerged as the news director for *Vice News*. These new hires were on top of the vast *IBT* diaspora that already permeated much of the wider world of media. Former staffers were toiling away at local newspapers, TV stations, magazines, and websites across the country. To me, it all seemed like a fortunate fringe benefit of having worked for a content-churning, labor-churning company. You couldn't throw a rock at a journalism conference without hitting someone who had *IBT* on their résumé.

But as the weeks wore on and no concrete leads materialized, my confidence in the benefit of my scattershot social network began to falter. The truth was, I was never very good at connecting with other human beings, professionally or otherwise, and now I feared the awkward social skills that hindered me in school were coming back to bite me again. I reflected back on a life of tenuous connections and surface-level friendships and thought, as I so often did, about how desperately I wished I could be a different kind of person. I thought of the Bird, who knew every waiter and waitress in town and could get us PPX status at even the stingiest of restaurants. She would have had twenty thousand leads by now. And of Joe, who seemed to be the most popular guy in Seattle just weeks after moving there. He was convinced that we Zara brothers would have gone so much further in life if we had grown up in a real city, if we had realized the value of networking sooner than we did. That's one point Joe and I always agreed on. But realizing the value of networking is not the same as being good at it.

Fred and I rarely engaged in the kind of drawn-out philosophical discussions that I shared with Joe. By contrast, we could go for long stretches without talking to each other, only to jump right in where we'd left off as if no time had passed—usually with an inside joke that only the two of us would understand. But in the summer of 2016, we were talking a bit more than usual, in part because he had been devastated by the mass shooting at the Pulse nightclub, where forty-nine people were senselessly gunned down. It was like Orlando's 9/11, Fred said; it produced a dark cloud of sadness and grief around the normally sunny city. The shooting happened so close to his house that he had to drive around police barriers and dodge news vans for months to get to and from work.

One afternoon, Fred called me. He was particularly distraught over a Facebook altercation he'd had with Lazer. Neither of us heard much from Lazer in those days—we had no idea where he was living or what he was doing for work—but he occasionally emerged online. Fred had posted something about the Pulse shooting and Lazer commented under the post, in all caps, that Fred had clearly been brainwashed. The shooting was a hoax, he insisted, the victims merely "crisis actors": FREDDY, DON'T BE A SHEEP. FREDDY, WAKE UP.

"I don't even know what to say to that," Fred told me later. "I drove by three fucking funerals this week."

I couldn't remember the last time I'd spoken to Lazer. It might have been when I was working at *Show Business Weekly* and he called me out of the blue. He told me he'd recently had some kind of revelation, that he'd stopped using dope, even though the scratchy sound of his voice over the phone said otherwise. He said he was going back to school to study mortuary science because that's what made him happy. He kept going on about happiness, how it was important to do what made you happy, which I thought was uncharacteristic of the Lazer I remembered. The detached punk rocker who shocked old ladies in church would never in a million years have fallen victim to such clichéd notions about happiness. But maybe people change. During our phone call, he expressed interest in coming to visit me in New York, maybe going out for a drink or a slice. "Anytime," I said. It's one of those things you agree to that you know will never happen.

After the Facebook altercation, Fred told me, he unfriended Lazer. "I'm done with him," he said. "I don't need people like that in my life." We talked for a bit longer about the past, or, more specifically, about those dispiriting moments when the past and present collide. It felt quaint in the chaotic context of 2016 to even try to verbalize how bleached hair and spiked bracelets could have been so transgressive and radical, but there was no mold for that in our insular corner of Trenton, New Jersey, in 1984. Lazer *was* the mold. Fred and I wondered what types of trauma had paved the road from spirited creative expression to ridiculous conspiracy theories. Neither of us had a good answer. It was easy enough to blame Facebook and the scattershot nature of social networks, but we both knew something else was going on.

Finally, I got a bite. Not just *a* bite but maybe *the* bite.

A digital-media company with very deep pockets was looking for a senior reporter to cover the business of law. At *IBT,* I had amassed a mountain of stories about lawsuits: Copyright lawsuits. Antitrust lawsuits. Mergers. Forced arbitration. I had a Rolodex of legal experts at the ready and tons of impressive clips. Even better, the company that was hiring was not pie-in-the-sky elite like the *Times* or *Bloomberg,* but it was well known and respected enough that it would be considered an upward move for my career. Plus, the HR person answered my e-mail personally when I reached out about the opportunity. *This could be it.*

After I applied through the company's website as instructed, the HR person followed up with the request I feared was coming. "Please confirm that you meet the minimum bachelor's degree requirement," she wrote. I had impressed her with my enthusiastic cover letter, but there was no fooling the online portal. Without a college degree, I wasn't an experienced journalist with skills that perfectly matched the job description. I was just another applicant with a red flag. I looked down at the e-mail and noticed in her signature that she had a PhD. A fucking PhD. The HR person was a fucking doctor. What the hell was the world coming to?

In a lot of ways, the exchange with this HR doctor was not unlike those I might have had with any number of recruiters back when I first arrived in New York. But it felt different, because now I was different. I had worked full-time in New York City media for more than a decade. I had managed a weekly newspaper for five years. I had navigated a fast-paced digital newsroom during a period of incredible growth. I had hundreds of clips and years of experience in editorial management. I'd reported stories from Kenya, Paris, Mexico. I'd led a team of journalists across more than a dozen beats. Why was I still being reduced to this one thing? What more did I have to prove?

Anger at the situation gave way to despair and ultimately depression as I crawled into bed that night. Out of Ambien and wide awake, I stared up at the violent darkness of our bedroom ceiling, my senses assaulted by visual snow and tinnitus, permanent reminders of the damage I had inflicted on my body over the years. I started to fear that I would never get past another gatekeeper again, that I would become a casualty of online job portals that were programmed to weed me out. It used to be that you could avoid them with a personal e-mail to HR, but now these portals were everywhere. Even if you had a personal contact, companies still demanded that you apply through automated processes because nothing was more important than doing things by the book.

Hours of insomnia went by as I got stuck in a feedback loop of self-defeating thought patterns. Mistakes revisited. Threads retraced. Again and again, I kept going back to that annoying rhetorical question: Had I failed school or had school failed me? On nights like this, the answer came to me with perfect clarity. I didn't like it, but there it was.

Lying next to me in bed, the Bird started twitching, intermittently at first and then with more force and frequency. She often acted out her dreams, especially the bad ones. Some nights she'd howl in terror without ever fully waking up, but usually she'd just thrust her legs forward and kick away the demons, the ones she never liked to talk about during the day, the abuse and poverty and instability that occupied the furthest depths of her mind. She had been through so much in her life, fought for the right to be herself in ways I could never imagine. In my manicured version of our future, I was slowly but surely working us toward a place where the bad dreams could no longer touch her. Now I was worried that I would fail her just as I had failed school. I draped my arm around her fetal-positioned body and squeezed, trying to absorb the shock of the twitches as they came.

CHAPTER 34

Learning Curve

I LET THE BIRD TALK me into going to Fire Island, where some friends had rented a beach house. It was not my first choice for a summer getaway—the sun and my pasty skin didn't exactly get along—but with me not working and bills piling up, I couldn't afford to be choosy. I spent most of the weekend under a large umbrella thinking about my next move, my options. I was constantly writing pitches in my head, scouring my environment for leads and angles and ideas, hoping they might lead to at least more freelance. *Has anyone done a serious deep dive on the history of beach umbrellas? Ugh—try again.*

One of our beach-house companions was a computer programmer who was also looking for work. He was a few years older than me and complaining about the blatant ageism in the tech industry. I would be forty-six in November and I was starting to wonder if I had to add age to my list of things to worry about. *Keep pitching,* I told myself. It's easier to stay positive when the sun is out, even if you're hiding in the shade. Then I found myself wondering if debt collectors could track you down on vacation.

The next week, I e-mailed a former colleague, Marcus Baram, who had previously been the managing editor of *IBT.* Marcus and I had gotten along well during his two years there. He was an old-fashioned newshound who'd cut his teeth on papers like the *Daily News* and the *Voice* and who loved nothing more than to dig into public documents, fire off FOIA requests, and extract nuggets of newsworthiness out of just about any piece of information. I don't think he ever slept. Tall and energetic with a prominent brow and thick black hair, he'd bounced around relentlessly from cubicle to cubicle, tossing endless story leads to reporters. His ideas weren't always fully formed, but he had a nose for accessible and timely hooks that could be quickly executed with a bit of legwork. We both got excited about the same things: The rush of a scoop. Being a pain in the ass to powerful companies. One of our finest collaborative moments was when he suggested I call Arby's and ask them to comment on being the constant butt of Jon Stewart's jokes. They did, and the story went viral.

Marcus left *IBT* during the Peter Goodman era, in part to promote a biography he'd completed about Gil Scott-Heron. We crossed paths again at the IRE conference in Philadelphia, where we geeked out over our shared love of spy equipment and all the data-mining tools there for investigative journalists. "I'm like a kid in a candy store here," Marcus said, inspecting the fake can of shaving cream with the tiny tape recorder inside. After his book came out, Marcus landed a full-time gig as a senior news editor for *Fast Company*, the business magazine that focuses on leadership and innovation. We hadn't spoken for a while, but I had him on my list of *IBT* alumni who took freelance pitches, part of that vast *IBT* diaspora. I pitched him a terrible idea for a story about debt collectors, which he rightly turned down because it was garbage, but then he surprisingly sent me an e-mail wondering if I'd come by the *Fast Company* office at 7 World Trade Center to discuss a longer-term freelance opportunity. *Fast Company* had recently launched an online breaking-news product, a kind of news stream that could publish quick hits. It was looking to grow its digital presence. Marcus needed a freelance editor to help him get it off the ground.

Having covered media for so long, I knew that *Fast Company* was highly beloved in certain corners of tech and business. The magazine had been founded in 1995 and became an early darling of the dot-com boom. It positioned itself as a "handbook for the business revolution" and took on an almost cult-like status, more manifesto than magazine, with breathless stories about being your own personal brand and the chaotic serenity of Michael Bloomberg's office design. It sold a timely dream—that "work is personal" and that everyone can be a CEO in the new economy—and readers, for a long time, were all in. After the dot-com boom went bust, *Fast Company*'s brand of rah-rah techno-evangelism seemed a little passé. It struggled to reinvent itself in the early 2000s and nearly went out of business until it was rescued by Joe Mansueto, the billionaire entrepreneur who founded the financial services firm Morningstar and who also happened to be a longtime *Fast Company* reader.

Vanity purchases on that scale do not always end well for legacy media brands—ask *Newsweek*—but the billionaire-owner story turned out very differently for *Fast Company*. Joe was less interested in micromanaging a media empire than in being a good steward of a beloved magazine, keeping the name alive and running the business in a sustainable way. In that sense, *Fast Company* was the spiritual opposite of *IBT*. It didn't go on massive hiring sprees and cycles of mass layoffs every six months. Best of all, it had a product that high-level people enjoyed reading. CEOs loved it. Celebrities loved it. Even the Bird was a fan, often picking up copies for long trips and fawning over the design coverage. When I told her I had an interview there, she beamed. "That's the airport magazine!"

Maybe it was the beta-blocker, but I was surprisingly not very nervous when I walked into 7 World Trade Center for the first time, even though it was clearly a thousand steps above any place I'd ever worked. The tall glass skyscraper was the first to rise over what people used to call Ground Zero, and everything about it felt sleek and modern, right down to the large marble lobby and talking elevators that somehow automatically knew which floor you were going to. At the magazine's headquarters on the twenty-ninth floor, you were greeted by a futuristic sky café and breathtaking panoramic views of Lower Manhattan. *Fast Company* occupied one half of the floor, and *Inc.* magazine, also owned by Joe Mansueto, occupied the other half; from its windows, you could gaze down at the red Jeff Koons sculpture that looked like a giant balloon animal gone horribly wrong. Glass offices lined the perimeter, and when you walked through the floor, the entire horizon seemed to move with you as if you were in some kind of virtual-reality fantasy land.

I met Marcus in the futuristic sky café. He remarked that I looked different, more professional than he remembered. I was wearing a jacket and tie. And no hat. Never a hat when I'm trying to make an impression. I learned that a long time ago. Unless I'm outside somewhere. Then hats are fine, but only cool hats. Marcus and I were joined by his boss, Anjali, who ran the entire *Fast Company* website. Anjali seemed to really like Marcus and her questions mostly revolved around how I was going to help him get this news-stream thing off the ground. Then she made it clear that the editing gig was freelance and that there were no full-time staff positions available at the moment. I guess that was in case I got any ideas. I didn't, though. Everything about *Fast Company* felt out of my league.

Like every other good thing that's ever happened in my career, timing and luck played a role. The news stream took off, driven in part by crazier-than-usual election-year politics. Everyone was paying more attention to news in the fall of 2016 because the world felt like it was on fire. Higher-ups at *Fast Company* decided they wanted to turn the news stream into its own vertical and they were going to need someone who understood digital news to run the section. SEO was getting a lot more sophisticated, but many of the basic tenets that I'd learned from Wilson four years earlier still held up. I did what I could to drive traffic to the stream and once again became addicted to Chartbeat. Around that same time, someone on staff left—unusual, since most people seemed to genuinely like working there—and suddenly there was an opening.

I was going on my third month as a contractor when Anjali unexpect-edly called me into her office and asked if I wanted to come on board full-time. She said I was a good presence in the newsroom, calm under pressure, a perfect counterbalance to Marcus's can't-sit-still style. I'm always surprised when people say something like that to me because I'm usually internalizing enough anxiety to power a small city, but I think I understand why. Anjali was astute, more than any other manager I'd ever worked with, serious and straightforward when she needed to be but also likely to start giggling uncontrollably at some silly joke as if she were at a sleepover. And she was compassionate, concerned with work-life balance and long-term career development, things that usually got pushed aside. If she saw me staying late, she'd yell "Zara, what are you still doing here?" over and over until I promised to go home.

When Anjali told me the salary they were offering, my jaw dropped. I stared out the window of her office for a moment, trying to play it cool, fixing my gaze on the crown of the Woolworth Building, its green roof and Gothic spikes. The number was far higher than the Bird's symbolic eighty K, so much so that I assumed I must have misheard it. I didn't actually believe it was real until I saw the offer in writing. The job also had health benefits, life insurance, and a 401(k), which I knew was a thing but never expected to have.

As thrilled as I was, I was also very aware that I was once again being hired by a company that had never seen my résumé. *Fast Company* had the Ivy League in its DNA. Its cofounders had both worked for the *Harvard Business Review*. Its top editor at the time had gone to Brown, and its second in command had gone to Columbia. For God's sake, the media kit boasted that 84 percent of *Fast Company*'s readers were college graduates. I assumed the other 16 percent were Stanford dropouts who ran billion-dollar start-ups. If my past was untellable before, now I would need to guard it with my life.

The learning curve at *Fast Company* was much steeper than I'd expected. It wasn't so much figuring out what my new colleagues knew but what they cared about or, really, what they took seriously. People talked about funding rounds and incubators, carbon offsets and flat management structures. Private spaceflight was seen as inevitable and self-driving cars just around the corner. Cultish companies like Goop and Casper and Drybar were suddenly at the center of my radar, as was any celebrity who owned his or her own line of cruelty-free fragrances. Every product was either plant-based or DTC or both. At one of our editorial meetings, there was an entire discussion about whether or not we should do a feature on Guy Fieri. I mean, the name sounded familiar, but it wasn't until I googled him on my phone under the table that I realized they were talking about that chef with the bleached hair.

Being at a magazine that people actually liked also changed the dynamic of networking events. Gone were the days of people refusing to take my business card. Now CEOs wanted to tell me about their sustainable-seafood start-ups, and publicists needed five minutes of my time to unveil the next frontier in sleep science. My in-box was flooded with urgent e-mails about genius start-up founders who were disrupting industries that definitely needed disrupting, like paper towels. Revolutions happened every hour, every minute, and every single one of them was a world-changing idea.

The irony of this professional whiplash was not lost on me. Weeks earlier I had been worried I'd never get past another gatekeeper again, and now I was suddenly thrust into a gatekeeper role of a most peculiar type, tasked with fielding endless pitches from PR reps and trying to distinguish between genuinely innovative ideas and snake oil. I thought back to when I'd arrived in New York eleven years earlier, how I so badly wanted to escape the anonymity of service jobs and *be* what I did, like a real professional. If I could fit in here, I might just become a personal brand. That seemed to be *Fast Company*'s whole thing.

CHAPTER 35

Where Do We Belong?

I SPENT ELECTION NIGHT 2016 IN a dimly lit laundry room, but it was not as bad as it sounds. The laundry room was actually in a beautiful Tribeca condo that was filled with attractive, very well-dressed one-percenters who had gathered for a catered party to celebrate what everyone assumed would be Hillary Clinton's big night. Isabel, the Bird's old boss, lived there, and the Bird and I were both invited as guests. It was my first week on staff at *Fast Company,* and as the new news editor, I naturally had to work on the biggest news night of the year. I brought my laptop to the party and used Isabel's washing machine as my makeshift standing desk, occasionally dipping into the crowd to grab a flute of champagne from the bar or some finger foods from the nice people with the silver trays. With work to focus on, I was in my element, scanning social media for news, looking for viral gold, chatting on Slack with writers and with Marcus and Anjali, assigning stories, writing some myself. Everybody was suddenly mad about the Libertarian candidate Gary Johnson. Was that a quick hit? *Writing it up!* Hearkening back to my old drinking-game days, I was eager to show *Fast Company* what I could do, how I could draw traffic to the website, because that's what I thought mattered most. I wanted to prove that I could be useful on this historic night. I was as blind to the possibility of an upset as my college-educated colleagues; we were all expecting the same landslide. We might have come from different backgrounds, but we all lived and worked in the same bubble.

The party unfolded as I imagine parties just like it unfolded in a lot of coastal cities that night. The festive and giddy energy that marked the start of the evening curdled into a boil of anxiousness, then genuine worry. Indiana. Kentucky. West Virginia. By the time Ohio and Florida came into the picture, there was dread in the air, stretches of silence pierced by gasps and *Oh, shit*s. I was too focused on Chartbeat to notice, too self-satisfied that our news stream was killing it. At some point, I heard someone playing "Let It Be" on Isabel's piano, and a handful of party guests joined together in somber song, definitely not a good sign. The Bird came into the laundry room to ask when I would be finished working. It was now close to midnight. "I want to go home," she said. We collected our coats and said our goodbyes as I scanned a giant untouched cake in the shape of a stuffed pig with Donald Trump's head on it, a mound of orange and yellow icing. *Gross,* I thought.

We took a cab back to our apartment uptown, passing the Javits Center and watching the cars exiting the parking lot. Later that night, I handed off the news section to our West Coast editor. But sleep wouldn't come, so I went into the map room, opened my laptop back up, and checked into Slack to see what the hell was happening with the election. (The map room is what the Bird and I called our spare bedroom, one of our first projects as a couple. It's the perfect place to work because neither one of us ever gets tired of looking at maps.)

Before I knew it, the sun was coming up. I had no idea how long I'd been sitting there reading news, occasionally staring up at our Peters world map and trying to process what was happening. The Bird came into the room and looked at me. "Bird, is it really true?" she asked.

I nodded. She started crying and went back to bed.

The Bird had never really called herself a feminist before Hillary Clinton ran for president. Maybe she wanted a degree of distance from a word that she felt had too much baggage. Or maybe she didn't want to lose her edge, the freedom to openly say "slag" on dating websites, the part of herself that used her sexuality to her advantage when she was in her twenties and poor. But watching the raw sexism of the 2016 campaign unfold changed her view. After she left the map room that morning, I cried for her. And for my mom, who had been waiting her entire life to vote for a woman president. My mom, who hadn't seen college as an option because women just didn't do that in those days, who'd put her working life on hold to raise three boys, who'd had the guts to divorce my dad, who'd retired with barely enough to survive on. She was seventy-three and in the hospital with a brain infection when the election was called.

New Yorkers sometimes compare the morning after the 2016 election to the morning after 9/11. I wouldn't know. I was still in Orlando on 9/11, working in the frame shop at Jo-Ann Fabrics. My only sense then that anything was different was that the store was eerily quiet and people kept coming in to buy eight-dollar posters of the World Trade Center, as if we were going to sell out forever and they would become collectors' items.

On my long subway commute down to the *Fast Company* office the day after the election, I became unusually aware of my fellow riders, their differences, every race and color, every religion, all packed together in a single car. That's a normal day on a New York City subway and one of the things I love about this city. How bad can things be, really, if we can all share the space on a tiny car? Now I wondered if I still had a right to be here. I wondered if my fellow subway riders were looking at me, a white male, suspiciously, if they thought the previous night was my fault.

Over the following days and weeks, our news team was tasked with filtering the implications of this new era through a *Fast Company* lens. But my job also necessitated that I pay more attention to news as a holistic entity, including the parts I wanted to tune out. I developed an unhealthy focus on the endless election autopsies that were identifying college as a pivotal voter fault line, educational attainment (or lack thereof) as a key determinant of the most shocking election outcome in history. The headlines came one after another, hot takes and postmortems and prescriptives, buoyed by data and demographics and exit polls:

America's Educational Divide Put Trump in the White House

Education Mattered in 2016

Trump Won Because Voters Are Ignorant, Literally

Four years earlier, I'd spent a presidential election writing about drinking games and hoping that political pundits would lose interest in the white working class once it was all over, because the truth was it was acceptable to be proud of your working-class roots only once you'd left them behind, and without a formal education, I could never really do that. In my wishful-thinking version of things, the perceived corrosive influence of voters who matched my demographic profile would be at most a statistical blip. Now the narratives that had taken root in 2012 were more pervasive than ever, and the results were even more catastrophic: non-college-educated whites had handed the country to a malignant reality-TV star. I wanted to scream out, *No, not all of us!* But that would have given me away, outed me among my new colleagues in our shiny office on the twenty-ninth floor. It was easier to be complicit in the narratives by keeping my head down and my mouth shut, by letting the shame I felt for my background ossify along with the perception among educated pundits that I had legitimate reasons to feel ashamed.

I started to feel increasingly disconnected from the industry that I had worked so hard to infiltrate. The camaraderie that I had forged with my colleagues at *IBT* had taken years to build, and now I was back to square one in an elite magazine world that felt even more alien to me at a time when education and expertise and credentials were seen as the antidote to all that ailed our country. The unpolished precepts of punk rock, pride in being self-taught—these were not exactly things people wanted to hear about in a nation where the embrace of chaos had just taken such a consequential turn.

Faced with this professional out-of-body experience, I did what I always do: I dove into the details and particulars of my job and tried to make myself *of* this new world by learning as much as I could about it. I attended all the *Fast Company* events. I used terms like *thought leader* and *upskill* and *experience economy* in earnest. I interviewed high-level people about their productivity hacks and entrepreneurial aha moments and side hustles. I printed out research papers to read during my long commutes up and down the island and finally figured out what the hell a blockchain was. I continued to fight through cycles of anxiety, doubling up on beta-blockers on days when self-doubt felt insurmountable and reveling in those moments when I could sit with my laptop in front of a large window, gaze upon an eye-popping view of the sun setting over New York Harbor, and feel like I had earned the right to be there on that twenty-ninth floor.

The *Fast Company* ethos seemed to hinge on a paradox that work should be both a meaningful part of your existence and yet completely separate from your sense of self-worth. Being what you did, or aspiring to that, was no longer in vogue. You weren't supposed to be too busy or work too hard or want things too much because those were all symptoms of unfair systems. Here was a paradox I was still trying to wrap my head around. Either the future-of-work people had it wrong or my motivation for moving to New York was shallow and selfish. What if that was all that was left once I peeled away the professional identity I wasn't supposed to be clinging to?

CHAPTER 36

Thirty Years of Magical Thinking

MY FIRST EMOTION WHEN I read the discharge summary was bemusement. "'Final diagnosis: schizotypal personality disorder,'" I read out loud to the Bird, who was standing next to me in our kitchen when I opened the envelope. "Ooh, that doesn't sound good," she said. It didn't sound good, but what did it matter now? Apparently, I had been given that diagnosis after my stay in the mental hospital back in 1987. No one ever told me about it, or, if someone did, I don't remember it. I'm not sure why I contacted the hospital all those years later. Maybe I was hoping for some clue, some insight into my frame of mind at the time of my academic collapse. The hospital stay had taken place just a few weeks after I got kicked out of high school. Maybe the psychiatric evaluation I'd undergone contained some long-forgotten detail that would help explain why I failed so miserably. Unfortunately, the details of the evaluation were gone forever. The hospital informed me that medical records were purged after about twenty years. The discharge summary I held in my hand, with that final diagnosis, was all that remained.

"Now, don't go googling that," the Bird said. I nodded compliantly, but of course there was no way I was not going to immediately do just that.

Even though I knew this diagnosis that some psychiatrist slapped on me as a sixteen-year-old after a three-day evaluation could never be an accurate picture of me now, it somehow was. Or it was at least plausible. Looking up the signs and symptoms of schizotypal personality disorder, I kept seeing things that had plagued me for my entire life: "Being a loner and lacking close friends outside of the immediate family," said the Mayo

248

Clinic. "They are very anxious in social situations, especially unfamiliar ones," explained the Merck Manuals. "Spending more time in a situation does not ease their anxiety." People with the condition also tended to have "odd" speech patterns and behavior—like talking backward, maybe, or peeing in a roommate's Che mug—and "odd" thoughts and perceptions. And believing I could will away my physical flaws by staring into a mirror definitely seemed to fall into the realm of "magical thinking," another tell-tale sign. Schizotypal personality disorder is sometimes discussed as being on a schizophrenia spectrum, but it's not the same as schizophrenia and typically doesn't involve psychosis or losing touch with reality. And even though I'd never heard of this condition, it apparently affects almost 4 percent of the American population. It's more common in males and tends to show up in adolescence or early adulthood. Many people diagnosed with the condition experience major depressive episodes—like the one that got me locked up in the hospital—and they also seem to be at an increased risk for substance abuse.

What type of sorcery is this? I thought to myself as I stared at the twenty-five open tabs cluttering up my laptop screen.

At a certain point, I stopped reading and asked myself how deep into this rabbit hole I was willing to go. Was this going to be just another passing health obsession, like the time I'd convinced myself that I deserved to be stricken with liver disease and spent weeks reading the medical literature on the significance of pale nail beds? Or was that masochistic episode of hypochondria itself another sign of a personality disorder that no one ever bothered to tell me I had? The distinction mattered, I thought, because maybe—just maybe—knowing I had it might have made a difference. Maybe it would've set me on a different path, away from City Gardens and heroin, toward treatment, toward college, toward something better. Maybe I'd feel more deserving of the career I had now, not always teetering on the brink, terrified of the next layoff. Maybe the twenty-ninth floor wouldn't feel like a giant Monopoly game that I was still learning how to play.

I sat across from our new editor in chief, Stephanie Mehta, and tried to explain in the best possible terms what we did on the news team and how my role as the editor played into it. The late-winter sun hung low in the sky, peering through the south-facing window of her office that overlooked the reflecting pools of the old Twin Towers. We were surrounded by an opulent display of flower arrangements that had arrived to welcome her to her new gig. Stephanie was friendly but down to business, TV-ready, with short bangs and a glossy-magazine style, the kind of new boss you want desperately to impress. This was early 2018 and I'd been there for almost two years. I felt a level of competence and ease with my job that I'd never felt before, having absorbed the DNA of the brand, having synthesized its devotion to tech and business and channeled it into a high-output source of digital news. Our section got lots of traffic, although at *Fast Company*, we preferred to say we were "exceeding our audience goals," and everyone on the team got along like peaches and cream.

Still, a lot went down in the chaotic weeks prior to our first meeting. In January, the previous editor left abruptly after an eleven-year tenure. I learned about his departure not from a company memo but on Twitter—never a good sign of workplace stability—and then our second and third in command jumped ship shortly after that. Our parent company was restructuring, looking for ways to cut redundancies and improve efficiencies and do all the things that companies say they're going to do right before the ax falls. I was again in a newsroom that was quietly unionizing, this time with the Writers Guild of America, East. I was more eager to sign the card this time around—and I eventually did—but early negotiations were adding a component of uncertainty to an already tense set of circumstances.

To me, it all felt familiar, too familiar, a rerun of a reboot on a continuous loop that someone had forgotten to turn off. *When does it start to get more stable?* I thought to myself. Here I was, once again, at a job I loved, my existence there the result of a mind-blowing mix of unlikely timing and luck, faced with the possibility that it could come to an end. Not for nothing, but it wasn't an especially good time for me to be fired. The Bird and I were planning a two-week trip to Turkey and Uzbekistan to celebrate our anniversary in May, and the plane tickets were already booked. Hell, I was just getting used to the idea of being the kind of person who jets off to Turkey and Uzbekistan.

The fickle nature of the media business was exhausting enough in its own right, and yet as I was sitting there in the entirely familiar position of trying to navigate another change in leadership, I wasn't overly preoccupied with whether or not my next paycheck would be my last. All I could think about during that first meeting with Stephanie was what I always thought about: *Please don't ask me about my background.* Thirteen years in journalism and I still had no good answer to the basic question of where I went to school, nor could I fathom even having a conversation about it without blushing like a spoiled radish. Intellectually, I understood that education would always be seen as a defining characteristic in our society, that I couldn't control how people in my industry would perceive me when they found out I had a GED and not a J-school degree, and yet the thought of those snap judgments remained as unbearable to me as it had when I'd first arrived in New York. I started to wonder if the only way out of this self-defeating mental trap was doing exactly what I feared most—talking about it—because even though I sometimes felt like the only degreeless person left in the white-collar world, I knew I couldn't possibly be.

One gray Sunday afternoon, I called my mom and asked her point-blank about the diagnosis of schizotypal personality disorder, but she knew nothing about it. "They just told us you were not a danger to yourself, so we checked you out," she said.

"Not a danger to myself? What does that mean?"

"That's what they told us."

"How did they even know that?"

"They must have had their ways."

Pressing my mom for granular details was a generally complicated process, especially when emotions were involved. She hadn't been quite the same since the brain infection that landed her in the hospital back during the 2016 election. Her tendency to overexplain the connections between things—always a facet of her personality—became more pronounced and her explanations less linear, and it was easy to lose the plot.

It didn't help that neither of us liked talking about certain parts of our past, especially *that* part. The night in 1987 when I smashed my head into a mirror, the night they sent me to the institution—those were ancient wounds from another life, better off buried under thirty years of scar tissue. Whenever my teenage years came up, my mom would respond with a series of monologues about how she regretted putting me in the hospital in the first place, regretted letting the school system label me *emotionally disturbed,* regretted being absent, regretted not fighting harder when the high school kicked me out. She regretted so much that my desire to better understand her choices as a parent felt trivial in comparison, as if my pressing her for granular details was the ultimate act of selfishness. When details fade from your memory, emotions are all you have left. I went into the call feeling angry, righteous, eager to demand answers about a pivotal moment in my adolescence: *Why wasn't I told about this thing that some doctor said I had?* I guess that's because it would have been easier to blame my academic failures on an untreated personality disorder than to take ownership of the personal choices that had contributed to them. The story I tell myself about education is that no one ever instilled in me how important it was or explained why it mattered. But what if people had tried to and I just hadn't listened? On the phone with my mom that Sunday, I realized that her guilt would always be greater than my anger.

Our conversation ended the same way those conversations always did. She said she was sorry for how things had unfolded back when I was a teenager, and I said she had no reason to be sorry because it all worked out in the end. "I like my life, Ma." It always seemed to make us both feel better when I put it like that. "I like my life."

A few months later, I e-mailed the psychiatrist who'd signed off on my final diagnosis. I asked if he'd be interested in speaking with me. He'd ended up becoming a pretty big deal in the world of mental health, a top professor at an Ivy League university, and I discovered that he had written some well-known research papers on the link between mental health and substance abuse. If nothing else, I thought, he might offer insights into the condition he said I had and whether it could have been connected to my struggles with addiction. Of course, I knew he probably wouldn't remember our encounter from 1987, but I didn't think I had anything to lose by reaching out to the guy. He never wrote back, though, which makes me wonder if he was either creeped out by my request or just never got the e-mail. I probably shouldn't have sent it on a Monday.

CHAPTER 37

Higher Learning

FAST COMPANY WAS THE FIRST magazine to do a major cover story on Mark Zuckerberg. It was May 2007, and Facebook was barely three years into its history, just another Silicon Valley start-up with plenty of hype and a hazy business model. The editor who approved the cover story was Bob Safian, Stephanie's predecessor, an unassuming but savvy spotter of future trends. Bob often talked about how *Fast Company* just got lucky with this early profile of a twenty-two-year-old start-up founder who went on to become one of the world's most influential people. "I wish I could say we saw that coming," Bob later said. He was humble that way. Of course, *Fast Company* was known for exactly those kinds of prophetic moments, a chronicler of meritocratic myths that placed great leaders and shrewd entrepreneurship at the center of every noteworthy revolution. On the cover of the May 2007 issue, Mark Zuckerberg is practically bathed in a beatific glow, fresh-faced with a toothy smile and his trademark hoodie, the whimsical *Fast Company* logo obscured behind his thick curly locks. He's clearly poised for world domination, a prototype of an archetype of a new kind of power broker. That profile of him is still online and it's perhaps this digital version that best sums up what made Mark Zuckerberg's backstory so compelling, even before his name was known to most people.

"Hacker. Dropout. CEO," the story's headline reads.

All these years later, it's hard to think of anyone who better personifies the trope of the superstar dropout. It's a club that includes Ralph Lauren and Rachael Ray, Jan Koum and Jay-Z, literary legends like Robert Frost, punk-rock poets like Patti Smith, and famous inventors like Thomas

Edison. America loves their stories. America loves *them*. In a meritocracy, there is no higher reward than to cast a smug eye on an ultra-successful career and say, *I did it my way*. And that Frank Sinatra, hoo-boy, he dropped out of high school too. It's weird to realize how much my feelings about these types of maverick dropouts have changed. For people without college degrees, the mythology that gets built around them can be like catnip, affirmation that college is not a prerequisite for high achievement. No matter how hopeless I felt about my prospects over the years, I could always latch on to Fran Lebowitz or Paul Thomas Anderson or Anna Wintour, study their career trajectories as a way of satisfying my confirmation bias.

Outliers make great headlines—it's one of the first things you learn in the news business. Boring statistics, by contrast, often take time to sink in. When I first started working in journalism, I developed the compulsive habit of looking up the résumés and backstories of fellow journalists whose work I admired, peers I wanted to emulate. I'd come across an aspirational profile or a deep dive or an investigative piece, then I'd search the author's name on LinkedIn or Wikipedia. I'd always feel a tinge of sadness when I inevitably came across his or her alma mater, as if the confirmation bias I was trying desperately to cling to was being peeled away. Then I would meet people for whom college had been a way out of poverty or a path to escape the limitations of their socioeconomic status or a chance to access a professional network. I'd meet people for whom higher education wasn't a threat to their sense of self-worth but the backbone of it. And in those moments, I would be reminded that what I'd missed out on was so much more than an algorithmic signal for some piece of job-recruiting software.

It took years working in journalism for me to understand the true damage caused by the word *dropout,* as if leaving Harvard to run a successful start-up was on the same spectrum as slipping through the cracks of an underfunded school system. For every Mark Zuckerberg, there are thousands, millions, of people without the means or advantages or opportunities to choose school at all and millions more for whom learning in a classroom is just not the right choice. Some are successful, others are barely scraping by, and some are like me, just hoping no one will ask.

* * *

The midday sun was getting more furious by the minute, bouncing off the shiny tiles of the promenade and turning the park into a giant oven. We knew if we kept wandering this wide-open area at the center of Tashkent, we were goners. "It looks like it goes on forever," the Bird said, agog at the sight of endless green lawns, rows of dribbling fountains, soaring white columns, and sculptures of storks. Leave it to the Soviets to construct such an imposing public square with no place to find shade. Or who knows — maybe it was the Russian Empire that first settled on this layout. Or Genghis Khan, or the Arabs. The thing about Uzbekistan, we were learning on our first day there, was that every inch of it contained almost too much history to comprehend. The park in which we now stood had been renamed Independence Square in 1991. At its center was a large, globe-shaped monument with the country's modern-day borders emblazoned on its golden surface. A giant statue of Lenin had once stood in the same spot, and at some point in the 2000s, when the strongman president Islam Karimov was in charge, a sculpture of a "happy mother" holding her baby was added. The space was as pristine as it was awe-inspiring, clearly built for show, right down to the green-suited police officers who guarded the entrances of Tashkent's elaborately designed but sparsely used subway. Their job was either to keep us safe from what appeared to be nonexistent street crime or to make sure we didn't take selfies, not that we would ever do such a thing. Weirdly, we saw almost no other people in or near the park. Maybe the Uzbeks weren't impressed by impeccable landscaping and walls of red granite. Or maybe they just had the good sense to stay out of the heat.

That's when the Bird pointed out a building in the distance, pasty white with elongated windows, shields of dark blue tint. It was the Hyatt Regency, a luxury hotel, exactly the indoor destination we needed. If we started walking up the hot sidewalk with the wavy-shaped bricks right now, it would surely be late enough for a cocktail when we got there.

Once at the hotel, we ordered two gin and tonics and settled down at a shaded outdoor table overlooking the street. I raised a glass to Bobir, my old comrade from the frame shop whose vivid stories of growing up here during a time of frenetic transition were one of the big reasons I wanted to come. I never saw him again after my last day in the shop, and over the years he's blended into the aggregation of people I wish I hadn't lost touch with. Once, when I was working insane hours at *Show Business Weekly,* he left an odd voice mail on my phone, identifying himself but not giving a reason for his call. "Hello, this is Bobir from gallery," he said. "Maybe you remember me? Okay, that's all." I've always regretted not calling him back. At the time, I was still fetishizing the idea that being too busy to return calls was the most elevated thing you could be, a mindset that I've never fully been able to shed. That's probably why the Bird always insisted that we take a full two weeks off on these big trips. "They can survive without you," she'd say, ignoring my requests to shorten my time away from work. Of course they can. My biggest fear is that they'll figure that out one day.

We sipped our drinks slowly that afternoon, phones out of sight, watching the action unfold on the sidewalk in front of us, enjoying the mundane in a faraway city. The past and future dissolved around the edges of our quiet little moment until the moment itself was the only thing left.

I like my life.

It's not just an empty platitude I tell my mom to make her feel better. It's one of those things that occur to you when the moment is just right, like on a hot day in May 2018 when you're people-watching in Tashkent with your wife. She doesn't believe in soul mates or an afterlife and I don't know if I do either, so our moments together will have to be enough.

(Major events, good and bad, were just around the corner. The world was about to change overnight. A pandemic would soon make the effortlessness and innocence of these trips seem like remnants of a forgotten age. It would force our society to reevaluate the role of higher education in a more urgent way. It would turn the office culture that I had wanted so badly to be a part of on its head, reducing the big editorial meetings I once found so exhilarating to Zoom calls and Slack threads. It would rob the working world of a living dimension, flatten it until the differences between blue and white collars were even more stark. Eighteen months into the pandemic, the Bird landed her dream job as a designer and art director for one of the biggest advertising agencies on Broadway. They had seen her online portfolio, loved her enthusiastic cover letter, and asked her to apply. She was two months shy of her fifty-sixth birthday when she got the offer. Later, I watched her wrestle, as I did, with the alien-like sensation of trying to assimilate into a corporate environment, saw how she worried that the topic of education would come up with her colleagues. It's going to come up, I told her. Work is always changing and our ideas about work have to change with it.)

Our last stop in Uzbekistan was Samarkand, an ancient city that was once part of the Silk Road. The heart of the city was a massive square called the Registan that contained three medieval madrassas, Islamic schools, facing a giant courtyard. Each building had its own towering archway and an intricate facade of geometric patterns and shapes. You could get lost staring at it. Turquoise domes extended upward, shimmering against a backdrop of endless sky that turned white at dusk, contrasting with a blanket of sharp-edged clouds. The corners of the complex had very tall, cylinder-shaped towers. Seen from a distance, they reminded me of the old smokestack at the Roebling factory, how its slender silhouette used to pierce the horizon like a giant cigar when we were driving around the potholed streets of Trenton. Six years earlier, it had been in such a state of disrepair that it had to be torn down brick by brick.

The Registan came alive most strikingly in the evenings, as cooler air swept in and people from all over Samarkand would flock to the grounds to enjoy the sunset. The Bird and I visited three evenings in a row. On our final day there, we stopped by an ornately designed ice cream kiosk that sat on the outer edge of the complex, apparently a favorite destination for local families. I got a small cup of plain vanilla, no cone, no toppings, my go-to order. I know it's boring, but I like to make things easy on the people who have to scoop it.

After our ice cream, we sat down on the flat steps and stared quietly at the golden complex. The sun had gone down and the lights from the dormitory cells of the madrassas were glowing in unison, long rows of pointed arches like candles aflame. Overwhelmed by this beautiful gem of antiquity, the Bird and I said nothing, but we were surely both thinking the same thing: *Here's a view we'll never see again. What are the chances, after all, that we'll ever return to this remote part of Central Asia?* Our moment of pensive silence was interrupted by a girl's voice. "May we take our picture with you?" We looked up to see two teenagers holding phones. They identified themselves as students who were looking to practice their English. Perhaps we were the only Westerners on the steps that night. One of the teenagers said she was planning to attend university in the United States, and when she described the recent approval of her student visa, she could hardly contain her excitement. "I'm going to live in Chicago," she said, "and I'm going to study, and omigod, I'm even going to see New York." She stood next to us and posed as her friend snapped a photo. Then she thanked us for our time. We wished her luck in her studies, and they disappeared just as quickly as they had arrived. *What an unlikely encounter,* I thought after they were gone. *What a nice way to start an adventure.*

Acknowledgments

I am indebted first and foremost to my wife, Christina, who did not spit-laugh her Prosecco all over the table at Thai Market when I told her over dinner one night that I wanted to write a book about the value of education. She believed in this idea from the beginning and allowed me the most incredible honor of telling parts of her story along with mine. Thank you also to my parents, who showed me love above all else, and to my brothers, built-in best friends.

I'm so grateful for the team at Little, Brown, especially my two brilliant editors, Vanessa Mobley and Vivian Lee, who helped shape this book from start to finish, along with Morgan Wu, Jayne Yaffe Kemp, and the most incisive copy editor, Tracy Roe. Thank you to Aliya Farrukh Shaikh for the fact-checking and to my agent, Ryan Harbage, for connecting me with the perfect team to help bring this project to life.

No one works in a vacuum. I've been afforded the privilege of being a professional journalist through the grace and good faith of many colleagues who took a chance on hiring me, mentoring me, opening doors for me, or letting me in the room, only some of whom are mentioned in this book. I'd be remiss not to thank Marcus Baram, Ali Basye, Kathleen Davis, Peter Goodman, Anjali Khosla, Michael Learmonth, Stephanie Mehta, Jeffrey Rothfeder, Robert Safian, Meg Thompson, and Jennifer Wood by name, but there are many others. I owe a special thanks to Ellen Killoran, who described to me during our final conversation how she had fought to get me hired, despite my lack of a degree, simply because she liked my work. Acts like that, big and small, are the reason I was able to have a career.

Acknowledgments

Finally, I may not have had much of a traditional education to speak of, but in my brief time in classrooms I was fortunate enough to have had some incredible teachers, especially English teachers, whose warmth, patience, and clear-minded instruction gave me the best gift of all: small glimpses of my future self as a writer. I can trace my entire professional life back to their words of encouragement.

About the Author

Christopher Zara is an author and journalist who writes about culture, media, business, and technology. He is a senior editor at *Fast Company*, where he runs the digital news desk, and was previously a deputy editor at *International Business Times*, a theater critic for *Newsweek*, and managing editor of *Show Business Weekly*. Christopher lives on the Upper West Side with his wife, Christina D'Angelo, and their cat, Jimmy Carter McPickles, who is officially on the lease.

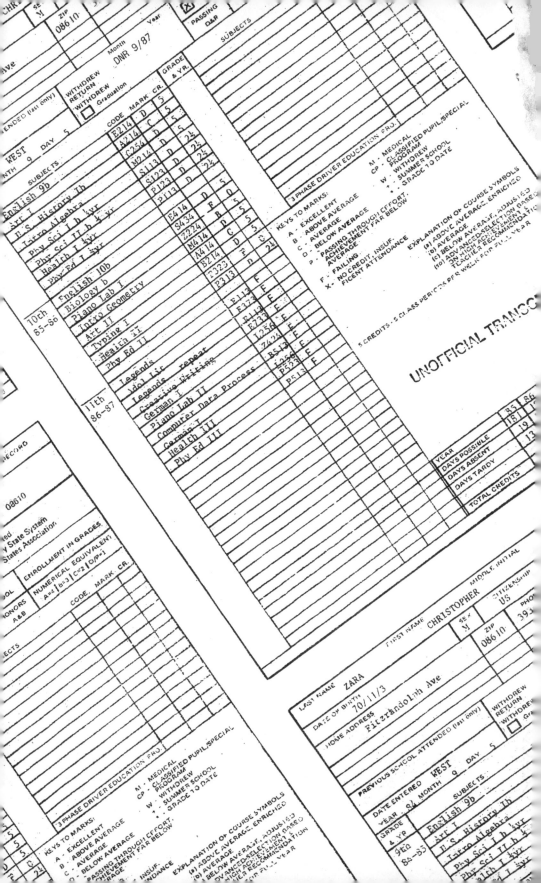

ZIP
08610

Month
DNR 9/87   Year

WITHDREW
RETURN
☐ WITHDREW
☐ Graduation

CODE	MARK	CR.
E214	D	5
A214	C	5
C254	D	5
M214	D	2½
S113	D	2½
S123	D	2½
P123	D	2½
P113		5
E414	D	0
S434	B	5
2224	C	5
M414	C	C
A414	D	5
B214	F	2½
2323	D	
P313		
E113	F	
E373	F	
E113	F	
E233	F	
1256	F	
2424	F	
BS13	F	
1256	F	
P523	F	

WEST   DAY 5
MONTH 9

SUBJECTS

English 9b
Art I
U.S. History Ib
Intro Algebra
Phy Sci II.b ½ yr
Phy Sci II.b ½ yr
Health I ½ yr
Phy Ed I ½yr

10th
85-86
English 10b
Biology b
Piano Lab I
Intro Geometry
Art II
Typing II
Health II
Phy Ed II

11th
86-87
Legends
Adol Lit   repeat
Legends
Creative Writing
German I
Piano Lab II
Computer Data Process
German I
Health III
Phy Ed III

	YEAR	85	86
	DAYS POSSIBLE	151	
	DAYS ABSENT	19	
	DAYS TARDY	13	
	TOTAL CREDITS		

08610
y State System
States Association

CODE	MARK	CR.

HONORS
A & B

LAST NAME   ZARA
FIRST NAME   CHRISTOPHER   MIDDLE INITIAL
DATE OF BIRTH   70/11/3
SEX   M
CITIZENSHIP   US
ZIP   08610
HOME ADDRESS   Fitzrandolph Ave
PHO   393

WITHDREW
RETURN
☐ WITHDREW
Gr

PREVIOUS SCHOOL ATTENDED (last only)

DATE ENTERED   WEST   DAY 5
YEAR 84   MONTH 9
GRADE   4 yr
9th

SUBJECTS
English 9b
Art I
U.S. History Ib
Intro Algebra
Phy Sci II.b ½ yr
Health I ½ yr

84-85